MASTERING
SPANISH

MASTERING SPANISH

Fourth Edition

Laurel H. Turk

DePauw University

Aurelio M. Espinosa, Jr.

Stanford University

D. C. HEATH AND COMPANY

Lexington, Massachusetts   Toronto

Preface

Mastering Spanish, Fourth Edition, is a program for students who have completed one year of college Spanish or its equivalent in secondary school. It is designed to further the development of the language through a comprehensive review of the basic grammatical elements essential for a good command of Spanish. The components of this program are a text, a workbook/testing program, an audio program, and a cultural reader.

The text consists of fifteen regular lessons, five *Repasos,* five short cultural sections called *Notas culturales,* a section on Spanish letter writing, four appendices, and end vocabularies. The maps and the illustrations supplement the material on the cultural background of the Spanish-speaking countries. Throughout the text, emphasis is placed on verb mastery, practical vocabulary, and the active use of the language.

Each lesson begins with the grammatical explanations; the number of grammatical points discussed in each lesson varies from four to seven, with ten shorter items in *Lección quince.* Forms of the present indicative tense are reviewed in *Lección primera,* commands in *Lección dos,* the preterit and imperfect tenses in *Lección cuatro,* the present perfect and pluperfect indicative tenses in *Lección cinco,* the future and conditional tenses in *Lección ocho,* the present subjunctive tense in *Lección nueve,* the present perfect subjunctive tense in *Lección once,* and the imperfect and pluperfect subjunctive tenses in *Lección doce.* The verb review is placed at the beginning of each lesson so that the exercises and drills may be taken up separately, or in conjunction with the grammatical explanations and other appropriate exercises which follow each discussion. The stress on verb forms is recognized as a necessity if the student is to gain a complete mastery of the language.

Throughout the text the headings as well as the directions are given in Spanish. The grammatical explanations are given in English to ensure comprehension. Additional expressions for use in the classroom are listed in Appendix B.

The grammatical explanations give a systematic, logical, and practical review of the fundamentals of Spanish structure. They emphasize general usage rather than exceptions. An important feature of the grammatical explanations is that each major structure is immediately followed by appropriate and adequate drills. Wherever feasible, these exercises are devised so that they may be done orally. The device of placing the exercises immediately after the grammatical summary enables the student to center his attention on the particular point under discussion and to review a maximum number of points in a relatively short time. This method of presentation also permits an easy division of each lesson into assignments. The sentences in the exercises are purposely short to encourage rapid drill work. The vocabulary of the drills is most often limited to words of high frequency, permitting the student to focus on the structure under consideration.

Each lesson concludes with a *Glosario* which contains all the idioms and expressions used in the explanations and exercises of the lesson and occasional words which the student may not have encountered in his previous study of Spanish.

Each *Repaso,* which follows a group of three lessons and offers additional oral drills and short English sentences to be expressed in Spanish, summarizes the major points taken up in the preceding lessons.

Following each *Repaso* is a short section called *Notas culturales.* These readings deal with general cultural items such as observations on the Spanish language in America, the Hispanic presence in the United States, some Spanish customs, Spanish-American foods, and excerpts from *El continente de siete colores,* by the well-known Colombian essayist, Germán Arciniegas. A series of questions to be answered in Spanish is included with each selection; written reports in Spanish are suggested in three of the *Notas culturales;* and English to Spanish sentences are given in the other two.

For those who may wish to carry on social or commercial correspondence in Spanish, some commonly used phrases and formulas and sample letters are given in the special section on letter writing, called *Cartas españolas.*

Appendix A contains a summary of Spanish pronunciation, including the basic principles of intonation, with an explanation of terms used, word stress, diphthongs, triphthongs, linking of words, punctuation, and capitalization; Appendix B includes a list of expressions used in the classroom, grammatical terms, punctuation marks, and the abbreviations and signs used in the text; Appendix C gives the cardinal and ordinal numerals, the days of the week, the months of the year, the seasons, dates, and ways to express the time of day; and Appendix D contains the regular verb paradigms and complete lists of irregular verbs used in the text, as well as a few additional verbs which may be encountered in later study of Spanish.

The Spanish-English vocabulary is intended to be complete, with the exception of a few proper and geographic names which are either identical in Spanish and English or whose meaning is clear, a few past participles used as adjectives when the infinitive is given, the words in the *Glosario* for *Notas culturales IV,* the Spanish examples translated in the *Cartas españolas,* and a few diminutives given in *Lección trece.* Idioms are listed under the most important word in the phrase, and, in most cases, cross listings are given. With few exceptions, irregular plural forms of nouns and adjectives are included only for those forms which are used in the plural in the text. The English-Spanish vocabulary contains only the English words used in the English-Spanish exercises.

In this edition of *Mastering Spanish,* the verb review formerly included in three opening lessons is now spread throughout eight regular lessons. The infinitives of many common verbs of each type and the forms of the various tenses are given in the lessons as a means of avoiding constant reference to Appendix D. Varied exercises follow each verb review section. The order of presentation of grammatical material has been reorganized and some of the explanations have been modified. The types of drill exercises in previous editions are largely unchanged, although individual exercises have been shortened, a few lengthened, and others rewritten.

The summary list of words and expressions included in the *Glosario* at the end of each lesson should serve as a valuable review for students and should help to avoid much vocabulary thumbing.

In this new edition five *Repasos* are included, one after each three lessons. The *Lecturas* of the preceding edition have been replaced with five *Notas culturales.* It is assumed that the instructor will make use of the summary of Spanish pronunciation and intonation which appears in Appendix A. In the oral exercises or in the supplementary readings all aspects of good pronunciation should be stressed.

Supplementary Materials

Workbook/Testing Program

The *Workbook* has been completely revised, and the exercises, which have been rewritten, differ from those in the text. A feature of the *Workbook* is the inclusion of five comprehensive tests, each of which covers a unit of three lessons.

Audio Program

As an aid to the instructor and student, an innovative audio program accompanies the text, covering most of the oral exercises and the *Notas culturales.* A comprehension exercise has been included in the audio program for each regular lesson and for the five comprehensive tests. For the first three lessons and for the comprehensive tests, the comprehension exercise consists of questions, using vocabulary contained in the corresponding lessons, to be answered in Spanish in complete sentences. Beginning with *Lección cuatro,* the comprehension exercises are based on the preceding *Notas culturales:* for *Lección cuatro—Lección seis,* they are based on *Notas culturales I;* for *Lección siete—Lección nueve,* they are based on *Notas culturales II,* etc. In each unit of three lessons the exercises consist of true-false statements, sentences to be completed in Spanish, and questions to be answered in complete Spanish sentences.

Cultural Reader

To develop reading comprehension and vocabulary skills and to promote classroom discussion, a cultural reader, *¿Qué me cuenta?* by Eduardo Zayas-Bazán and Gastón Fernández may be used with *Mastering Spanish. ¿Qué me cuenta?* is divided into fifteen lessons, each containing three reading selections, exercises, and activities that focus on a cultural theme.

In the preparation of this edition the authors wish to express their deep appreciation for the valuable suggestions and constructive criticism offered by colleagues who have used the earlier editions, and by the members of the staff of the Modern Language Department of D. C. Heath and Company.

L.H.T.

A.M.E., Jr.

Contents

MASTERING
SPANISH

LECCIÓN PRIMERA

Formas del presente de indicativo de los verbos regulares • Algunos verbos que tienen formas irregulares en el presente de indicativo • Otros verbos que tienen formas irregulares en el presente de indicativo • Verbos que cambian la vocal radical en el presente de indicativo • El artículo definido, el género y el número de los sustantivos • Usos del artículo indefinido

1 Formas del presente de indicativo de los verbos regulares

tomar	tomo	tomas	toma	tomamos	tomáis	toman
comer	como	comes	come	comemos	coméis	comen
vivir	vivo	vives	vive	vivimos	vivís	viven

Some common verbs with regular forms in the present indicative tense are:

comprar to buy
esperar to wait (for); to hope, expect
estudiar to study
explicar to explain
hablar to speak, talk

llevar to take, carry
mirar to look at, watch
necesitar to need
tomar to take, drink, eat
trabajar to work

aprender (a + *inf.*)[1] to learn (to)
comer to eat

comprender to understand
vender to sell

abrir to open
escribir to write

permitir to permit, allow, let
vivir to live

Remember that the present indicative tense (**yo**) **tomo** corresponds in English not only to the simple present tense, *I take,* but also to the emphatic, *I do take,* and to the progressive, *I am (I'm) taking.*

The present tense in Spanish is often used for the future tense in English to give the action a more vivid or immediate character: **Te veo mañana,** *I'll see you tomorrow.*

See pages 22–23 for the forms and uses of subject pronouns in Spanish.

EJERCICIOS

A. Repitan[2] la frase; luego, al oír un sujeto nuevo, substitúyanlo (*substitute it*) en la frase, cambiando la forma del verbo cuando sea necesario:

---

[1] The parentheses in an entry of this type are explanatory, that is, the preposition **a** is used after **aprender** before an infinitive. See Appendix B, pages 214–215, for the abbreviations used in the text.

[2] See pages 212–213 for some commands and other words and expressions which may be used in the classroom. Others may be found in the Spanish-English end vocabulary.

1. *Los estudiantes* toman café.
   (Yo, Carlos y yo, Tú, Usted, María y Diana)
2. *José* no comprende la frase.
   (Nosotros, Ustedes, Ella, Yo, Ramón y Luis)
3. ¿Escribes *tú* muchas cartas?
   (ustedes, Carolina, los muchachos, yo, usted)

B. Para contestar afirmativamente[1] en español:

1. ¿Hablan ustedes español en esta clase?
2. ¿Esperas tú el autobús?
3. ¿Necesitan ellos más tiempo?
4. ¿Compran ustedes muchas cosas?
5. ¿Aprenden ustedes a hablar bien?
6. ¿Come Luisa a las seis?
7. ¿Abren ustedes las puertas a veces?
8. ¿Escribo yo en la pizarra?
9. ¿Estudias tú mucho?
10. ¿Explica ella la lección?

2 Algunos verbos que tienen formas irregulares en el presente de indicativo

Some common verbs with irregular forms in the present indicative tense are:

decir *to say, tell*	**digo** **dices** **dice** decimos decís **dicen**
estar *to be*	**estoy** **estás** **está** estamos estáis **están**
haber *to have* (aux.)	**he** **has** **ha** **hemos** habéis **han**
ir (a + obj. or inf.) *to go (to)*	**voy** **vas** **va** **vamos** vais **van**
oír *to hear*	**oigo** **oyes** **oye** oímos oís **oyen**
poder *to be able, can*	**puedo** **puedes** **puede** podemos podéis **pueden**
querer *to wish, want*	**quiero** **quieres** **quiere** queremos queréis **quieren**
ser *to be*	**soy** **eres** **es** **somos** **sois** **son**
tener *to have* (possess)	**tengo** **tienes** **tiene** tenemos tenéis **tienen**
venir (a + obj. or inf.) *to come (to)*	**vengo** **vienes** **viene** venimos venís **vienen**

---

[1] Adverbs of manner are often formed by adding **-mente** to the feminine singular of adjectives.

3 Otros verbos que tienen formas irregulares en el presente de indicativo

In the present indicative tense, a number of verbs are irregular only in the first person singular: **caer,** *to fall* (**caigo**); **dar,** *to give* (**doy**); **hacer,** *to do, make* (**hago**); **poner,** *to put, place* (**pongo**); **saber,** *to know* (a fact), *know how* (**sé**);. **salir** (**de** + *obj.*), *to go out* (*of*), *leave* (**salgo**); **traer,** *to bring* (**traigo**); **valer,** *to be worth* (**valgo**); **ver,** *to see* (**veo**). Also irregular only in the first person singular are **conducir,** *to drive, conduct* (**conduzco**); **conocer,** *to know, be acquainted with* (someone or something) (**conozco**); **escoger,** *to choose* (**escojo**).

See Appendix D, page 231, for accented forms in the present indicative tense of **enviar,** *to send,* and **continuar,** *to continue;* also see pages 230–231 for forms of verbs ending in **-uir: huir,** *to flee.*

EJERCICIOS

A. Lean en español, supliendo (*supplying*) la forma correcta del verbo entre paréntesis en el presente de indicativo:

1. (decir) —¿Qué le _____ tú a Margarita? —Yo no le _____ nada.   2. (estar) —¿Dónde _____ yo ahora? —Usted _____ cerca de la mesa.   3. (poder) —¿_____ ustedes esperar unos minutos? —Sí, _____ esperar un rato.   4. (ir) —¿_____ usted a asistir a esta clase? —Sí, _____ a asistir a esta clase este semestre.   5. (venir) —¿Quién _____ a ayudar a Pablo? —Yo _____ a ayudarlo esta noche.   6. (tener) —¿_____ ustedes que buscar la cartera? —Sí, _____ que buscarla.   7. (querer) —¿_____ ustedes ir a clase? —Sí, _____ ir allá ahora.   8. (ser) —¿_____ tú estudiante? —Sí, _____ estudiante.   9. (hacer) —¿Qué _____ tú ahora? —No _____ nada.   10. (salir) —¿_____ yo de capa temprano? —Sí, tú _____ a las siete y media.   11. (conocer) —¿_____ tú a mi tía? —Sí, la _____ muy bien.   12. (saber) —¿_____ usted la lección? —Sí, la _____ bastante bien.   13. (enviar) —¿Les _____ ustedes flores a sus novias? —Sí, les _____ flores a menudo.   14. (traer) —¿Me _____ usted el boleto? —Sí, le _____ el boleto pronto.

B. Para expresar en español:

1. I know that Paul is not coming to class.   2. Are you (*pl.*) going to wait for the bus?   3. I want to buy the tickets soon.   4. I see that Margaret is near the door. 5. I'm putting the things on the table.   6. Joseph says that he drives well.   7. Do you (*fam. sing.*) want to attend this class?   8. Louise explains that she has to look for the purse.   9. I leave home early.   10. Can they wait a while?   11. Charles sends flowers to me often.   12. I am going to help Paul tonight.

4 Verbos que cambian la vocal radical (*Stem-changing verbs*) en el presente de indicativo

A. Verbs of Class I

cerrar	**cierro**	**cierras**	**cierra**	cerramos	cerráis	**cierran**
volver	**vuelvo**	**vuelves**	**vuelve**	volvemos	volvéis	**vuelven**
jugar	**juego**	**juegas**	**juega**	jugamos	jugáis	**juegan**

Certain verbs ending in **-ar** and **-er** have regular endings, but the stem vowel **e** becomes **ie** and **o** becomes **ue** when stressed, that is, in the three singular forms and in the third person plural. Verbs of this type are indicated: **cerrar (ie)**, **volver (ue)**. **Jugar** is the only stem-changing verb in which **u** becomes **ue**.

Some verbs of Class I are:

almorzar (ue)   to take (eat, have) lunch
cerrar (ie)   to close
comenzar (ie) (a + *inf.*)   to commence (to), begin (to), start (to)
contar (ue)   to count; to tell, relate
costar (ue)   to cost
devolver (ue)   to return, give back
empezar (ie) (a + *inf.*)   to begin (to), start (to)
encontrar (ue)   to encounter, find

envolver (ue)   to wrap (up)
jugar (ue)   to play (*a game*)
pensar (ie)   to think, believe; + *inf.* to intend
perder (ie)   to lose, miss (*something*)
recordar (ue)   to recall, remember
sentarse (ie)   to sit down
volver (ue)   to return, come back

EJERCICIO

Repitan la frase; luego, al oír un sujeto nuevo, substitúyanlo en la frase, cambiando la forma del verbo cuando sea necesario:

1. *Pablo* comienza a leer.
   (Yo, Carmen y yo, Tú, Usted y él, Ricardo)
2. *Nuestros amigos* almuerzan temprano.
   (Mi hermano, Diana y yo, Yo, Ustedes, Tú)
3. ¿Juegan *ustedes* al tenis?
   (tú, usted, Ramón y Luis, nosotros, yo)
4. *Juan* piensa esperar aquí.
   (Tú, Yo, Juan y yo, Uds., ella)
5. *Los muchachos* vuelven pronto.
   (Marta, Tú, Nosotros, Yo, Uds.)

B. Verbs of Class II

sentir	**siento**	**sientes**	**siente**	sentimos	sentís	**sienten**
dormir	**duermo**	**duermes**	**duerme**	dormimos	dormís	**duermen**

When the stem of certain -ir verbs is stressed, the stem vowel e becomes ie and o becomes ue, like Class I verbs, which end in -ar and -er. Later you will review forms in which the stem vowel e of these verbs becomes i and o becomes u. These verbs are designated: **sentir (ie, i), dormir (ue, u)**.

Some verbs of Class II are:

divertirse (ie, i)   to have a good time, amuse oneself
preferir (ie, i)   to prefer

sentir (ie, i)   to feel, regret, be sorry
dormir (ue, u)   to sleep

C. Verbs of Class III

pedir	**pido**	**pides**	**pide**	pedimos	pedís	**piden**

Class III verbs, which also end in -ir, change the stem vowel e to i (never to ie) in the same forms as Class II verbs. Such verbs are designated: **pedir (i, i)**.

Some verbs of Class III are:

pedir (i, i)   to ask for, request
repetir (i, i)   to repeat
seguir[1] **(i, i)**   to follow, continue

servir (i, i)   to serve
vestirse (i, i)   to get dressed, dress (*oneself*)

EJERCICIOS

A. Repitan la frase; luego, al oír un sujeto nuevo, substitúyanlo en la frase, cambiando la forma del verbo cuando sea necesario:

1. *Elena* no duerme mucho.
   (Elena y Clara, Yo, Nosotros, Ustedes, Él)
2. ¿Le pide *usted* a Margarita un favor?
   (Isabel, tú, nosotros, ustedes, yo)

B. Lean en español, supliendo la forma correcta del verbo entre paréntesis en el presente de indicativo:

1. ¿A qué hora (almorzar) _____ ustedes?   2. ¿Saben ellos si María (pensar) _____ acompañarlos?   3. A veces Ricardo (perder) _____ el autobús. 4. ¿Cuánto (costar) _____ ese coche?   5. Yo (devolver) _____ los libros a la

---

[1] See Appendix D, pages 229–230, for the first person singular present indicative tense of verbs with changes in spelling, including those ending in -guir: seguir (sigo).

biblioteca.   6. Ellas (sentir) _____ no estar aquí.   7. ¿Por qué no le (pedir)
_____ tú a Luis el lápiz y papel?   8. Yo (seguir) _____ trabajando en el
centro.   9. Mis amigos (preferir) _____ ir al concierto.   10. Los estudiantes
siempre (repetir) _____ las frases.   11. Mi hermano (vestirse) _____ rápidamente.   12. La joven (envolver) _____ las cosas.

C. Para expresar en español:

1. I remember the word.   2. Paul is beginning to speak Spanish.   3. Do you
(*pl.*) intend to go to the concert?   4. Mary and I return home at six o'clock.
5. The students have a good time.   6. I ask for books in the library.   7. Richard
says that you (*fam. sing.*) always sleep very well.   8. Do you (*pl.*) play tennis
often?   9. Do you (*fam. sing.*) prefer to leave home early?   10. Carmen is start-
ing to serve coffee.

5 El artículo definido, el género (*gender*) y el número de los sustantivos

A. The masculine forms of the definite article (*the*), used in Spanish to denote a
specific noun, are **el** (*singular*) and **los** (*plural*); the feminine forms are **la** and
las. Since Spanish nouns have many endings, learn the definite article with
each noun.

B. Nouns referring to male beings, most nouns ending in **-o,** days of the week, the
names of languages, certain nouns ending in **-ma, -pa, -ta,** and infinitives used as
nouns, are masculine:

| **el viernes** Friday | **el español** Spanish | **el mapa** map |

BUT: **la mano** hand
la radio[1] radio (*as a means of communication*)
la foto (*abbreviation of* **fotografía**) photo

Nouns referring to female beings and most nouns ending in **-a** (except those
ending in **-ma, -pa, -ta**) or in **-(c)ión, -dad, -tad, -tud, -umbre, -ie** are feminine:

| **la invitación** invitation | **la reunión** meeting | **la verdad** truth |

BUT: **el día** day
el avión (air)plane
el programa program

---

[1] **El radio,** *radio, radio set,* is gradually being used more widely, especially in Spanish America, than **la radio,**
radio, as a network or means of communication.

Some nouns ending in -a, particularly in -ista, are either masculine or feminine: el (la) artista, *artist* (man or woman).

The gender of other nouns must be learned by observation:

el deporte sport   **la gente** people   **el té** tea   **la leche** milk

Many nouns ending in -o, particularly those of relationship, have a corresponding feminine form ending in -a: **el hijo,** *son,* **la hija,** *daughter;* **el primo,** *cousin* (m.), **la prima,** *cousin* (f.); **el tío,** *uncle,* **la tía,** *aunt.*

Certain nouns denoting rank or relationship may be used in the masculine plural to refer to individuals of both sexes: **los muchachos,** *the boys, the boy(s) and girl(s);* **los hermanos,** *the brothers, the brother(s) and sister(s).*

C. In general, to form the plural of nouns, add -s to those ending in an unaccented vowel and -es to those ending in a consonant, including **y.** Most nouns ending in an unstressed syllable ending in -s and most family names do not change in the plural: **el (los) paraguas,** *umbrella(s),* **el (los) tocadiscos,** *record player(s),* **el (los) lunes,** *Monday(s);* **Ruiz** (family name), **los Ruiz,** *the Ruiz family.* **Los señores Ruiz** means *Mr. and Mrs. Ruiz.*

Singular	*Plural*
la amiga friend (*f.*)	**las amigas** friends
el jardín garden	**los jardines** gardens
la joven young woman	**las jóvenes** young women
el examen examination, test	**los exámenes** examinations, tests

Note that the accent mark is not written on the plural **jardines** and that it is added on the plurals **jóvenes** and **exámenes** to keep the stress on the same syllable as in the singular. Nouns ending in -z change the **z** to **c** before -es, and those ending in -ión drop the accent mark in the plural: **el lápiz, los lápices; la reunión, las reuniones.**

EJERCICIOS

A. Después de oír el sustantivo, repítanlo empleando el artículo definido; luego, repitan la frase en el plural.

MODELO: mapa   *el mapa, los mapas*

1. hijo 2. amiga 3. parque 4. mano 5. autobús 6. universidad 7. mes
8. ciudad 9. viaje 10. jardín 11. librería 12. país 13. día 14. noche
15. avión 16. miércoles 17. flor 18. foto 19. vez 20. examen

B. Repitan cada oración (*sentence*); luego, repítanla otra vez (*again*), cambiando los sustantivos al plural y haciendo los otros cambios necesarios.

MODELO: El amigo de ella trae su libro.   *El amigo de ella trae su libro.*
Los amigos de ellas traen sus libros.

1. La muchacha deja el lápiz en su cuarto.   2. El artista le explica el cuadro al estudiante.   3. La mujer siempre pasa por la calle el sábado.   4. La profesora de francés no sabe la canción.   5. El muchacho habla del plan para la próxima reunión.   6. El joven no puede aceptar mi invitación.   7. El profesor de español va a hablar sobre un problema social.   8. La estudiante mira la foto del parque nacional.

6   Usos del artículo indefinido

The indefinite article **un** (*m.*), **una** (*f.*), *a, an,* is regularly repeated before each noun in a series:

Inés tiene un reloj y una pulsera.   Inez has a watch and (a) bracelet.

The plural forms **unos, -as** mean *some, any, a few, several,* or *about* (in the sense of *approximately*). Normally *some* and *any* are expressed in Spanish only when emphasized:

Hay unas cintas sobre la mesa.   There are some tapes on the table.
Mi tío tiene unos cincuenta años.   My uncle is about fifty years old.

BUT: **¿Tiene usted dinero?**   Do you have any (some) money?
No tenemos que tomar notas.   We don't have to take (any) notes.

After **ser** the indefinite article is generally not used with *unmodified* predicate nouns which indicate profession, occupation, religion, nationality, rank, or political affiliation:

El padre de Isabel es abogado.   Betty's father is a lawyer.

BUT: **Mi tía es una buena profesora.**   My aunt is a good teacher (*f.*).

EJERCICIO

Lean en español, supliendo la forma correcta del artículo indefinido cuando sea necesario:

1. La muchacha tiene _____ disco y _____ cinta.   2. ¿Es _____ mexicana tu amiga?   3. Carolina es _____ colombiana muy simpática.   4. ¿Hay _____ carteles en la pared?   5. ¿Saca usted _____ fotos a menudo?   6. ¿Es _____ médico el señor Solís?   7. Dicen que es _____ médico distinguido.   8. Hay _____ quince muchachos en la reunión. 9. A veces Laura trae _____ revistas a clase.   10. Necesito comprar _____ cuaderno y _____ lápiz.

Glosario[1] (*Glossary*)

a clase   to class
a las (seis)[2]   at (six) o'clock
a las (siete) y media   at half past
   (seven), at (7):30
a menudo   often, frequently
¿a qué hora?   at what time?
a veces   at times
asistir a   to attend, be present at
ayudar (a + *inf.*)   to help (to)
el cartel   poster
cerca de *prep.*   near
dejar   to leave (*behind*)
después de *prep.*   after
esta noche   tonight
(estar) en el centro   (to be)
   downtown

jugar (ue) (a + *obj.*)   to play (*a game*)
Lección primera   Lesson One
los señores (Ruiz)   Mr. and Mrs.
   (Ruiz)
otra vez   again, another time
pasar por   to pass (go, come) by *or*
   along
profesor (de español)   (Spanish)
   teacher (*m.*)
profesora (de francés)   (French)
   teacher (*f.*)
sacar (fotos)   to take (photos)
salir de casa   to leave home
tener . . . años   to be . . . years old
tener que + *inf.*   to have to, must
   + *inf.*

---

[1] All the expressions used in the explanations and exercises of each lesson and occasional individual words
not used in the active vocabularies of Turk, Espinosa, and Haro, *Foundation Course in Spanish*, Heath, 1981,
or in Turk and Allen, *El español al día*, Book II, Heath, 1979, are given in this section for reference.
[2] Parentheses are used in the Glosarios and end vocabularies to indicate that other words or expressions
may be substituted; for example, in this expression another numeral could be used instead of **seis.**

LECCIÓN DOS

Formas de mandato correspondientes a **usted, ustedes** · Formas de mandato
correspondientes a **tú** · Palabras interrogativas y exclamaciones · La **a**
personal · El participio presente · Usos de **conocer** y **saber**

1 Formas de mandato (*Command forms*) correspondientes a **usted, ustedes**

Infinitive	Stem	Singular	Plural
tomar	tom-	tome Ud.[1]	tomen Uds.[1]
comer	com-	coma Ud.	coman Uds.
abrir	abr-	abra Ud.	abran Uds.
traer	**traig-**	**traiga** Ud.	**traigan** Uds.
cerrar (ie)	**cierr-**	**cierre** Ud.	**cierren** Uds.
volver (ue)	**vuelv-**	**vuelva** Ud.	**vuelvan** Uds.
pedir (i, i)	**pid-**	**pida** Ud.	**pidan** Uds.
seguir (i, i)	**sig-**	**siga** Ud.	**sigan** Uds.

In Spanish, the stem for the formal command forms of all verbs, except the five which
follow, is that of the first person singular present indicative tense. (In reality, the
formal command forms are those of the third person singular and plural of the present
subjunctive tense, which will be discussed later.) **Usted (Ud.)** and **ustedes (Uds.)**
are usually expressed with the verb and are placed after it; in a series of commands,
however, it is not necessary to repeat **usted** or **ustedes** with each verb.

Infinitive	1st Sing. Pres. Ind.	Singular Command	Plural Command
dar	**doy**	**dé** Ud.	**den** Uds.
estar	**estoy**	**esté** Ud.	**estén** Uds.
ir	**voy**	**vaya** Ud.	**vayan** Uds.
saber	**sé**	**sepa** Ud.	**sepan** Uds.
ser	**soy**	**sea** Ud.	**sean** Uds.

Remember that certain verbs ending in **-car, -gar, -zar** change **c** to **qu**, **g** to **gu**, and **z** to
c before the endings **-e (-é)**, **-en**: **busque(n) Ud(s)., llegue(n) Ud(s)., empiece(n) Ud(s).**

---

[1] In writing, **usted** and **ustedes** may be abbreviated to **Ud.** and **Uds.** or **Vd.** and **Vds.**

Some infinitives of these types given in Lección primera are: **almorzar (ue)**, **buscar,**
comenzar (ie), **empezar (ie)**, **jugar (ue)**, and **sacar.** Others are:

acercarse	to approach	**pagar**	to pay (for)
entregar	to hand (over, in), turn in,	**practicar**	to practice
	deliver	**tocar**	to play (*music*)

EJERCICIOS

A. Repitan la frase; luego, repítanla otra vez, cambiando el mandato al plural:

1. Pase Ud., por favor. 2. Espere Ud. unos minutos. 3. Aprenda Ud. las
palabras. 4. Escriba Ud. la composición. 5. Siéntese[1] Ud. allí. 6. No le[1]
permita Ud. entrar. 7. No siga Ud. cantando. 8. Traiga Ud. refrescos antes
de salir. 9. Ponga Ud. los cuadernos en la mesa. 10. No juegue Ud. aquí.

B. Para contestar afirmativa y luego negativamente[2] en español, cambiando el verbo
a la forma de mandato correspondiente a **usted** o **ustedes**, según los modelos.

MODELOS: ¿Abro la puerta?   *Sí, abra Ud. la puerta.*
  No, no abra la puerta.

  ¿Abrimos los libros? *Sí, abran Uds. los libros.*
  No, no abran los libros.

1. ¿Entro en el cuarto?	6. ¿Seguimos leyendo?
2. ¿Traigo las cosas?	7. ¿Vamos al café?
3. ¿Busco un regalo?	8. ¿Empezamos a cantar?
4. ¿Pago la cuenta?	9. ¿Ponemos las maletas aquí?
5. ¿Cierro la ventana?	10. ¿Salimos a tomar café?

C. Para expresar en español de dos maneras (*in two ways*): primero, empleando la
forma de mandato correspondiente a **Ud.**, y luego la forma correspondiente a
Uds.:

1. Look at the map. 2. Learn the words. 3. Repeat the sentence. 4. Leave at
six o'clock. 5. Don't arrive late. 6. Don't take the photos now. 7. Don't
continue singing. 8. Don't go to the library, please.

---

[1] For review of object pronouns and their position with respect to verbs used in commands, see section
3, B, page 24.

[2] When two or more adverbs in **-mente** are used in a series, **-mente** is added only to the last one.

2   Formas de mandato correspondientes a **tú**

Familiar singular commands are:

Affirmative	Negative	Affirmative	Negative
toma (tú)	no tomes (tú)	**vuelve** (tú)	no **vuelvas** (tú)
come (tú)	no comas (tú)	**pide** (tú)	no **pidas** (tú)
abre (tú)	no abras (tú)	busca (tú)	no **busques** (tú)

The affirmative singular command has the same form as the third person singular of the present indicative tense in all verbs except the nine which follow. This form is often called the singular imperative. The subject pronoun **tú** is omitted except for emphasis.

The negative familiar singular command is the second person singular of the present subjunctive tense. (See page 95)

The nine verbs which have irregular familiar singular command forms are:

decir	**di**	no **digas**	ser	**sé**	no **seas**
hacer	**haz**	no **hagas**	tener	**ten**	no **tengas**
ir	**ve**	no **vayas**	valer	**val** (vale)	no **valgas**
poner	**pon**	no **pongas**	venir	**ven**	no **vengas**
salir	**sal**	no **salgas**			

Note these examples of familiar singular commands of certain reflexive verbs:

levantarse	**levántate** (tú)	get up	no te **levantes**	don't get up
sentarse	**siéntate** (tú)	sit down	no te **sientes**	don't sit down
vestirse	**vístete** (tú)	get dressed	no te **vistas**	don't get dressed
ponerse	**ponte** (tú)	put on	no te **pongas**	don't put on
irse	**vete** (tú)	go away	no te **vayas**	don't go away

EJERCICIOS

A. Para contestar afirmativa y luego negativamente en español, cambiando el verbo a la forma de mandato correspondiente a **tú.**

MODELO: ¿Abro el libro?   *Sí, abre el libro.   No, no abras el libro.*

1. ¿Escribo la frase?
2. ¿Llevo los paquetes?
3. ¿Salgo al patio ahora?
4. ¿Sirvo los refrescos?

5. ¿Me siento aquí?
6. ¿Me pongo los[1] guantes?
7. ¿Me levanto de la silla?
8. ¿Me voy con Ana esta tarde?

---

[1] For the use of the definite article in Spanish for the possessive adjective in English, see Lección seis, page 58.

B. Para expresar en español empleando la forma correspondiente a **tú,** primero afirmativa y luego negativamente:

1. Write the composition. 2. Come with the other students. 3. Do that tomorrow. 4. Return the books today. 5. Leave early. 6. Get up before eight o'clock. 7. Sit down near the table. 8. Put on your gloves. 9. Look for the photos. 10. Pay the bill now.

3 Palabras interrogativas y exclamaciones

A. Interrogative words

1. **¿Quién? (***pl.* **¿Quiénes?)** *Who? Whom?* refers only to persons; it requires the personal (or distinctive) **a** when used as the object of a verb:

   ¿Quién entra?   Who is entering?
   ¿A quiénes vas a invitar?   Whom are you going to invite?

   Whose? can only be expressed by **¿De quién(es)?** and the verb **ser:**

   ¿De quién es la bicicleta?   Whose bicycle is it?

   All interrogatives bear the written accent mark in both direct and indirect questions:

   No sé quién grita.   I don't know who is shouting.

2. **¿Qué?** *What? Which?* is both a pronoun and an adjective; as an adjective, it may mean *Which?* For a definition, **¿Qué?** is used with **ser:**

   ¿Qué va a pasar esta tarde?   What is going to happen this afternoon?
   ¿Qué le envías a Luisa?   What are you sending (to) Louise?
   ¿Qué cartel traen Uds.?   Which poster are you bringing?
   ¿Qué es un examen?   What is an examination?
   —¿Qué es Ramón? —Es abogado.   "What is Raymond?" "He is a lawyer."

3. **¿Cuál? (¿Cuáles?)** *Which one (ones)? What?* asks for a selection, and is regularly used only as a pronoun. With **ser,** use **¿Cuál(es)?** for *What?* unless a definition or identification is asked for:

   ¿Cuál de los cuadros prefieres?   Which (one) of the pictures do you prefer?
   ¿Cuál es la capital de Chile?   What (i.e., Which city) is the capital of Chile?

4. Other interrogative words are:

   ¿cómo? how? in what way?   **¿cuánto, -a?** how much?
   ¿cuándo? when?   **¿cuántos, -as?** how many?

¿**dónde?**   where?

¿**adónde?**   where? (*with verbs of motion*)

¿**por dónde se va . . . ?**   how (i.e., by what route) does one go . . . ?

¿**para qué?**   why? for what purpose?

¿**por qué?**   why? for what reason?

¿**qué clase de . . . ?**   what kind of . . . ?

¿**qué tal?**   how are you? how goes it?

¿**Cuántas personas hay aquí?**   How many people are there here?

¿**Adónde van ellos?**   Where are they going?

¿**Cómo se puede hacer eso?**   How can one do that?

¿**Cómo te gusta el café? ¿Con azúcar?**   How do you like your coffee? With sugar?

The last sentence refers to one's taste. *How do you like . . . ?* in the sense of *What do you think of . . . ?* is expressed by ¿**Qué le (te) parece . . . ?**

—¿**Qué te parece este coche?** —**Me gusta mucho.**   "How do you like this car?" "I like it very much."

B. Exclamations

1. ¡**Qué** + *a noun!* means *What a (an) . . . !* When an adjective follows the noun, either **más** or **tan** must precede the adjective:

¡**Qué lástima (sorpresa)!**   What a pity (surprise)!

¡**Qué libro más (tan) interesante!**   What an interesting book!

When the adjective precedes the noun, **más** or **tan** is omitted; before plural nouns ¡**qué!** means *what!*

¡**Qué buena idea!**   What a good idea!

¡**Qué bonitas flores!**   What beautiful flowers!

¡**Qué** + *an adjective or adverb!* means *How!*

¡**Qué guapo es!**   How handsome he is!

¡**Qué bien tocan todos!**   How well (they) all play!

¡**Qué suerte tienes!**   How lucky (fortunate) you are!

NOTE: In the last example, **suerte** is a noun in Spanish, but an adjective in English; the expression means literally *What luck you have!*

2. All interrogatives may be used in exclamations if the sense permits:

¡**Quién dice eso!**   Who says that!

¡**Cuántas flores tiene ella!**   How many flowers she has!

With verbs, ¡**cuánto!** means *how . . . !*

¡**Cuánto me alegro de verte!**   How glad I am to see you!

¡**Cuánto lo sentimos!**   How we regret it (sorry we are)!

EJERCICIOS

A. Para leer en español supliendo **¿qué?** o **¿cuál(es)?**:

1. ¿_____ pasa en la calle ahora? 2. ¿A _____ hora termina el partido de fútbol? 3. ¿_____ muchachos juegan mejor? 4. ¿_____ de ellos se gradúan este año? 5. ¿_____ otro deporte te gusta? 6. ¿_____ clases tienes hoy? 7. Allí vienen dos jóvenes extranjeros. ¿_____ es Luis Sierra? 8. ¿_____ es el señor Martínez, abogado o médico? 9. ¿A _____ de los cafés prefieres ir? 10. ¿_____ de tus amigos te acompañan?

B. Escuchen cada frase; luego, cámbienla a una exclamación, usando **¡qué!** o **¡cuánto!**.

MODELOS: La noche es muy bonita.   *¡Qué noche más (tan) bonita!* or
¡Qué bonita es la noche!
Siento mucho no saberlo.   *¡Cuánto siento no saberlo!*

1. La tarde es mala.
2. Lola tiene suerte.
3. El parque es grande.
4. Miguel es guapo.
5. Es una sorpresa agradable.
6. Doña María es simpática.
7. Juegas bien al tenis.
8. El jardín es bonito.
9. La muchacha está triste.
10. Me alegro de estar aquí.
11. Nos divertimos allí.
12. Los niños son muy felices.

4 La **a** personal

When the direct object of the verb is a definite person (or persons), or a personified object, the personal or distinctive **a** (not translated in English) regularly introduces the object, except after **tener**:

Vemos a Pepe en el jardín.   We see Joe in the garden.
¿Conoce usted a mis padres?   Do you know my parents?
Temen a la muerte.   They fear death.

BUT: **Tengo ocho primos.**   I have eight cousins.

The personal **a** is also used when the direct object is **quien(es)**, *whom,* **¿quién(es)?**, *whom?* or one of the indefinites or negatives[1] **alguien** and **nadie**, and **alguno, -a**, and **ninguno, -a**, when the last two refer to persons:

¿Esperas a alguien?   Are you waiting for someone?
No veo a ninguno de ellos.   I don't see any (one) of them.

---

[1] See Lección siete, pages 80–82, for discussion of the indefinites and negatives.

The distinctive **a** may also be used before a geographical proper name, unless the name is preceded by the definite article. In current usage the **a** is being omitted more and more in such constructions:

> **Visitan (a) México a menudo.**   They visit Mexico often.
> **Desean ver el Cuzco.**   They want to see Cuzco.

Because of the flexible word order in Spanish, the distinctive **a** is required occasionally to avoid ambiguity when both the subject and the direct object refer to things:

> **La paz sigue a la guerra.**   Peace follows war.

EJERCICIOS

A. Lean en español, supliendo la **a** personal cuando se necesite (*it is needed*):

1. Juan y yo buscamos _____ Margarita. 2. ¿Llamas _____ tu hermana?
3. ¿Ayudas _____ alguien? 4. ¿_____ quiénes esperan ustedes? 5. Jorge conoce bien _____ Madrid. 6. Ana tiene _____ una amiga en Colombia.
7. Conocemos _____ la señora López. 8. Pablo quiere visitar _____ el Uruguay. 9. No veo _____ nadie en la calle. 10. Nosotros saludamos _____ la profesora.

B. Para expresar en español:

1. Whom do you (*fam. sing.*) see? 2. Which article do you (*formal sing.*) want to read? 3. Whose bracelet is this? 4. At what time do the girls leave?
5. Which one of the cities does John prefer? 6. How many students can come to the meeting? 7. We don't know why Mary is going to the bookstore.
8. What a beautiful day! 9. What pretty flowers! 10. How handsome the boy is! 11. What is Diane's father? 12. How sorry I am to arrive late!

5 El participio presente

The present participle, which in English ends in *-ing*, is regularly formed in Spanish by adding **-ando** to the stem of **-ar** verbs, and **-iendo** to the stem of **-er** and **-ir** verbs. The present participle always ends in **-o**:

> tomar   tomando, *taking*   comer   comiendo, *eating*   vivir   viviendo, *living*

Some verbs which have irregular present participles are:

caer	**cayendo** *falling*	oír	**oyendo** *hearing*
creer	**creyendo** *believing*	poder	**pudiendo** *being able*
decir	**diciendo** *saying, telling*	traer	**trayendo** *bringing*
ir	**yendo** *going*	venir	**viniendo** *coming*

In stem-changing verbs, Class II and Class III, the stem vowel **e** becomes **i**, and **o** becomes **u**, in the present participle. Examples:

sentir	**sintiendo**	*feeling*	dormir	**durmiendo**	*sleeping*
pedir	**pidiendo**	*asking (for)*	servir	**sirviendo**	*serving*

One of the principal uses of the present participle is with **estar** to express the progressive forms of the tenses, that is, to stress that an action is (was, has been, etc.) in progress at a given moment:

¿Qué estás haciendo ahora?   What are you doing now?

EJERCICIO

Repitan la frase; luego, repítanla otra vez, cambiando el verbo a la forma correcta del presente de indicativo del verbo **estar** seguida del (*followed by the*) participio presente.

MODELO: Ricardo trae el paquete.   *Ricardo está trayendo el paquete.*

1. Mi hermano lee la revista.   2. Nosotros miramos el mapa.   3. Luisa escribe una composición.   4. Varios estudiantes escuchan discos.   5. Mi mamá duerme la siesta.   6. Nuestra hermana sirve refrescos.   7. Pepe come con sus amigos.   8. Carlos dice algo interesante.

6   Usos de **conocer** y **saber**

Conocer means *to know* in the sense of *to be acquainted with someone, to know (be familiar with) something, to meet* (for the first time):

Yo conozco a aquella señorita.   I know that young lady.
El señor Solís conoce bien la ciudad.   Mr. Solís knows the city well.

Saber means *to know* in the sense of *to have knowledge of, know facts;* followed by an infinitive it means *to know how to, can* (mental ability):

Ya sé quién es.   I already know who he is.
Sabemos que Luis viene pronto.   We know that Louis is coming soon.
Roberto sabe tocar la guitarra.   Robert knows how to (can) play the guitar.

EJERCICIO

Para leer en español, completando las frases con la forma correcta de **conocer** o **saber:**

1. Yo _____ que Margarita es peruana.   2. Quiero _____ si Juan _____ a María Gómez.   3. Nosotros deseamos _____ a Miguel Valdés muy pronto.

4. ¿_____ tú dónde vive ese joven?   5. Nuestra profesora _____ bien el arte mexicano.   6. Mi tío _____ que yo no _____ bien el país.   7. Los estudiantes _____ hablar bien el español.   8. Ana _____ jugar al tenis.

Glosario

alegrarse (de + *obj. or inf.***)**   to be glad (of, to)
antes de *prep.*   before
la **cuenta**   account, bill
dormir (ue, u) la siesta   to take a nap
entrar (en + *obj.***)**   to enter, come (go) in
graduarse (*like* **continuar)**   to graduate
irse   to go away, leave

partido de fútbol   football game
pasar   to pass; to spend (*time*); to happen, go on
pase Ud.   come in
por favor   please (*after request*)
salir a   to come *or* go out on (to, into)
saludar   to greet, say hello to
tener (mucha) suerte   to be (very) fortunate *or* lucky
visitar   to visit, call on

LECCIÓN TRES

Los pronombres personales · Usos de los pronombres personales que designan el sujeto · Posición del pronombre como objeto del verbo · Las formas preposicionales y la construcción redundante · Los pronombres y verbos reflexivos · Posición respectiva de dos pronombres, uno como objeto directo y otro como objeto indirecto · Usos de **gustar** y **querer (a)**

1 Los pronombres personales

Singular

Subject of Verb	Object of Preposition	Direct Object of Verb
yo I	**mí** me	**me** me
tú you	**ti** you	**te** you
él he	**él** him, it (*m.*)	{ **lo, le**[1] him
ella she	**ella** her, it (*f.*)	{ **lo** it (*m., neuter*)
usted you	**usted** you	**la** her, it (*f.*)
		{ **lo, le** you (*m.*)
		{ **la** you (*f.*)

Plural

nosotros, -as we	**nosotros, -as** us	**nos** us
vosotros, -as you	**vosotros, -as** you	**os** you
ellos they	**ellos** them	**los, les**[2] them
ellas they (*f.*)	**ellas** them (*f.*)	**las** them (*f.*)
ustedes you	**ustedes** you	{ **los, les**[2] you (*m.*)
		{ **las** you (*f.*)

2 Usos de los pronombres personales que designan el sujeto

The subject pronouns, except the formal forms for *you* (**usted** and **ustedes**), are omitted unless needed for clearness, emphasis, or when a pronoun is combined with a noun or another pronoun to form a compound subject. **Usted** and **ustedes,** which require the third person of the verb in Spanish, are regularly expressed, although excessive repetition should be avoided. The subjects *it* and *they,* referring to things, are rarely expressed in Spanish, and the impersonal subject *it* is always omitted.

In general, the familiar forms **tú** and **vosotros, -as,** are used when speaking to children, relatives, or close friends with whom one is on a first-name basis. In most of Spanish America, **ustedes** is used for the plural of *you,* both familiar and formal (this practice is followed in this text, except in Lección quince):

Vamos al café ahora.   We are going (Let's go) to the café now.

---

[1] In Spanish America **lo** is more frequently used than **le** as a direct object, meaning *him, you* (formal m.).
[2] In Spain the form **les** is often used instead of **los** as a direct object referring to masculine people.

Indirect Object of Verb	*Singular* Reflexive Object of Verb
me (to) me	**me** (to) myself
te (to) you	**te** (to) yourself
le (se) {(to) him, it (to) her, it (to) you	**se** {(to) himself, itself (to) herself, itself (to) yourself

	Plural
nos (to) us	**nos** (to) ourselves
os (to) you	**os** (to) yourselves
les (se) {(to) them (to) you	**se** {(to) themselves (to) yourselves

Ella lee y él escribe.   She is reading, and he is writing.
Él y ella están en la biblioteca.   He and she are in the library.
Ellas son felices.   They (*f.*) are happy.
Juan y yo buscamos a Carlos.   John and I are looking for Charles.
Ustedes hablan bien el español.   You (*pl.*) speak Spanish well.
Tú hablas mejor que él.   You (*fam. sing.*) speak better than he.

3   Posición del pronombre como objeto del verbo

A. All object pronouns (direct, indirect, and reflexive) are regularly placed immediately before the verb, including the auxiliary verb **haber** in the compound tenses (three major exceptions are explained in B, C, D, below):

Diana no me llama a menudo.   Diane doesn't call me often.
Los he visto[1] en la calle.   I have seen them in the street.

---

[1] See Lección cinco, pages 48–49, for the forms of the present perfect and the pluperfect indicative tenses.

B. Object pronouns are placed after, and are attached to, affirmative commands. (In commands the formal **usted(es)** is regularly expressed, but the familiar **tú** is used only for emphasis.) Note that an accent mark must be written on the stressed syllable of a verb of more than one syllable when a pronoun is added:

> **Tráigalos usted en seguida.**   Bring them at once.
> **Hágame usted el favor de esperar.**   Please wait.
> **Tómalo (tú), por favor.**   Take it, please.

> BUT: **Dame el periódico, por favor.**   Give me the newspaper, please.
> **Hazme (tú) el favor de leer la carta.**   Please read the letter.

In negative commands, however, object pronouns precede the verb and are placed between the negative and the verb:

> **No les escriba usted hoy.**   Do not write to them today.
> **No me digas eso.**   Don't tell me that.
> **No te pongas el vestido nuevo.**   Don't put on the new dress.

C. Object pronouns are usually attached to an infinitive:

> **Empiezo a leerlo.**   I'm beginning to read it.
> **Vamos a sentarnos ahora.**   We are going to (Let's) sit down now.

However, object pronouns may precede conjugated forms of certain verbs and verbal expressions, such as **ir a, querer, poder, saber,** followed by an infinitive:

> **Lo voy a hacer** or **Voy a hacerlo.**   I am going to do it.
> **La quieren ver** or **Quieren verla.**   They want to see her (it).
> **Usted se puede sentar** or **Usted puede sentarse.**   You may (can) sit down.

D. Object pronouns are attached to the present participle, except in the progressive forms of the tenses, in which case they may be attached to the participle or placed before the auxiliary. An accent mark must be written over the stressed syllable of the participle when a pronoun is attached:

> **Dándome los libros, Pepe sale.**   Giving me the books, Joe leaves.
> **Están estudiándolos** or **Los están estudiando.**   They are studying them.

EJERCICIOS

A. Repitan cada frase y luego substituyan el sustantivo en cursiva (*in italics*) con el pronombre correspondiente, según el modelo.

MODELO: Jorge solicita *una beca*.   *Jorge solicita una beca*.   *Jorge la solicita*.

1. ¿Dónde pasa Ud. *las vacaciones?*
2. Llamamos *a nuestros amigos*.
3. Mi hermano compra *el coche*.
4. No practican mucho *el español*.
5. ¿No va Ud. a ver *la película?*
6. Elena busca *a su hermana*.

B. Para contestar empleando formas de mandato afirmativas y negativas, substituyendo el sustantivo con el pronombre correspondiente.

MODELO: ¿Hago *el trabajo?* *Sí, hágalo Ud.* *No, no lo haga Ud.*

1. ¿Traigo *el disco* ahora?
2. ¿Llamo *a los muchachos?*
3. ¿Escribo *la carta?*
4. ¿Aprendo *la canción?*
5. ¿Cierro *las ventanas?*
6. ¿Busco *a mi amigo?*

C. Después de escuchar cada frase, repítanla dos veces, substituyendo el sustantivo con el pronombre correspondiente.

MODELO: Estoy tomando *café.* *Estoy tomándolo.* *Lo estoy tomando.*

1. Estoy estudiando *la lección.*
2. ¿Estás escribiendo *las cartas?*
3. Estamos tomando *refrescos.*
4. Ellas están visitando *a María.*
5. Uds. no están mirando *el mapa.*
6. Inés está buscando *a sus amigos.*

D. Después de escuchar cada frase, repítanla dos veces, substituyendo el sustantivo con el pronombre correspondiente.

MODELO: Voy a hacer *el viaje.* *Voy a hacerlo.* *Lo voy a hacer.*

1. Puedo traer *las revistas.*
2. ¿Vas a pasar *el día* aquí?
3. No queremos dejar *los paquetes* allí.
4. Pepe no desea tocar *la guitarra.*

4 Las formas preposicionales y la construcción redundante

A. The prepositional forms are used only as objects of prepositions. They are the same as the subject pronouns, except for **mí** and **ti:**

Corren hacia mí.   They are running toward me.
¿No quieres charlar con él (ella)?   Don't you (*fam. sing.*) want to chat with him (her)?

When used with **con**, the forms **mí, ti,** and the reflexive **sí** (see section 5, pages 26–27) become **conmigo, contigo, consigo**, respectively:

No van conmigo (contigo).   They aren't going with me (with you [*fam. sing.*]).

B. The prepositional phrases **a mí, a ti, a él,** etc., are used in addition to the direct or indirect object pronoun for emphasis:

Yo la veo a ella, pero no a Felipe.   I see her but not Philip.
Dame a mí la foto, por favor.   Give me the photo, please.

Since the indirect objects **le** and **les** have several meanings, the prepositional forms are often used for clearness. They are also frequently added for courtesy when the direct object pronouns meaning *you* (formal) are used:

Yo le doy a ella las flores.   I'm giving her the flowers.
Mucho gusto en conocerlo (-la) a Ud.   (I'm) very pleased to meet (know) you.

C. When a noun is expressed as the indirect object of the verb in Spanish, the corresponding indirect object pronoun is normally added. With forms of **gustar,** the prepositional form must be used:

Le traigo a Ana la cinta.   I'm bringing Ann the tape.
A Marta le gusta (Le gusta a Marta) el disco.   Martha likes the record.

The prepositional form must also be used when the verb is understood:

Le enseño la foto a él, pero no a ella.   I'm showing him the photo, but not her.

The prepositional form is also used to express a <u>direct</u> object pronoun when the verb is understood: **¿A quién ves? ¿A él?**   *Whom do you see? Him?*

EJERCICIO

Repitan cada frase; luego, substituyan el sustantivo en cursiva con el pronombre correspondiente, según el modelo.

MODELO: Corren hasta *la esquina.*   *Corren hasta la esquina.*   *Corren hasta ella.*

1. Van al río con *Ricardo.*   2. Charle Ud. un poco con *Marta.*   3. Los regalos son para *mis padres.*   4. No hablen Uds. más acerca de *las muchachas.*   5. Ella trabaja en *la tienda.*   6. Hay muchos cuadros en *los cuartos.*   7. No pueden entrar sin *el profesor.*   8. En *la ciudad* hay varios parques.

5   Los pronombres y verbos reflexivos

A. Reflexive pronouns, which are used when the subject acts upon itself, may be direct or indirect objects:

Lucía se sienta.   Lucy sits down.
Vamos a lavarnos las manos.   We are going to (Let's) wash our hands.
Levántese Ud.   Get up.
Estamos desayunándonos.   We are eating breakfast.

The prepositional pronouns **mí, ti, nosotros, -as, vosotros, -as,** and **sí** (third person singular and plural) may be used reflexively: **para mí,** *for myself*; **para sí,** *for himself, herself, yourself* (formal), *itself, themselves* (m. and f.), *yourselves*: **Ella se lo lleva consigo,** *She takes it with her(self)*.

EJERCICIO

Para expresar en español:

1. Sit down here; sit down near him.   2. Are you (*formal sing.*) buying it for yourself, or for her?   3. Jane cannot bring the guitar with her.   4. We want to wash our hands at once.   5. I always get up early in order to eat breakfast with you (*fam. sing.*).   6. Are you (*pl.*) going to take your friends with you to the concert?

B. Reflexive verbs are much more frequent in Spanish than in English. A few verbs are always used reflexively in Spanish, while others may be used either as transitive or intransitive verbs, although with different meanings. Two common verbs which are regularly reflexive in Spanish are:

atreverse (a)   to dare (to)   **quejarse (de)**   to complain (of, about)

Many intransitive verbs in English (that is, verbs that cannot take a direct object) are expressed in Spanish by using the reflexive pronoun with a transitive verb. Note the following verbs:

acercar to bring . . . near	**acercarse (a)** to approach, draw near (to)
acostar (ue) to put to bed	**acostarse (ue)** to go to bed
despertar (ie) to awaken (*somebody*)	**despertarse (ie)** to wake up (*oneself*)
divertir (ie, i) to amuse	**divertirse (ie, i)** to have a good time
lavar to wash (*something*)	**lavarse** to wash (*oneself*)
levantar to raise, lift (up)	**levantarse** to get up, rise
sentar (ie) to seat	**sentarse (ie)** to sit down

Some verbs may be transitive or intransitive in English. These verbs are expressed intransitively in Spanish by making them reflexive. See **lavar,** listed above, and **concentrar** and **vestir (i, i),** listed below. Other examples are:

abrir to open (*something*)	**abrirse** to open (*by itself*), be opened
cerrar (ie) to close (*something*)	**cerrarse (ie)** to close (*by itself*), be closed
desarrollar to develop (*something*)	**desarrollarse** to develop, evolve

With certain verbs the reflexive is translated *to become, get,* or *to be* plus an adjective. A few examples are:

alegrar to make glad
concentrar to concentrate, bring together
vestir (i, i) to dress (*somebody*)

alegrarse (de) to be glad (of, to)
concentrarse to concentrate, be concentrated
vestirse (i, i) to dress (*oneself*), get dressed

Other common verbs whose meaning is changed when used reflexively are:

dormir (ue, u) to sleep
hacer to do, make
hallar to find
llamar to call

poner to put, place

dormirse (ue, u) to fall asleep
hacerse (+ *noun*) to become
hallarse to be found, be
llamarse to call oneself, be named
ponerse to put on (*clothes*); (+ *adj.*) to become

EJERCICIOS

A. Repitan cada frase; luego, al oír un sujeto nuevo, cambien la frase, según el modelo.

MODELO: *Yo* me duermo en seguida.   *Yo me duermo en seguida.*
(José)   *José se duerme en seguida.*

1. *Ana* se pone los guantes.   (Ana y yo)
2. *Yo* voy a sentarme cerca de ella.   (Ricardo)
3. *La niña* se viste despacio.   (Tú)
4. *Roberto* siempre se divierte mucho.   (Roberto y yo)
5. *Jorge* está lavándose la cara.   (Tú)
6. *Juan y José* se despiertan tarde.   (Nosotros)
7. *Diana* se alegra de verlos.   (Ustedes)
8. *Nosotros* no nos quejamos del profesor.   (Carlos)
9. *Él* no se atreve a hacer eso.   (Él y yo)
10. *Ella y yo* vamos a acercarnos al coche.   (Yo)

B. Para expresar en español:

1. They wash the car; they wash their hands.   2. He sleeps six hours; he goes to sleep late.   3. Put (*formal sing.*) the shoes here; put on your shoes.   4. Does Joe's mother dress him? Does he get dressed quickly?   5. Mary raises her hand; Mary gets up.   6. I awaken James; he does not wake up early.   7. Call (*fam. sing.*) the boy; what is his name?   8. Our parents approach the house; we are glad to see them.

6 Posición respectiva de dos pronombres, uno como objeto directo y otro como objeto indirecto

When two object pronouns are used together, the indirect object pronoun always precedes the direct. When both are in the third person, the indirect pronoun (**le, les**) becomes **se**. Since **se** may mean *to him, to her, to you* (formal), *to it, to them,* the prepositional forms are often required in addition to **se** for clarity. A reflexive pronoun precedes any other object pronoun:

> **Pepe nos lo enseña.**   Joe shows it to us.
> **Llévenselo ustedes a ellos.**   Take it to them.
> **Ella puede leérsela a ustedes.**   She can read it to you.
> **No se lo escribas (tú) a ella.**   Don't write it to her.
> **Dándomelo, Margarita se sienta.**   Giving it to me, Margaret sits down.

Remember that an accent mark must be written on the stressed syllable of the verb when two object pronouns are attached to an infinitive, an affirmative command form, or a present participle.

EJERCICIOS

A. Lean en español; luego, contesten las preguntas afirmativamente, substituyendo los sustantivos en cursiva con los pronombres correspondientes, según los modelos.

> MODELOS: ¿Le da Pepe *las cosas a Luisa?*   *Sí, Pepe se las da a ella.*
> ¿Se lava Jorge *la cara?*   *Sí, Jorge se la lava.*

1. ¿Le llevan ustedes *el dinero a los muchachos?*
2. ¿Le escribes *las cartas a Luis?*
3. ¿Está enseñándoles Carlota *los cuadros?*
4. ¿Se están poniendo ellos *los zapatos?*
5. ¿Te estás lavando *las manos?*
6. ¿Vas a leerles *el cuento a los niños?*

B. Para expresar en español:

1. Bring (*pl.*) the package to me; don't take it to her.   2. Louis reads it (*m.*) to us; can you (*fam. sing.*) read it to them also?   3. They are writing (*progressive*) it (*f.*) to Charles; write (*pl.*) it to him.   4. Joe puts on his gloves; he is putting (*progressive*) them on.   5. I want to give them (*f.*) to you (*pl.*), not to him.   6. Don't talk (*pl.*) to Paul about them (*m.*), please.   7. Please (*formal sing.*) send the package to her; send it to her today.   8. Please (*fam. sing.*) wash your face; wash it now, please.

7   Usos de **gustar** y **querer** (a)

A. The English verb *to like,* usually referring to things, is regularly expressed in Spanish by **gustar,** meaning *to please, be pleasing* (*to*). The subject in English (*I, he, you,* etc.) becomes the indirect object in Spanish, and the direct object in English becomes the subject of the Spanish verb; e.g., instead of *She likes the hat,* say *The hat is pleasing to her:* **Le gusta a ella el sombrero.** Normally only the third person singular and plural forms of **gustar** are used. The direct objects *it* and *them* are not expressed in Spanish; the subject, when expressed in Spanish, usually follows the verb:

> **Me (Nos) gusta la foto.**   I (We) like the photo.
> **¿No le gusta a Ud.?**   Don't you like it?
> **Le gustan a ella las blusas.**   She likes the blouses.
> **Me gusta más este coche.**   I prefer this car (I like this car better).

Remember that when a noun is the indirect object of **gustar,** the indirect object pronoun must also be used (see section 4, C, page 26):

> **A Pepe le gustan (Le gustan a Pepe) los discos.**   Joe likes (the) records.

B. **Querer (a)** means *to like, love, feel affection for, a person:*

> **Queremos mucho a Juanita.**   We like Jane very much (We are very fond of Jane).

Vista general de Caracas, Venezuela

EJERCICIO

Repitan cada oración; luego, substituyan las palabras entre paréntesis en la frase, cambiando la forma del verbo cuando sea necesario:

1. Me gusta *la canción*.   (las canciones)
2. Nos gustan *estos estilos*.   (este estilo)
3. A Marta le gustan mucho *los vestidos*.   (ese vestido)
4. ¿Le gusta a Ud. *aquella tienda*?   (aquellas tiendas)
5. ¿No te gusta más *este cartel*?   (estos carteles)
6. No les gusta *esa revista*.   (esas revistas)

Glosario

acerca de *prep.*   about, concerning
la **beca**   scholarship
¿cómo se llama (él)?   what is (his) name?
charlar   to chat
divertirse (ie, i) mucho   to have a very good time
dos veces   two times, twice
en seguida   at once, immediately
gustarle a uno más   to prefer, like better (best)
hacer el (un) viaje   to make *or* take the (a) trip

hágame Ud. (*formal sing.***) el favor de** + *inf.*   please + *verb*
háganme Uds. (*pl.***) el favor de** + *inf.*   please + *verb*
hazme (tú) (*fam. sing.***) el favor de** + *inf.*   please + *verb*
mucho gusto en conocerlo (-la)   (I'm) very glad *or* pleased to know (meet) you (*formal sing.*)
solicitar   to solicit, apply for
un poco   a little; a little while

Repaso primero

A. Formas de verbos en el presente de indicativo. Den la forma del verbo que corresponda a cada sujeto:

1. *yo*   poner, decir, hacer, enviar, dormir
2. *tú*   ser, ir, oír, continuar, cerrar
3. *él*   preferir, pedir, jugar, volver, comenzar
4. *nosotros*   ser, querer, salir, servir, jugar
5. *ustedes*   sentir, pedir, perder, devolver, almorzar

B. Para contestar negativamente en español:

1. ¿Compras (Compra usted) papel en la biblioteca?
2. ¿Empiezas (Empieza usted) a leer el libro?
3. ¿Quieren ustedes esperar un rato?
4. ¿Puedes (Puede usted) ir al café ahora?
5. ¿Sales (Sale usted) de casa antes de las ocho?
6. ¿Juegan ustedes al tenis a menudo?

C. Para contestar afirmativa y luego negativamente en español, cambiando el verbo a la forma de mandato correspondiente a **tú:**

1. ¿Cierro la puerta?
2. ¿Sirvo el café?
3. ¿Salgo al patio?
4. ¿Me siento aquí?
5. ¿Me pongo los zapatos?
6. ¿Me voy esta tarde?

D. Para contestar afirmativamente, cambiando el verbo a la forma de mandato correspondiente a **usted;** luego, repitan la contestación (*answer*), substituyendo las palabras en cursiva con el pronombre, según los modelos.

MODELOS: ¿Tomo *el libro?*   *Sí, tome Ud. el libro.   Sí, tómelo Ud.*
   ¿Tomamos *las cosas?*   *Sí, tomen Uds. las cosas.   Sí, tómenlas Uds.*

1. ¿Traigo *los boletos?*
2. ¿Toco *el disco* ahora?
3. ¿Busco *la revista?*
4. ¿Ponemos *los paquetes* aquí?
5. ¿Practicamos *las canciones?*
6. ¿Pagamos *la cuenta?*

E. Para contestar negativamente, según el modelo.

MODELO: ¿Estás tomando *café?* *No, no estoy tomándolo, pero voy a tomarlo pronto.*

1. ¿Estás escribiendo *la carta?*   3. ¿Estás escuchando *las cintas?*
2. ¿Estás buscando *el cuaderno?*   4. ¿Estás contando *el dinero?*

F. Lean en español, colocando el pronombre correctamente con cada verbo:

1. (me) Laura escribe. Quiere escribir. Escribe tú. No escribas.
2. (nos) Pablo mira. Está mirando. Va a mirar. Miren Uds.
3. (lo) Yo hago. Puedo hacer. Estoy haciendo. No hagas.
4. (te) Tú lavas. Estás lavando. Lava tú. No laves.
5. (se) Ud. sienta. Puede sentar. Siente Ud. No siente Ud.

G. Lean en español; luego, substituyan los sustantivos en cursiva con los pronombres correspondientes:

1. Yo le doy *el regalo a Diana.*   4. Voy a leerle *el artículo a Luisa.*
2. No le lleve Ud. *las cosas a Juan.*   5. Estamos lavándonos *las manos.*
3. ¿Puedes traerle *las flores a Ana?*   6. No le vendas *el coche a tu amigo.*

H. Formas del presente de indicativo. Para expresar en español:

1. He has lunch, sits down in his room, and begins to write a letter.
2. They miss the bus, return home, and play in the patio.
3. Mary loses her purse, finds it in the street, and counts the money.
4. Do you (*fam. sing.*) remember the song? Do you intend to call Mr. Solís?

I. Usos de **gustar** y **querer** (a). Para expresar en español:

1. I like this watch. 2. Do you (*fam. sing.*) like it? 3. We like George's guitar.
4. Mary likes to write articles. 5. Doesn't she like (**las**) roses? 6. We don't like
this magazine. 7. Charles likes Helen. 8. Whom does Caroline like?

J. Usos de las palabras interrogativas y las exclamaciones. Para expresar en español:

1. Whom does Charlotte call? 2. Which (ones) of the boys are going to the
meeting? 3. Why don't you (*pl.*) want to play tennis with us? 4. Whose pencil
is this? 5. How glad I am to see you (*pl.*)! 6. What a surprise! 7. How pretty
Betty is! 8. What a beautiful dress!

K. Expresiones. Para expresar en español:

1. The boys help John often. 2. Can you (*fam. sing.*) go to the concert with us
tonight? 3. They leave home at eight o'clock. 4. We want to take a trip soon.
5. Do you (*pl.*) have to leave at once? 6. John is taking (*progressive*) a nap.
7. They are very lucky. 8. Mr. and Mrs. Ruiz visit Mexico at times. 9. Come
in (*formal sing.*) and sit down near me. 10. Please (*pl.*) bring the pencils and the
notebooks to me, not to him. 11. I know that the girls are going to be downtown
tonight. 12. Mary often listens to the radio after class.

Notas culturales I

Observaciones sobre el español de América

Como la lengua traída a América por los españoles se ha desarrollado° bajo condiciones geográficas e históricas muy diversas, es natural que no se hable una lengua absolutamente uniforme¹ desde México hasta° la Argentina. En realidad, la expresión "el español de América" agrupa modalidades° que no sólo difieren del español peninsular—sobre todo° de la lengua corriente en el norte y centro de España—, sino que° difieren notablemente entre sí.°

    Las diferencias se manifiestan especialmente en la pronunciación. Cubanos, mexicanos, argentinos, puertorriqueños, etc., aun hablando y escribiendo con arreglo a° las mismas normas, pronuncian de distintas maneras.°

    En cuanto a° las diferencias de pronunciación, algunos de los rasgos° del español de América son bien conocidos en todos los países hispánicos y se admiten sin protesta ni reparo° en el trato° corriente de españoles e hispanoamericanos. Tres de estos rasgos son los siguientes:

    1. Como en el sur de España (y fuera de° España en las Islas Canarias, las Filipinas y entre los judíos sefarditas),² no se distinguen la s³ y la z: la confusión de palabras como casar° y cazar° es general.

se ha desarrollado *has developed*

desde ... hasta *from ... to*

agrupa modalidades *brings together types* / **sobre todo** *above all, especially*

no sólo ... sino que *not only ... but*

entre sí *among themselves*

con arreglo a *according to*

de distintas maneras *in different ways*

En cuanto a *As for*

rasgos *characteristics*

reparo *objection* / **trato** *relations*

fuera de *outside (of)*

casar *to marry* / **cazar** *to hunt*

---

¹ **que no se hable . . . uniforme,** *that an absolutely uniform language not be spoken.* (The subject frequently follows the Spanish verb. Also, note the use of **se** with **hable** to substitute for the passive voice; see Lección cinco, page 54. There are several uses of this construction in this section. For the use of the subjunctive mood after impersonal expressions, see Lección diez, page 111.)

² **los judíos sefarditas,** *the Sephardic Jews* (= the Jews who are descendants of the former Jews of Spain and Portugal).

³ For the names of the letters of the Spanish alphabet, see Appendix A, page 202.

34

2. En extensas zonas de América, como también en el sur de España, la **ll** se pronuncia como **y: caye** en lugar de° **calle.**

en lugar de *instead of, in place of*

3. La **s** americana (representando **s** y **z**) se pronuncia en general contra los dientes, como la inglesa, a diferencia de° la española, que es alveolar.[1]

a diferencia de *unlike*

Otros rasgos, en cambio,° aunque se encuentren° también en algunas partes de la Península, pertenecen más bien° al lenguaje familiar y vulgar° y deben evitarse° en el uso culto.° Algunos ejemplos siguen.

en cambio *on the other hand* / aunque se encuentren *even though they may be found* / pertenecen más bien *belong rather* / vulgar *popular* / deben evitarse *should be avoided* / culto *cultured*
habla *speech*

1. En el habla° del Caribe, como también en el sur de España, se aspira[2] la **s** final de sílaba o de palabra: **loh campoh** en lugar de **los campos.**

2. En la misma zona, como en el sur de España, se reduce la **j** española a° una **h** aspirada: **hugar** por **jugar.**

reducirse a *to be reduced to*

3. En la misma zona se confunden° la **r** y la **l** en posición final o en combinación con otra consonante: **comel** por **comer; solpresa** por **sorpresa.**

confundirse *to become confused (mixed)*

4. En algunas partes de América, la **y** (procedente de **y** y **ll**) ha adquirido° el sonido de la **z** inglesa en *azure.*

ha adquirido *has acquired*

Gramaticalmente, el español de América es, en general, idéntico al de° España y las diferencias tienen poca importancia. El fenómeno más interesante es la conservación del arcaísmo **vos**[3] por **tú** en extensas zonas del sur y oeste de América: en la Argentina, el Uruguay, el Paraguay, la América Central y el sur de México (Chiapas). Las regiones que emplean **vos** conservan con él las antiguas formas de plural de segunda persona **cantás** por **cantáis, tenés** por **tenéis, sos** por **sois,** etc., que fueron desechadas° por el español normal en el siglo XVI.

idéntico al de *identical to that of*

fueron desechadas *were cast aside*

El vocabulario del español de América tiene gran interés; abunda en palabras y acepciones arcaizantes,° y la formación de palabras nuevas es muy intensa. La abundancia de palabras indígenas, junto con el interés por el neologismo y los extranjerismos,[4] da carácter especial al vocabulario americano. En las Antillas, el suroeste de los Estados Unidos, México y la América Central, el influjo de Norteamérica ha introducido° muchas palabras inglesas.

arcaizantes *obsolescent*

ha introducido *has introduced*

---

[1] alveolar = a sound made by the tongue touching above and behind the upper front teeth.

[2] **se aspira,** *is aspirated* (= is pronounced as an *h* sound, as in *hat*).

[3] The archaic pronoun **vos,** used in popular speech in parts of Spanish America instead of **tú,** takes the plural form of the verb but is singular in meaning.

[4] **junto con . . . extranjerismos,** *along with the interest in neologisms* (= the use of new words or of new meanings for established words) *and foreignisms* (= the use of foreign words or idioms in Spanish).

PREGUNTAS

Para contestar en español en oraciones completas:

1. ¿Se habla una lengua absolutamente uniforme desde México hasta la Argentina?
2. ¿Qué agrupa la expresión "el español de América"?   3. ¿En qué partes de España es corriente la modalidad de lengua que llamamos "el español peninsular"?
4. ¿Podemos hablar de una pronunciación uniforme del español en Hispanoamérica?
5. ¿Cuál es uno de los rasgos de la pronunciación hispanoamericana que se admite en el trato corriente de españoles e hispanoamericanos?   6. ¿Observa el profesor la pronunciación peninsular de la **z,** o la pronunciación hispanoamericana?

7. ¿Cómo se pronuncia la **ll** en extensas zonas de América y de España?   8. ¿En qué difiere la pronunciación de la **s** española de la hispanoamericana?   9. ¿Cómo se pronuncia la **s** final de sílaba o de palabra en el habla del Caribe?   10. ¿En qué regiones se reduce la **j** española a una **h** aspirada?   11. ¿En qué regiones se confunden la **r** y la **l** en posición final o en combinación con otra consonante?
12. ¿Cómo se pronuncia la **y** (de **y** y **ll**) en algunas partes de América?

13. ¿En qué zonas de América se conserva el arcaísmo **vos** por **tú?**   14. En lugar de **cantáis** y **sois,** ¿qué formas conservan las regiones que emplean **vos?**   15. ¿En qué siglo fueron desechadas de la lengua normal las formas como **cantás** y **sos?**

16. ¿Se encuentran palabras y acepciones arcaizantes en el vocabulario de Hispanoamérica?   17. ¿Hay palabras de origen indígena en el español de América?
18. ¿En qué zonas de América se han introducido muchas palabras inglesas?

EJERCICIO ESCRITO

Escriban un breve informe (*report*), de unas setenta y cinco palabras, sobre uno de los temas siguientes:

1. Algunos rasgos de la pronunciación del español de América.
2. Un arcaísmo gramatical que se conserva en extensas zonas del sur y oeste de América.
3. Observaciones sobre el vocabulario del español de América.

LECCIÓN CUATRO

Formas del pretérito de indicativo de los verbos regulares   ·   Algunos verbos
que tienen formas irregulares en el pretérito de indicativo   ·   Otros tipos de verbos
que tienen formas irregulares en el pretérito de indicativo   ·   Usos del pretérito
de indicativo   ·   Formas del imperfecto de indicativo   ·   Usos del imperfecto de
indicativo   ·   Verbos con significados especiales en el pretérito   ·   Usos de
preguntar y **pedir**

1   Formas del pretérito de indicativo de los verbos regulares

tomar	tomé	tomaste	tomó	tomamos	tomasteis	tomaron
comer	comí	comiste	comió	comimos	comisteis	comieron
vivir	viví	viviste	vivió	vivimos	vivisteis	vivieron

EJERCICIO

Repitan la frase; luego, al oír un sujeto nuevo, substitúyanlo en la frase, cambiando
la forma del verbo cuando sea necesario:

1. *Yo* no esperé a Tomás.
   (Tú, Usted, Los estudiantes, Luisa y yo, Ella)
2. *Los jóvenes* comieron temprano.
   (José y yo, Yo, Diana y Marta, Tú, Carlota)
3. *Mis tíos* vivieron en la Argentina.
   (El señor Díaz, Yo, Mi hermano y yo, Tú, Usted)

2   Algunos verbos que tienen formas irregulares en el pretérito de indicativo

Some common verbs are:

decir	**dije**	**dijiste**	**dijo**	**dijimos**	**dijisteis**	**dijeron**
hacer	**hice**	**hiciste**	**hizo**	**hicimos**	**hicisteis**	**hicieron**
querer	**quise**	**quisiste**	**quiso**	**quisimos**	**quisisteis**	**quisieron**
venir	**vine**	**viniste**	**vino**	**vinimos**	**vinisteis**	**vinieron**
andar	**anduve**	**anduviste**	**anduvo**	**anduvimos**	**anduvisteis**	**anduvieron**
estar	**estuve**	**estuviste**	**estuvo**	**estuvimos**	**estuvisteis**	**estuvieron**
poder	**pude**	**pudiste**	**pudo**	**pudimos**	**pudisteis**	**pudieron**
poner	**puse**	**pusiste**	**puso**	**pusimos**	**pusisteis**	**pusieron**
saber	**supe**	**supiste**	**supo**	**supimos**	**supisteis**	**supieron**
tener	**tuve**	**tuviste**	**tuvo**	**tuvimos**	**tuvisteis**	**tuvieron**
traer	**traje**	**trajiste**	**trajo**	**trajimos**	**trajisteis**	**trajeron**
dar	**di**	**diste**	**dio**	**dimos**	**disteis**	**dieron**
ir, ser	**fui**	**fuiste**	**fue**	**fuimos**	**fuisteis**	**fueron**
ver	**vi**	**viste**	**vio**	**vimos**	**visteis**	**vieron**

In the forms listed, note that:

1. Four verbs have **i**-stems and six have **u**-stems. There are no written accents on any of the forms, and in the first eleven verbs the first person singular ends in **-e** and the third person singular ends in **-o.**
2. The third person singular of **hacer** is **hizo;** the third person plural ending of **decir** and of **traer** is **-eron.**
3. **Ir** and **ser** have the same forms.

EJERCICIOS

A. Repitan la frase; luego, repítanla otra vez, cambiando la forma del verbo al pretérito de indicativo:

1. Yo no hago nada por la tarde. 2. Pepe y yo no vemos a nadie. 3. Laura no quiere ir al cine. 4. Los chicos no pueden quedarse. 5. ¿Adónde vas en avión? 6. ¿Quién te trae muchos regalos? 7. Mi hermana tiene que volver en autobús. 8. Mis amigos no dicen eso. 9. Ella pone todos los paquetes sobre la mesa. 10. Ramón oye el timbre.

B. Para contestar negativamente en español:

1. ¿Estuviste en el centro anoche?
2. ¿Trajo Ud. muchas fotos a casa?
3. ¿Pudiste trabajar ayer por la mañana?
4. ¿Fueron Uds. de compras?
5. ¿Vio Luis el partido de fútbol?
6. ¿Vinieron Uds. a clase el sábado?
7. ¿Les dijiste la verdad a tus amigas?
8. ¿Dieron ellos un paseo?

3 Otros tipos de verbos que tienen formas irregulares en el pretérito de indicativo

A. All verbs ending in **-car, -gar, -zar.** See Lección dos, pages 12–13, and Appendix D for changes in spelling before the ending **-é:**

buscar	**busqué**	buscaste	buscó	buscamos	buscasteis	buscaron
llegar	**llegué**	llegaste	llegó	llegamos	llegasteis	llegaron
empezar (ie)	**empecé**	empezaste	empezó	empezamos	empezasteis	empezaron

B. Certain verbs ending in **-er** and **-ir** preceded by a vowel replace unaccented **i** by **y** in the third person singular and plural of the preterit. Accents must be written on the other four forms. **Caer,** *to fall,* and **leer,** *to read,* have the same changes as **creer,** *to believe,* and **oír,** *to hear:*

creer	creí	**creíste**	**creyó**	creímos	**creísteis**	**creyeron**
oír	oí	oíste	**oyó**	oímos	oísteis	**oyeron**

C. Verbs ending in **-ducir** and **-uir** (except **-guir**) have irregular forms in the preterit tense and also in the present indicative. In Appendix D, review the forms of the models **conducir** and **huir,** pages 230–231.

D. Stem-changing verbs, Class II and Class III,[1] change **e** to **i** and **o** to **u** in the third person singular and plural of the preterit:

	3rd Singular	3rd Plural
sentir	**sintió**	**sintieron**
dormir	**durmió**	**durmieron**
pedir	**pidió**	**pidieron**

SPECIAL NOTE: Remember that the stem vowel of stem-changing verbs, Class I, does not change in the preterit tense.

4   Usos del pretérito de indicativo

The preterit tense, sometimes called the past definite, is a narrative tense. It expresses a single past action or state, the beginning or end of a past action, or a series of acts viewed as a complete unit in the past, regardless of the length of time involved. Duration is often defined by an adverb or adverbial expression; for example, **nunca** regularly requires the preterit:

> **Te llamé hace unos minutos.**   I called you a few minutes ago.
> **Empecé a escuchar la cinta.**   I began to listen to the tape.
> **Luis hizo tres viajes a México el año pasado.**   Louis made three trips to Mexico last year.
> **Diana pasó cuatro semanas allí.**   Diane spent four weeks there.
> **Ella nunca creyó lo que le dije.**   She never believed what I told her.

EJERCICIOS

A. Escriban cada frase, cambiando la forma del verbo al pretérito de indicativo; luego, lean la frase nueva en voz alta (*aloud*):

1. Yo no almuerzo hasta la una.   2. Llego tarde al partido.   3. Me acerco rápidamente al estadio.   4. Pago cuatro dólares por mi billete (boleto).   5. Le entrego el dinero al empleado.   6. Entro y busco un asiento.   7. Empiezo a sacar fotos del partido.   8. Saco ocho o diez fotos.   9. Por la mañana juego al golf. 10. Por la tarde toco unos discos primero.   11. Luego, busco mi libro de español.

---

[1] See Appendix D, pages 232–234, for all stem-changing verbs used in the text.

12. Por fin comienzo a estudiar.   13. Leo bien toda la lección.   14. Practico todas las palabras y las expresiones.   15. A las cinco conduzco mi coche despacio a casa de Ramón.   16. Lo invito a comer conmigo en un restaurante.

B. Repitan la frase; luego, repítanla otra vez, cambiando la forma del verbo al pretérito de indicativo:

1. Yo me despierto tarde.   2. Ellos empiezan a entrar en la clase.   3. La chica pierde el autobús.   4. ¿No cierras tu cuaderno?   5. Laura le devuelve el libro a Enrique.   6. ¿Se sienta Carlos en la sala de clase?   7. María se divierte mucho. 8. ¿Sigue Ud. por este camino?   9. Mi mamá duerme la siesta.   10. Mis hermanos se visten rápidamente.   11. ¿Le pide Ud. a Ana alguna cosa?   12. ¿Repiten ellos las frases?

C. Para contestar afirmativamente:

1. ¿Buscaste a tu amiga?
2. ¿Jugaste al fútbol el sábado?
3. ¿Tocaste la guitarra ayer?
4. ¿Condujo Ud. el coche al centro?
5. ¿Le pidió Ud. algo a Juan?

6. ¿Durmieron Uds. bien?
7. ¿Oyeron Uds. la orquesta?
8. ¿Se puso Ud. el abrigo?
9. ¿Leyó Ud. la revista?
10. ¿Sirvió Carlota café?

D. Para expresar en español:

1. John has a good time; he had a good time last night.   2. Ann asks for a bracelet; she asked for a bracelet.   3. My mother serves refreshments; she served coffee.   4. The teacher repeats the question; he repeated the question. 5. I arrive home at five o'clock; I arrived home early.   6. I practice every day; I practiced an hour and a half.   7. I drive my car often; I drove it downtown today. 8. Henry continues working in the restaurant; he continued working there.

5   Formas del imperfecto de indicativo

A. Regular verbs in the imperfect indicative tense:

tomar	tomaba	tomabas	tomaba	tomábamos	tomabais	tomaban
comer	comía	comías	comía	comíamos	comíais	comían
vivir	vivía	vivías	vivía	vivíamos	vivíais	vivían

B. Three verbs which are irregular in the imperfect indicative tense:

ir	iba	ibas	iba	íbamos	ibais	iban
ser	era	eras	era	éramos	erais	eran
ver	veía	veías	veía	veíamos	veíais	veían

EJERCICIO

Repitan la frase; luego, repítanla otra vez, cambiando la forma del verbo al imperfecto de indicativo:

1. Felipe está en su cuarto   2. No queremos llegar tarde.   3. Yo no sé nada de la película.   4. Es un día muy hermoso.   5. Los vemos todos los días.   6. Ellos van al parque a menudo.   7. A veces los visitamos.   8. Carlos piensa ir a México.   9. Damos un paseo todas las tardes.   10. Siempre tomas café allí.

6   Usos del imperfecto de indicativo

A. General use of the imperfect tense

The imperfect tense, frequently called the past descriptive, describes past actions, scenes, or conditions which were continuing for an indefinite time in the past. The speaker transfers himself mentally to a point of time in the past and views the action or situation as though it were taking place before him. There is no reference to the beginning or end of the action or situation described:

Era un día frío del mes de febrero. El mar ofrecía un color azul obscuro. La madre y su hijo iban tristes y silenciosos por la playa. Cuando se hallaban a mitad del camino más o menos, vieron a lo lejos dos personas que venían hacia ellos.	It was a cold day in the month of February. The sea was a dark blue color. The mother and her son were going along the beach sad and silent. When they were more or less half way, they saw in the distance two people who were coming toward them.

B. Specific uses of the imperfect indicative tense

1. To describe what was happening at a certain time, often equivalent to *was* (*were*) plus the present participle in English:

   Luisa escribía (estaba escribiendo) y María leía (estaba leyendo).   Louise was writing and Mary was reading.

2. To indicate repeated or habitual past action, equivalent to *used to, would,*[1] *was* (*were*) *accustomed to* plus an infinitive:

   Iban a la iglesia todos los domingos.   They went (used to go, would go) to church every Sunday.

---

[1] Do not confuse *would* meaning a habitual action with *would* used as a conditional. **¿Podría (yo) hablar contigo?** *Could I (Would I be able to) talk with you?* (See Lección ocho, pages 87–88.)

3. To describe the background or setting in which an action took place or to indicate that an action was in progress when something else happened (the preterit indicates what happened under the particular circumstances described):

Pepe escuchaba discos cuando yo volví de la biblioteca.   Joe was listening to records when I returned from the library.
Llovía cuando Miguel salió de casa.   It was raining when Michael left home.

4. To describe a mental, emotional, or physical state in the past; thus, the verbs *to believe, know, wish, feel, be able,* etc., are usually expressed by the imperfect rather than the preterit tense in Spanish (see section 7, below):

Yo creía que estabas enferma.   I believed that you were ill.
Ana quería ir a la reunión con él.   Ann wanted to go to the meeting with him.

5. To express indirect discourse in the past:

Pablo dijo que conocía a Jaime.   Paul said that he knew James.
Luis me preguntó si yo podía ir con él.   Louis asked me if (whether) I could go with him.

6. To express time of day in the past:

¿Qué hora era cuando volviste?   What time was it when you returned?
Eran las nueve de la mañana.   It was nine o'clock in the morning (9:00 A.M.).

7 Verbos con significados (*meanings*) especiales en el pretérito

Certain common verbs, such as **saber, conocer**[1]**, tener, querer, poder,** often have special meanings when used in the preterit tense. In general, the imperfect tense indicates existing knowledge, desire, ability, etc., while the preterit tense indicates that the act was or was not accomplished. Contrastive examples are:

Sabíamos que José estaba en Chile.   We knew that Joseph was in Chile. (*Mental state*)
Supimos ayer que él estaba allí.   We found out (learned) yesterday that he was there.

---

[1] **Conocer** may be used in all tenses to mean *to recognize.*

Él conocía bien a Diana.   He knew Diane well.
Él la conoció el mes pasado.   He met her (made her acquaintance) last month.

Carlos quería llamar a Margarita.   Charles wanted to call Margaret.
Carlos quiso llamarla.   Charles tried to call her.

Ana no quería quedarse en casa.   Ann didn't want (was not willing) to stay at home.
Ella no quiso quedarse allí.   She refused to (would not) stay there.

Lupe tenía una carta cuando la vi.   Lupe had a letter when I saw her.
Lupe tuvo dos cartas hoy.   Lupe received (got) two letters today.

Le dije que yo podía buscar la llave.   I told him that I could look for the key (i.e., I was able to look, capable of looking, for the key).
La busqué pero no pude hallarla.   I looked for it but couldn't find it (i.e., I did not succeed in finding it).

EJERCICIOS

A. Repitan cada frase; luego, cambien cada verbo al imperfecto de indicativo:

1. Felipe necesita otro cuaderno.   2. Carmen quiere charlar conmigo todos los días.   3. Pepe y yo no sabemos eso.   4. ¿Puedes tocar la guitarra a veces? 5. Vamos al café a menudo.   6. Son las once de la noche.   7. Hay varios estudiantes en la calle.   8. Yo veo al señor Solís casi todas las tardes.

B. Repitan cada frase; luego, cambien el primer verbo al pretérito y el segundo al imperfecto de indicativo:

1. Miguel dice que quiere cenar con Elena.
2. Ana me pregunta si yo voy al centro con ella.
3. Carlota contesta que no sabe la canción.
4. Mi primo nos escribe que puede venir a visitarnos pronto.
5. Yo sé que la amiga de María no vive aquí.
6. ¿Ves a la muchacha que piensa tocar los discos?

C. Lean cada frase en español, cambiando cada infinitivo en cursiva a la forma correcta del pretérito o del imperfecto de indicativo:

1. Luis *estar* en su cuarto anoche cuando yo *llamar* a la puerta.
2. Él *estudiar* su lección cuando yo *abrir* la puerta.
3. Luis me *decir* que *querer* enseñarme un artículo.
4. Él me *preguntar* si yo *tener* tiempo para leerlo.
5. Yo *sentarme* y él me *entregar* el artículo.
6. Al leerlo, yo *ver* que *estar* bien escrito y que *ser* muy interesante.
7. Mientras yo *estar* leyéndolo, Ramón *llamar* por teléfono.
8. Luis *levantar* el auricular y *contestar* en español.

9. Los dos *charlar* unos minutos y luego Luis *colgar* el auricular.
10. Su amigo *querer* saber si Luis *poder* ir al teatro el sábado.
11. Al poco rato yo *mirar* el reloj y *ver* que *ser* tarde.
12. *Ser* las diez y yo *tener* que irme en seguida.

D. Para escribir en español:

1. Michael told me a few minutes ago that he wanted to eat lunch with Helen.
2. Ann asked me whether I was going downtown with her today.   3. My cousin
(*m.*) finally wrote us that he could come to visit us soon.   4. Charlotte answered
that she could not sing the song because she did not know it well.   5. Did you
(*fam. sing.*) see the girl who intended to play the records?   6. "What time was
it when you (*pl.*) arrived home?" "It was three P.M."   7. John was putting on his
topcoat when I entered his room.   8. When my father was young, he took a
trip to Mexico by bus.   9. Mary often called Jane by telephone when she lived
here.   10. Yesterday afternoon I sat down in the stadium and began to take
photos of the game.

8   Usos de **preguntar** y **pedir**

Preguntar means *to ask* (a question); **preguntar por** means *to ask for* (*about*), *in-quire about*:

> **Ana me preguntó si yo podía ir.**   Ann asked me if (whether) I could go.
> **Te llamé para preguntar por la película.**   I called you to ask about the film.

Pedir (i, i) means *to ask* (a favor), *ask for* (something), *to request* (something of someone)
(the use of **pedir,** *to ask* or *request someone to do something,* will be discussed later):

> **Le pedí a ella el diccionario.**   I asked her for the dictionary.
> **Ella no nos pidió nada.**   She didn't ask us for anything.

With both these verbs (also with **decir** and a few other verbs), the person of whom
something is asked is the indirect object. The neuter pronoun **lo** is used to complete
the sentence if a direct object is not expressed:

> —¿**Pueden ellos acompañarnos?**   —**Pregúnteselo Ud. (a ellos).**   Can they
> accompany us?" "Ask them (lit., Ask it of them)."
> —¿**Le dijiste eso a María?**   —**Sí, se lo dije.**   "Did you tell Mary that?"
> "Yes, I told her."

EJERCICIO

Para expresar en español:

1. I asked Joe whether he was going shopping.   2. He asked the clerk for a
topcoat.   3. Whom did you (*formal sing.*) ask for the dictionary? Inez?   4. Did

you (*fam. sing.*) ask John about the tape?   5. "Is Mary going with us?" "I must ask her (it)."   6. "Did you (*fam. sing.*) tell Jane what you intend to do?" "Yes, I told her (it)."   7. We took a walk this afternoon.   8. John left yesterday morning.   9. We always had time to talk with them.   10. It was ten P.M. when I returned.   11. Did you (*fam. sing.*) go shopping with her?   12. Mr. Díaz made the trip by bus, not by plane.

Glosario

a casa de (Ramón)   to (Raymond's) house
a la iglesia   to church
a lo lejos   in the distance
al poco rato   after (in) a short time (while)
alguna cosa   something, anything
el **año pasado**   last year
el **auricular**   receiver (*telephone*)
ayer por la mañana (tarde)   yesterday morning (afternoon)
colgar (ue)   to hang (up)
dar un paseo   to take a walk
el **empleado**   employee, clerk
en autobús   by (in a) bus
en avión   by (in a) plane
eran las nueve de la mañana   it was nine o'clock in the morning (9:00 A.M.)
eran las tres de la tarde   it was three o'clock in the afternoon (3:00 P.M.)
hace unos minutos   a few minutes ago

hasta la una   until one o'clock
invitar (a + *inf.*)   to invite (to)
ir al centro   to go downtown
ir de compras   to go shopping
lo que   what, that which
llamar por teléfono   to telephone, call by (on the) telephone
llegar tarde   to arrive (be) late
más o menos   more or less, approximately
por fin   finally, at last
por la mañana (tarde)   in the morning (afternoon)
la **sala de clase**   classroom
son las once de la noche   it is eleven o'clock in the evening (11:00 P.M.)
tener tiempo para   to have time to
toda la lección   all the lesson, the whole (entire) lesson
todas las tardes   every afternoon
todos los días (domingos)   every day (Sunday)
(traer) a casa   (to bring) home

LECCIÓN CINCO

1 Formas del participio pasado

Past participles are regularly formed by adding **-ado** to the stem of **-ar** verbs and **-ido** to the stem of **-ar** and **-er** verbs:

| tomar | **tomado** | *taken* | comer | **comido** | *eaten* | vivir | **vivido** | *lived* |

The following verbs have irregular past participles:

abrir	**abierto** *opened*	poner	**puesto** *put, placed*
cubrir	**cubierto** *covered*	romper	**roto** *broken*
decir	**dicho** *said*	ver	**visto** *seen*
escribir	**escrito** *written*	volver	**vuelto** *returned*
hacer	**hecho** *done, made*	devolver	**devuelto** *given back*
ir	**ido** *gone*	envolver	**envuelto** *wrapped (up)*

There is a written accent mark on the following past participles: caer, **caído,** *fallen;* creer, **creído,** *believed;* leer, **leído,** *read;* oír, **oído,** *heard;* traer, **traído,** *brought.*

2 Formación de los tiempos compuestos (*compound*)

The auxiliary verb **haber** is used with the past participle to form the compound or perfect tenses. The present tense of **haber** plus the past participle form the present perfect tense, and the imperfect of **haber** plus the past participle form the pluperfect tense, often called the past perfect tense in English.

Present Perfect		Pluperfect	
Singular	*Plural*	*Singular*	*Plural*
he	hemos	había	habíamos
has } tomado	habéis } tomado	habías } comido	habíais } comido
ha	han	había	habían

Él y yo lo hemos hecho fácilmente. He and I have done it easily.
Ella no se lo ha puesto. She has not put it on.

Ellos ya lo habían visto.   They had already seen it.
¿No la había tomado Ud.?   Hadn't you (Had you not) taken it?

APLICACIÓN: Lean en español, teniendo en cuenta el significado (*bearing the meaning in mind*):

1. he abierto; yo había abierto   2. hemos escrito; habíamos escrito   3. ella ha vuelto; ella había vuelto   4. Ud. ha puesto; Ud. había puesto   5. Uds. lo han roto; Uds. lo habían roto   6. tú te has levantado; tú te habías levantado   7. lo he envuelto; lo habíamos envuelto   8. ¿Lo has traído? ¿Los habías leído?

Remember that: (1) following forms of **haber,** the past participle always ends in **-o;** (2) the form of **haber** and the past participle are seldom separated; (3) negative words precede the form of **haber;** (4) pronoun objects precede the form of **haber** or come between the negative and the form of **haber.**

NOTE: The past participle is often used as an adjective, in which case it agrees with the noun or pronoun it modifies in gender and number: **La taza está rota,** *The cup is broken.* See section 3, A, 4, for the use of **estar** with the past participle.

EJERCICIOS

A. Repitan la frase; luego, repítanla dos veces, cambiando la forma del verbo al pretérito perfecto (*present perfect*) y al pluscuamperfecto (*pluperfect*) de indicativo:

1. Yo veo a Pablo.
2. Ana me escribe una carta.
3. Elena no abre la puerta.
4. Carlos cubre la mesa.
5. Ana y yo vamos a la playa.
6. ¿Qué haces tú?
7. Ustedes lo envuelven.
8. Mis amigos no vuelven a casa.
9. Nos ponemos el traje.
10. Luis no me devuelve el dinero.
11. ¿No los trae usted?
12. ¿Oyes la guitarra?

B. Para contestar negativamente en español, siguiendo los modelos.

MODELOS: ¿Cerraste la puerta?   *No, todavía no he cerrado la puerta.*
　　　　　　¿Salió Ana de casa?   *No, todavía no ha salido de casa.*

1. ¿Abriste el cuaderno?
2. ¿Escribiste el artículo?
3. ¿Recibió Ud. la tarjeta?
4. ¿Envolvió José el paquete?
5. ¿Trajo Elena el vaso?
6. ¿Vieron Uds. la película?
7. ¿Fueron Uds. al cine?
8. ¿Oyeron Uds. la orquesta?
9. ¿Devolvió él los libros?
10. ¿Hicieron ellos el trabajo?

C. Para expresar en español:

1. Paul has not returned the money to his friend yet.   2. We have not had time to go shopping this week.   3. Mary's sister had already written two letters in Spanish.   4. We said that we had seen them (*m. pl.*) yesterday morning.   5. I

know that Martha has put on her new dress.   6. We thought that the boys had gone to the beach.   7. My sister found the bracelet that she had lost (on) Sunday. 8. My aunt called saying that she had missed the plane yesterday.

3   Usos de **estar** y **ser**

A. **Estar** is used:

1. To express location or position, whether temporary or permanent:

Los jóvenes están en casa.   The young people are at home.
¿Dónde has estado?   Where have you been?
Guadalajara está en México.   Guadalajara is in Mexico.

2. With an adjective to indicate a state or condition of the subject, which may be relatively temporary, accidental, or variable:

¿Está caliente[1] el café?   Is the coffee hot?
Las muchachas han estado ocupadas.   The girls have been busy.
Yo sabía que él estaba enfermo.   I knew that he was ill.

3. With the present participle to express the progressive forms of the tenses:[2]

Están esperando el autobús.   They are waiting for the bus.
¿Qué estás haciendo ahora?   What are you doing now?
Pepe estaba descansando en su cuarto.   Joe was resting in his room.
Hemos estado escuchando discos.   We have been listening to records.

4. With the past participle to describe a state or condition resulting from a previous action (in this construction the past participle, which is used as an adjective rather than as a verb, agrees with the subject in gender and number):

Están sentados en el patio.   They are seated in the patio.
La carta está bien escrita.   The letter is well written.
El almuerzo ya estaba preparado.   Lunch was already prepared.

NOTE: Certain verbs, like **encontrarse (ue), hallarse, verse, quedar(se),** are often substituted for **estar:**

¿Dónde nos encontramos ahora?   Where are we now?
La puerta ya se encontraba (se hallaba) abierta.   The door was already open.
Ella quedó sorprendida al saber eso.   She was surprised upon knowing (to know) that.

---

[1] Remember that in a question a predicate adjective normally follows the verb immediately.
[2] The progressive forms of **ir, salir,** and **venir** are rarely used.

B. **Ser** is used:

1. With a predicate noun or pronoun, or an adjective used as a noun, and, less commonly, with an adverb, an infinitive, or a noun clause, to establish an identity with the subject:

Él es abogado y ella es escritora.   He is a lawyer and she is a writer.
Soy yo; es ella.   It is I; it is she.
Allí es donde Juan trabaja.   There is where John works.
Ver es creer.   Seeing is believing.
Lo bueno es que la clase es pequeña.   What is good is that the class is small.

2. With an adjective to express an essential quality or characteristic of the subject that is relatively permanent. This includes adjectives of color, size, shape, nationality, and the like, and also the adjectives **joven, viejo, rico, pobre, feliz:**

Roberto es colombiano.   Robert is a Colombian.
El semestre va a ser interesante.   The semester is going to be interesting.
Estas casas son grandes (pequeñas).   These houses are large (small).
No somos viejos (jóvenes).   We are not old (young).
Aquel señor no es rico (pobre).   That gentleman is not rich (poor).

3. With the preposition **de** to show origin, possession, or material, and with the preposition **para** to indicate for whom or what a thing is intended:

¿De dónde es Carmen?   Where is Carmen from?
¿Es de Diana esta cámara?   Is this camera Diane's?
Estas pulseras no son de oro.   These bracelets are not (of) gold.
¿Para quién es este periódico?   For whom is this newspaper?

4. In impersonal expressions:

Es necesario (mejor) tomar esos cursos.   It is necessary (better) to take those courses.
No es fácil recordar eso.   It is not easy to remember that.

5. To express time of day:

¿Qué hora es?   What time is it?
Es la una y media.   It is half past one (1:30).
Son las once en punto.   It is eleven o'clock sharp.

NOTE: The verb is always plural in expressing time of day, except when followed by **la una,** *one o'clock.*

6. With the past participle to express the passive voice:

Las blusas fueron hechas por Clara.   The blouses were made by Clara.
La comida fue preparada por ella.   The meal (food) was prepared by her.

The passive voice (when the subject of the verb is acted upon by an agent) is formed by the verb **ser** and the past participle. The past participle agrees with the subject in gender and number. The agent *by* is usually expressed by **por;** **de** is used, however, when the action represents a mental or emotional act:

Ella es estimada de todos.   She is esteemed by all.

When a person receives the action of the verb, as in the last example, the third person plural active construction is replacing the passive construction in modern usage:

Todos la estiman.   All esteem her (She is esteemed by all).
Ellas saludaron a Enrique.   They greeted Henry (Henry was greeted by them).

C. **Ser** and **estar** with certain adjectives:

The meaning of some adjectives varies according to whether they are used with **ser** or **estar.** In general, the use of **ser** indicates that the adjective expresses an essential quality or characteristic of the subject, while **estar** indicates a temporary or subjective idea, often expressed as *look, feel, taste,* etc., in English. A few examples which show the contrasts are:

With **ser**	With **estar**
Inés es buena. Inez is good. *(Characteristic)*	**Inés está buena.** Inez is well. *(In good health)*
Pepe es malo. Joe is bad. *(Characteristic)*	**Pepe está malo.** Joe is ill. *(In poor health)*
Él es enfermo. He is sickly. *(Characteristic)*	**Él está enfermo.** He is sick (ill). *(Temporary condition)*
Ella es bonita. She is pretty. *(Characteristic)*	**¡Qué bonita está ella hoy!** How pretty she is (looks) today! *(Appearance)*
La nieve es fría. Snow is cold. *(Characteristic)*	**El té está frío.** The tea is cold. *(Changeable, temporary condition)*
Laura es lista. Laura is clever. *(Characteristic)*	**Laura está lista.** Laura is ready. *(Temporary condition)*
Ana es joven. Ann is young. *(Age regarded as characteristic)*	**Ana está joven hoy.** Ann is (looks) young today. *(Appearance)*

EJERCICIOS

A. Para contestar negativa y luego afirmativamente en español, según el modelo.

MODELO: ¿Es ella escritora?   *No, ella no es escritora.*
¿Profesora?   *Sí, ella es profesora.*

1. ¿Es abogado el padre de Pablo? ¿Ingeniero?
2. ¿Vive allí su amigo? ¿Aquí?
3. ¿Son largos los artículos? ¿Cortos?
4. ¿Es de Cuba aquel estudiante? ¿De la Argentina?

5. ¿Son nuevas las guitarras? ¿Viejas?

6. ¿Es fácil la lección? ¿Difícil?

7. ¿Están cerradas las puertas? ¿Abiertas?

8. ¿Estaba contenta la muchacha? ¿Triste?

9. ¿Eran las tres cuando ella llegó? ¿Las cinco?

10. ¿Era pequeño el parque? ¿Grande?

B. Para expresar en español:

1. Our friends are young.   2. This magazine is for Richard.   3. My sister is not ready yet.   4. Ann and I are listening (*progressive*) to records.   5. We know that it is necessary to practice a lot.   6. Carlos López is from Mexico.   7. The young lady is very charming.   8. This coffee is not very cold.   9. This watch is not gold.   10. Joseph's brother is not very ill.   11. Is this camera Robert's? 12. Our friends say that the gentleman is very wealthy.

C. Para completar con la forma correcta de **estar** o **ser** en el presente de indicativo, menos en 17 y 18:

1. ¿Qué _____ la tía de Luisa? ¿_____ escritora?   2. Ricardo _____ de España; _____ español.   3. Lima, que _____ una ciudad muy grande, _____ en el Perú.   4. —¿Qué hora _____? —Creo que _____ las dos y media.   5. _____ mejor decir que nosotros no _____ ni ricos ni pobres. 6. Aunque aquella señora _____ rica, nunca _____ muy contenta.   7. La novia de Felipe _____ rubia; se dice que _____ muy simpática.   8. —¿Cómo _____ tú? ¿_____ muy cansado?   9. Los Andes, que _____ montañas muy altas, siempre _____ cubiertos de nieve.   10. El profesor Sierra no _____ en su oficina hoy porque _____ enfermo.   11. —¿Qué _____ haciendo tú ahora? —Yo _____ escuchando un disco mexicano.   12. _____ fácil aprender el diálogo porque _____ bastante corto.   13. ¿Para quién _____ estas cartas que _____ escritas en portugués?   14. ¿Cuál _____ la fecha de hoy? Y, ¿_____ miércoles o jueves?   15. Aquella chica que _____ sentada en el patio _____ mi prima.   16. Hoy _____ un día muy hermoso; por eso mi mamá _____ trabajando en su jardín.   17. Las puertas _____ (*pres.*) cerradas. ¿Por quién _____ (*pret.*) cerradas?   18. Este edificio _____ (*pret.*) construido por el señor Solís. _____ (*pres.*) bien construido.

4 La construcción reflexiva para expresar el sujeto indefinido *one, they, you, we, people,* y para expresar la voz pasiva

A. To express an indefinite subject, corresponding to *one, they, people, we, you* (indefinite) in English, **se** is used in Spanish with the third person singular of the verb:

Se dice que ella es artista.   They say (People say, One says, We say, It is said) that she is an artist.

No se puede entrar.   One (People, You) cannot enter.

With a reflexive verb, and occasionally with other verbs, **uno** is used:

Uno se levanta tarde los domingos.   One gets up late on Sundays.
No se (Uno no) puede hacer eso.   One cannot do that (That cannot be done).

As in English, the third person plural of the verb may also be used to indicate an indefinite subject:

Dicen que el señor Díaz ya ha salido.   They say (It is said) that Mr. Díaz
has already left.

B. If the subject of a passive sentence is a thing and the doer of the action is not expressed, **se** may be substituted for the passive voice. In this case, the verb is in the third person singular or plural, depending on whether the subject is singular or plural. The reflexive verb normally precedes the subject in this construction:

Allí se habla español.   Spanish is spoken there.
Se abren las tiendas a las diez.   The stores are opened at ten o'clock.
Se escribieron los artículos ayer.   The articles were written yesterday.
Se han publicado algunos en el periódico.   Some have been published
in the newspaper.
Aquí no se cobran cheques.   Checks are not cashed here.

When the subject is singular, as in **Allí se habla español,** the construction may be considered as an indefinite subject, or as a passive sentence: *People speak (They speak, One speaks) Spanish there,* or *Spanish is spoken there.*

EJERCICIOS

A. Después de escuchar cada frase, repitan la frase, cambiándola a la construcción reflexiva, según los modelos.

MODELOS: Cierran la puerta a las cinco.   *Se cierra la puerta a las cinco.*
Aquí no venden libros.   *Aquí no se venden libros.*

1. En el Brasil hablan portugués. 2. No compran zapatos en esta tienda.
3. Cantan muchas canciones populares. 4. No conocen muy bien la música española. 5. Ven un avión grande en el aeropuerto. 6. No abren los edificios hasta las diez. 7. Necesitan mucho dinero para viajar. 8. Abren la biblioteca a las ocho. 9. Estudian español en la mayor parte de las universidades.
10. Durante el primer año toman cursos de inglés.

B. Para expresar en español, usando **se** o **uno** como sujeto indefinido:

1. We (One) cannot do that easily. 2. They say that it is going to rain.
3. How do they do that in Spain? 4. People know that Mr. Solís is in Argentina.
5. One enters through this door. 6. At times one dresses slowly.

5 Observaciones sobre el uso de algunos verbos

Tomar means *to take* in the sense of *to take* (in one's hand), *to take, have, eat,* or *drink* (food, meals, beverages, etc.):

>**Elena, toma el vaso, por favor.**   Helen, take the glass, please.
>**¿Tomas café para el desayuno?**   Do you take (have) coffee for breakfast?
>**Él tomó el avión de las tres.**   He took the three o'clock plane.

Llevar means *to take* (*along*), *take* or *carry* (someone or something to some place):

>**Jorge llevó a su novia al baile.**   George took his girlfriend to the dance.
>**Yo tomé la maleta en la mano y la llevé al coche.**   I took the suitcase in my hand and took (carried) it to the car.

Llevarse means *to take* (*carry*) *away* (often *with oneself*):

>**Él compró una camisa y se la llevó.**   He bought a shirt and took it with him.

Quitar means *to take away* (*off*), *remove from;* **quitarse** means *to take off* (from oneself):

>**Yo quité el libro de la mesa.**   I took (removed) the book from the table.
>**Pepe se quitó los zapatos.**   Joe took off his shoes.

Sacar means *to take out, take* (photos), *get* (a license):

>**Ana sacó muchas cosas de la cartera.**   Ann took many things from her purse.
>**Yo saqué varias fotos en el parque.**   I took several photos in the park.
>**Carlos sacó la licencia.**   Charles got the license.

A few verbs and expressions which include other uses of the English verb *to take* are:

>**almorzar (ue)**   to take (have, eat) lunch
>**dar un paseo (una vuelta)**   to take a walk *or* stroll
>**desayunarse**   to take (have, eat) breakfast
>**despedirse (i, i) (de)**   to take leave (of), say goodbye (to)
>**dormir (ue, u) la siesta**   to take a nap
>**hacer un viaje (una excursión)**   to take *or* make a trip (an excursion)
>**tardar (mucho) en**   to take (very) long to, be (very) long in, delay (long) in
>**tener lugar**   to take place

EJERCICIOS

A. Para contestar afirmativamente en español en oraciones completas:

1. ¿Cuándo diste un paseo? ¿Ayer por la mañana?
2. ¿Cuándo dormiste la siesta? ¿Ayer por la tarde?
3. ¿Adónde llevaron ellos las cosas? ¿A casa?

4. ¿Cuándo hizo Ud. una excursión? ¿El domingo?
5. ¿Qué se quitó Ud.? ¿El abrigo?
6. ¿Qué autobús tomó Ud.? ¿El autobús de las ocho?
7. ¿Adónde llevó Pablo a Marta? ¿Al concierto?
8. ¿Quién se lavó la cara? ¿Usted?
9. ¿Quiénes se desayunaron tarde? ¿Ustedes?
10. ¿Cuál de ellas tardó mucho en salir? ¿Isabel?

B. Para expresar en español:

1. Mr. Sierra took the two-o'clock plane.   2. Did you (*fam. sing.*) take Diane to the dance?   3. My father took a trip to Spain.   4. Why didn't Paul take a walk with you (*fam. sing.*)?   5. I believe that she took a nap.   6. I took some photos at (on) the beach.   7. He took his watch in his hand.   8. I took off my shoes; I took them off.   9. Please (*fam. sing.*) take the photo.   10. Please (*formal sing.*) cash the check this morning.

C. Después de repasar las expresiones para *Time of day,* Appendix C, page 219, expresen en español:

1. It is a quarter after one.   2. It is ten A.M.   3. It is four P.M. sharp.   4. It is ten minutes to two (*two ways*).   5. They intend to stay until five o'clock.   6. He will leave at twenty minutes before (to) nine.   7. They want to return at seven o'clock.   8. It was eleven P.M.   9. It was half past twelve.   10. It has already struck eight.

Glosario

el **avión de las tres**   the three-o'clock plane
cobrar un cheque   to cash a check
construido, -a *p.p. of* **construir** *and adj.*   constructed, built
construir (*like* **huir**)   to construct, build
el **curso de inglés**   English course
en el aeropuerto   at (in) the airport
(**estar**) **en casa**   (to be) at home
la **mayor parte de**   most (of), the greater part of

lo bueno   what is good, the good thing (part)
ni . . . ni   neither . . . nor, (not) . . . either . . . or
para el desayuno   for breakfast
por eso   therefore, because of that, that's why
sacar la licencia   to get the license
(**son las once**) **en punto**   (it is eleven o'clock) sharp
todavía no he cerrado la puerta   I still haven't closed the door (I haven't closed the door yet)

LECCIÓN SEIS

1 Usos del artículo definido

The definite article **el** (*pl.* **los**) or **la** (*pl.* **las**) is used in Spanish, as in English, to denote a specific noun. In addition, the definite article in Spanish has a number of other important functions. Some of the special uses in Spanish are:

A. With abstract nouns and with nouns used in a general sense, indicating a whole class:

> **La vida en México es interesante.**   Life in Mexico is interesting.
> **Me gustan las rosas.**   I like roses (i.e., all roses).

B. With titles (except before **don, doña, san, santo, santa**) when speaking about, but not directly to, a person:

> **El profesor Solís nos mira.**   Professor Solís is looking at us.

> BUT: **Buenas tardes, señora López.**   Good afternoon, Mrs. López.
> **Don Carlos Díaz vive en Santa Fe.**   Don Carlos Díaz lives in
> Santa Fe.

C. With days of the week and seasons of the year, except after **ser,** and with dates, meals, hours of the day, and modified expressions of time:

> **El lunes es el primer día de la semana.**   Monday is the first day of
> the week.
> **Van a salir el domingo.**   They are going to leave (on) Sunday.
> **Lupe volvió el quince de agosto.**   Lupe returned (on) August 15.
> **Llegarán tarde para el almuerzo.**   They will arrive (be) late for lunch.
> **Ya son las nueve.**   It is already nine o'clock.
> **Vi a la señorita Ortiz la semana pasada.**   I saw Miss Ortiz last week.

> BUT: **Hoy es martes.**   Today is Tuesday.
> **Es otoño.**   It is autumn (fall).

D. With parts of the body, articles of clothing, and other things closely associated with a person, in place of the possessive adjective when the reference is clear:

> **Marta se lavó las manos.**   Martha washed her hands.
> **Jorge no se quitó los zapatos.**   George didn't take off his shoes.
> **He perdido el reloj.**   I've lost my watch.
> **Ella tiene el pelo rubio.**   She has blond hair (Her hair is blond).

E. With the name of a language, except after **de** and **en** or immediately after **hablar** (and often after verbs such as **aprender, comprender, escribir, estudiar, practicar, saber**):

> **El español no es fácil.**   Spanish isn't easy.
> **Carlos habla bien[1] el francés.**   Charles speaks French well.

> BUT: **Éste es un libro de español.**   This is a Spanish book.
> **¿No habla usted portugués?**   Don't you speak Portuguese?
> **Estudiamos inglés y español.**   We study English and Spanish.

F. With names of rivers and mountains, with proper names and names of places when modified, and with the names of certain countries and cities:

> **El Amazonas está en el Brasil.**   The Amazon (River) is in Brazil.
> **Conocemos la España moderna.**   We know modern Spain.

Some commonly used names of countries and cities which are preceded by the definite article in conservative literary usage (but which are often used without the article in journalistic and colloquial use) are:

(el) Canadá	**(el) Brasil**	**(el) Paraguay**	**(el) Callao**
(los) Estados Unidos	**(el) Ecuador**	**(el) Perú**	**(el) Cuzco**
(la) Argentina	**(la) Florida**	**(el) Uruguay**	**(la) China**

The article is seldom omitted in the case of **La Habana** and **El Salvador,** which means *The Savior.*

G. In certain set phrases:

> **a (en) la escuela**   to (at, in) school
> **a la iglesia**   to church
> **al poco rato**   after (in) a short time (while)

NOTE: Special use of the definite article **el.** Feminine nouns which begin with stressed **a-** or **ha-** require **el** in the singular, instead of **la,** when the article immediately precedes the noun: **el agua,** *the water,* **el hambre,** *hunger;* but **las aguas,** *the waters,* **la amiga,** *the (girl)friend.*

Recall the two contractions of the masculine singular definite article: **a** + **el** = **al;** **de** + **el** = **del.** Examples: **al cine,** *to the movie;* **el cuarto del chico,** *the boy's room.*

EJERCICIOS

A. Lean en español, supliendo el artículo definido cuando sea necesario:

1. Buenos días, _____ señor Molina. _____ señor López no ha venido hoy.
2. Hoy es _____ jueves. Siempre tengo tres clases _____ jueves.

---

[1] When any word other than the subject pronoun comes between forms of **hablar** and the other verbs given in this subsection and the name of a language, the article is used.

3. Ellos hablan _____ español. Dicen que _____ español no es fácil.
4. Piensan ir a _____ España. Quieren conocer _____ España moderna.
5. Tomás toma _____ café aquí. No le gusta _____ café frío.
6. A María le gustan _____ rosas. Su novio le manda _____ flores a veces.
7. _____ profesor Martín ha vuelto. Lo vi _____ semana pasada.
8. Juanita y yo vamos a _____ iglesia _____ domingos.

B. Para expresar en español:

1. I like music a lot. 2. Mrs. Blanco has arrived. 3. The boys have already eaten lunch. 4. Today is Tuesday. 5. Does Ann have blond hair? 6. They have put on their gloves. 7. The card is written in French. 8. Do you (*fam. sing.*) speak Spanish well? 9. Jane doesn't speak Portuguese. 10. Mr. Solís is from Argentina. 11. The water is not very cold. 12. Our Spanish teacher is going to talk about Mexican art.

2   Omisión del artículo indefinido en español

You found in Lección primera, page 9, that the indefinite article is omitted in Spanish after **ser** in certain cases when it is used in English. The indefinite article is also omitted in Spanish:

A. Often before nouns, particularly in interrogative and negative sentences, after prepositions, and after certain verbs (such as **tener** and **buscar**), when the numerical concept of *a, an (one)* is not emphasized:

> **¿Busca usted abrigo ahora?**   Are you looking for a topcoat now?
> **Roberto salió sin paraguas.**   Robert left without an umbrella.
> **Luisa no tiene coche.**   Louise doesn't have a car (has no car).

B. With adjectives such as **otro, -a,** *another,* **tal,** *such a,* **cien(to),** *a (one) hundred,* **mil,** *a (one) thousand,* **cierto, -a,** *a certain,* **medio, -a,** *a half,* and with **¡qué!** *what a, an!* in exclamations:

> **Quiero otra taza de café.**   I want another cup of coffee.
> **Cierta muchacha me dijo eso.**   A certain girl told me that.
> **¡Qué ciudad!**   What a city!

EJERCICIO

Lean en español, supliendo el artículo indefinido cuando sea necesario:

1. Jaime no tiene _____ reloj.
2. ¿Deseas _____ ensalada para el almuerzo?

3. Mi padre necesita _____ coche más grande.
4. ¿Busca usted _____ maleta esta mañana?
5. Hoy tengo que comprar _____ cuaderno y _____ otro lápiz.
6. Nunca hemos oído tal _____ cosa.
7. Margarita no quiere _____ pulsera nueva.
8. _____ estudiante dejó el cuaderno aquí.

3 Las formas, la concordancia (agreement) y la posición de los adjetivos

A. Forms and agreement of adjectives

An adjective, which limits or describes a noun or a pronoun, must agree with either one in gender and number, whether the adjective modifies the noun or pronoun directly or is in the predicate. An adjective which modifies two or more singular nouns is put in the plural; if one noun is masculine and the other feminine, the adjective is regularly masculine plural. (The adjective should stand nearest the masculine noun.) Adjectives form their plurals in the same way as nouns (see Lección primera, page 8).

The feminine singular of adjectives ending in -o is formed by changing final -o to -a. Adjectives of nationality that end in a consonant and adjectives that end in -án, -ón, -or (except the comparatives mejor, peor, mayor, menor, and such words as interior, exterior, superior, and a few others which are comparatives in Latin) add -a for the feminine. Other adjectives have the same form for the masculine and feminine:

| Singular | | Plural | |
Masculine	Feminine	Masculine	Feminine
rojo	roja	rojos	rojas
mexicano	mexicana	mexicanos	mexicanas
español	española	españoles	españolas
francés	francesa	franceses	francesas
hablador[1]	habladora	habladores	habladoras
mayor	mayor	mayores	mayores
feliz	feliz	felices	felices
joven	joven	jóvenes	jóvenes
cortés	cortés	corteses	corteses

Note the addition of the written accent: joven-jóvenes; the dropping of the accent: cortés-corteses and francés-francesa, franceses, francesas; and the change in spelling: feliz-felices.

---

[1] hablador, -ora, *talkative.*

B. Position of adjectives

Limiting adjectives (articles, unstressed possessives, demonstratives, numerals, indefinites, and other adjectives which show quantity) usually precede the noun.

Adjectives which distinguish or differentiate a noun from others of the same class (adjectives of color, size, shape, nationality, adjectives modified by adverbs, past participles used as adjectives, and the like) regularly follow the noun:

veinte estudiantes españoles   twenty Spanish students
algunas muchachas mexicanas   some Mexican girls
una pluma y un lápiz rojos   a red pen and pencil
un niño muy feliz   a very happy little boy
muchas (pocas) cosas interesantes   many (few) interesting things

When two or more adjectives modify a noun, each occupies its normal position; if they follow the noun, the last two are regularly connected by **y.** Two or more singular adjectives may modify a plural noun:

el distinguido (famoso) autor mexicano   the distinguished (famous) Mexican author
las pinturas española y mexicana   the Spanish and Mexican paintings

Certain common adjectives (**bueno, mejor, mayor, malo, peor,** and less frequently **pequeño, joven, viejo,** and a few others) often precede the noun, but they may follow the noun to place more emphasis on the adjective than the noun:

una buena muchacha *or* **una muchacha buena**   a good girl
un joven artista *or* **un artista joven**   a young artist

Other adjectives have a different meaning when they precede or follow a noun. In addition to **grande** (see C, 2, which follows), other examples are:

un traje nuevo   a new suit (*brand-new*)
un nuevo estudiante extranjero   a new foreign student (*another student*)

el hombre pobre   the poor man (*not rich*)
el pobre hombre   the poor man (*a man to be pitied*)

un amigo viejo   an old friend (*elderly*)
un viejo amigo   an old friend (*of long standing*)

él mismo   he himself
el mismo día   the same day

Descriptive adjectives may also precede the noun when they are used figuratively, or when they express a quality that is generally known or is not essential to the recognition of the noun. In such cases there is no desire to single out or to differentiate. Also, when a certain quality has been established with reference to the noun, the adjective precedes the noun.

Whenever an adjective is changed from its normal position, the speaker or writer gives a subjective or personal interpretation of the noun. An adjective placed before the noun loses much of its force and expresses its quality as a matter of course. When an adjective follows a noun, it indicates a distinguishing quality and it assumes the chief importance. In English this result is attained by a slight pause and the stress of voice:

un magnífico (famoso) cuadro mexicano   a magnificent (famous) Mexican picture
los altos Andes   the high Andes
la blanca nieve   the white snow

C. Shortened forms of adjectives

1. A few adjectives drop the final **-o** when they precede a masculine singular noun: **bueno, malo, uno, primero, tercero, postrero** (*last*), **alguno, ninguno. Alguno** and **ninguno** become **algún** and **ningún,** respectively:

el primer mes   the first month
el tercer día   the third day
algún estudiante   some student

ningún jugador   no player
un buen (mal) coche   a good (bad) car

BUT: **los primeros días**   the first days
una buena idea   a good idea

2. Three common adjectives drop the last syllable under certain conditions:

a. **Grande** becomes **gran** before either a masculine or feminine singular noun, and usually means *great:*

un gran equipo   a great team

una gran ciudad   a great city

BUT: **dos grandes hombres**   two great men
esas grandes mujeres   those great women

When **grande** follows the noun, it regularly means *large, big:*

un país grande   a large country
estos edificios grandes   these large buildings

b. **Santo** (not **Santa**) becomes **San** before names of all masculine saints except those beginning with **Do-** or **To-:**

San Pablo   St. Paul

San Francisco   St. Francis

BUT: **Santo Tomás**   St. Thomas
Santo Domingo   St. Dominic

Santa María   St. Mary
Santa Inés   St. Agnes

c. **Ciento** becomes **cien** before all nouns, including **millones,** and before the adjective **mil,** but it is not shortened before numerals smaller than one hundred:

cien casas   100 houses
cien muchachos   100 boys
ciento cincuenta hombres   150 men

cien mil personas   100,000 persons

D. Use of prepositional phrases instead of adjectives

In Spanish a noun is rarely used as an adjective; instead, a prepositional phrase beginning with **de** or **para** is normally used. Such constructions may be considered compound nouns:

el fin de semana   the weekend
el partido (equipo) de fútbol   the
   football game (team)
el reloj de pulsera   the wristwatch
estas tazas para café   these coffee cups
la clase de inglés   English class
la residencia de estudiantes   the
   student residence hall, dormitory

un compañero de cuarto   a
   roomate
un programa de televisión   a
   TV program
un vaso para agua   a water
   glass
una casa de piedra   a stone
   house

EJERCICIOS

A. Repitan cada frase; luego, al oír un nuevo sustantivo, formen otra frase haciendo los cambios necesarios.

MODELO: Es una canción mexicana.   *Es una canción mexicana.*
                    canciones   *Son canciones (or unas canciones) mexicanas.*

1. Es un traje bonito.
   corbata
   sombreros
   blusas
   vestido
   chaqueta
2. Mi amigo es español.
   Mi amiga
   Los jugadores
   Las señoritas
   El estudiante
   La señora López

3. ¿Es hablador el joven?
   muchacha?
   estudiantes?
   mujeres?
   chico
   señores
4. Es un día hermoso.
   noche
   árboles
   rosas
   parque
   ciudad

B. Repitan cada frase; luego, cámbienla al singular:

1. sus buenos amigos   2. nuestras buenas amigas   3. los malos caminos
4. las niñas muy buenas   5. otras revistas españolas   6. nuestros hermanos menores   7. los primeros días buenos   8. esas grandes oportunidades   9. algunos jugadores mexicanos   10. aquellos grandes profesores   11. estos pobres chicos   12. los nuevos estudiantes   13. unos compañeros de cuarto   14. estas tazas para té   15. los programas de televisión   16. unos pueblos bonitos

C. Para contestar afirmativamente, según los modelos.

MODELOS: ¿Es rojo el vestido?   *Sí, es un vestido rojo.*
            ¿Son blancas las camisas?   *Sí, son camisas blancas.*

1. ¿Es buena la carretera?
2. ¿Es larga la excursión?
3. ¿Es muy grande el parque?
4. ¿Es estrecha la calle?

5. ¿Son cómodos los autobuses?
6. ¿Son altas las montañas?
7. ¿Son muy malos los caminos?
8. ¿Son hermosos los pájaros?

D. Para expresar en español:

1. several Spanish paintings   2. some foreign student (*m.*)   3. no large city
4. some great teacher (*f.*)   5. St. Paul and St. Mary   6. the same afternoon
7. two very happy children   8. a French girl   9. a red book and notebook
10. a radio program   11. some water glasses   12. this weekend   13. our stone
house   14. one hundred good players   15. the first year   16. the third building
17. the tennis team   18. our Spanish class   19. the famous Spanish author
20. few long trips

4   Repaso de los números

A. Después de repasar los números cardinales y sus usos (Appendix C, pages
   216–217), lean en español:

1. 18 muchachos   2. 21 países   3. 100 páginas   4. 116 ciudades   5. 200 preguntas   6. 365 días   7. 500 casas   8. 1,000 hombres   9. 150,000 personas
10. 1,000,000 de pesos   11. 5,000,000 de dólares   12. 10,000,000 de habitantes

B. Repasen los números ordinales y sus usos (Appendix C, pages 217–218); luego,
   expresen en español:

1. the first car   2. the first house   3. the first boys   4. the sixth lesson
5. Lesson Seven   6. the second street   7. the third trip   8. the tenth month
9. Charles the Fifth   10. Philip the Second   11. the eighth week   12. the third
question

C. Repasen el uso de los números para expresar fechas y los nombres de los meses
   (Appendix C, page 218); luego, lean en español:

1. January 1, 1983   2. May 2, 1979   3. October 12, 1492   4. September 29,
1547   5. July 4, 1775   6. February 22, 1789   7. December 10, 1810   8. June
29, 1903   9. March 31, 1905   10. April 15, 1817

D. Para contestar en español:

1. ¿Cuál es la fecha de hoy?   2. ¿En qué fecha nació Ud. (naciste)?   3. ¿Qué día de la semana es hoy?   4. ¿Qué día fue ayer?   5. ¿Qué día va a ser mañana?   6. ¿Tiene Ud. (Tienes) clases todos los días?   7. ¿En qué días tiene Ud. (tienes) clase de español?   8. ¿En qué días no tiene Ud. (tienes) clase?   9. ¿Cuántas clases tiene Ud. (tienes) hoy?   10. ¿Tiene Ud. (Tienes) clase por la tarde?   11. ¿Va Ud. (Vas) a la iglesia los domingos?   12. ¿Va Ud. (Vas) de compras los sábados?

Glosario

buenas tardes   good afternoon
buenos días   good morning (day)
el **compañero de cuarto**   roommate (*m.*)

él mismo   he himself
nacer   to be born
para el almuerzo   for lunch
la **semana pasada**   last week

Repaso dos

A. Formas del pretérito de indicativo. Para expresar en español:

1. I arrived, looked for, came, had (**tener**), was (**estar**).
2. They brought, said, believed, went, were (**ser**).
3. We could, wanted, gave, put, saw.
4. He made, heard, felt, asked for, slept.
5. You (*fam. sing.*) arrived, lived, asked for, went, read.

B. Lean en español, cambiando cada infinitivo en cursiva a la forma correcta del pretérito o del imperfecto de indicativo:

1. *Ser* las once de la mañana cuando yo *volver* del centro.   2. Cuando yo *ver* a Luisa, la *invitar* a almorzar conmigo.   3. Jaime le *preguntar* a Diana si ella *poder* ir al concierto con él.   4. Ramón *llamar* por teléfono a María, pero ella no *estar* en casa.   5. Él *querer* hablar con ella acerca de una composición que él *estar* escribiendo.   6. Al poco rato él *ir* al café, pero no *poder* encontrarla.   7. Los estudiantes *charlar* cuando la profesora *entrar* en la sala de clase.   8. Ellos *saber* que ella *ir* a darles un examen.   9. Miguel *pasar* despacio por la calle cuando yo lo *ver*. 10. Yo le *decir* que *querer* devolverle su libro de español.

C. Para contestar negativamente en español, siguiendo los modelos.

MODELOS: ¿Cerraste la puerta?   *No, todavía no he cerrado la puerta.*
           ¿Salió Ana de casa?   *No, todavía no ha salido de casa.*

1. ¿Abriste el cuaderno?
2. ¿Escribiste el artículo?
3. ¿Recibió Ud. la tarjeta?
4. ¿Envolvió José el paquete?
5. ¿Trajo Elena el vaso?

6. ¿Vieron Uds. la película?
7. ¿Fueron Uds. al cine?
8. ¿Oyeron Uds. la orquesta?
9. ¿Devolvió él los libros?
10. ¿Hicieron ellas el trabajo?

D. Para contestar afirmativamente en español, según el modelo.

MODELO: ¿Ha cubierto Ud. la mesa?   *Sí, ya está cubierta.*

1. ¿Ha preparado Ud. la comida?
2. ¿Has puesto las cosas allí?
3. ¿Has abierto las ventanas?

4. ¿Ha hecho Luisa la blusa?
5. ¿Han escrito ellos las cartas?
6. ¿Ha envuelto ella los guantes?

El Palacio del Presidente, Tegucigalpa, Honduras.

E. Lean en español, supliendo la forma correcta de **estar** o **ser**. Usen el tiempo presente, menos en 10, 12 y 13:

1. ¿_____ joven tu tío?   2. ¿_____ contentas tus hermanas?   3. Nuestros amigos mexicanos _____ muy simpáticos.   4. ¿_____ rico aquel hombre? 5. ¿Qué _____ aquellas dos mujeres?   6. Enrique y yo _____ estudiantes. 7. ¿_____ enferma la profesora?   8. Los chicos _____ jugando en el patio. 9. ¿De dónde _____ tú?   10. Yo no quiero _____ abogado.   11. _____ las diez y cuarto.   12. Las puertas _____ (*pret.*) abiertas por él.   13. Nosotros _____ (*pres. perf.*) durmiendo la siesta.   14. El almuerzo ya _____ preparado.

F. Usos de la construcción reflexiva y de la voz pasiva. Para expresar en español:

1. How does one say that in Spanish?
2. One can learn the song easily.
3. How is this done in Spain?
4. Books are bought in a bookstore.
5. One sits down in order to rest.
6. People know that Ann has left.
7. Mrs. Sierra prepared the meal.
8. The meal was prepared by her.
9. It (*f.*) is well prepared.
10. Joe wrote this letter.
11. The letter was written by Joe.
12. The letter is written in Spanish.

G. Repitan cada frase; luego, al oír un nuevo sustantivo, formen otra frase, haciendo los cambios necesarios:

1. un día hermoso   (noche)
2. un pueblo español   (ciudad)
3. el niño cortés   (niños)
4. su hermano mayor   (hermana)
5. mi amigo feliz   (amigas)
6. el equipo francés   (equipos)
7. un hombre hablador   (mujer)
8. ese camino largo   (calles)

H. Para expresar en español:

1. Good afternoon, Mrs. Solís. How are you (*formal sing.*) today?   2. They say that Miss Ortiz returned from Peru last week.   3. I got up at half past seven and it is already eight o'clock.   4. Today is Tuesday, the sixteenth of November, 1983.   5. It is said that French is not easy; therefore, it is necessary to practice a lot.   6. My Spanish teacher said that she is going to talk about Mexican music some day.   7. Are you (*fam. sing.*) looking for a suitcase now? And do you intend to go shopping tomorrow morning?   8. What a day! It is raining (*progressive*) now and John left without an umbrella.   9. There are several stone houses on this long street.   10. Bring (*formal sing.*) me a water glass and a coffee cup, please. 11. First we went to the football game and then we watched a good television program.   12. Mr. López made his first trip to Spain in August and he has to return there soon.   13. My cousin (*m.*) has written that there are nearly 35,000 students at his university.   14. This story which we are reading (*progressive*) was written by a famous Spanish author.   15. I saw Jane after class and I invited her to eat with me tonight.

Patio de la Misión de Santa Bárbara, Santa Bárbara, California.

Notas culturales II

La presencia hispánica en los Estados Unidos

Entre los muchos cambios que han ocurrido en la sociedad norteamericana durante los últimos treinta años, hay uno de interés especial. Se trata del° aumento extraordinario del número de hispanoparlantes° en nuestro país. Si incluimos los habitantes del Estado Libre Asociado° de Puerto Rico, se calcula que unos dieciocho millones de personas en los Estados Unidos tienen el español como lengua materna. Sólo cuatro naciones hispánicas tienen un número mayor de personas de habla española° que nuestro país: México, España, la Argentina y Colombia.

Aunque hay personas de habla española en todos los estados de nuestro país, la mayoría se ha concentrado° en tres grandes zonas: Nueva York y sus alrededores,° la Florida y los estados del suroeste.

En Nueva York la gran mayoría de los hispanos° son de origen puertorriqueño, aunque la ciudad también ha atraído personas de todo el mundo hispánico.° La inmigración de puertorriqueños se aceleró notablemente a partir de° la segunda guerra mundial, y en tiempos más recientes grupos de cubanos, colombianos y mexicanos también se han establecido en la gran metrópoli. Se calcula que unos dos millones de personas de habla española residen en la zona citada.

En la Florida la población hispanoparlante es predominantemente de origen cubano. Durante los últimos veinte años casi un millón de exiliados políticos han llegado al territorio norteamericano. En su mayoría° estos inmigrantes son de la clase media y de cierta preparación profesional y han logrado° establecerse en nuestro país sin grandes dificultades. Se cree que hoy día° un millón y medio de hispanos residen en la Florida.

Se trata del *It is a question of the*

hispanoparlantes *speakers of Spanish*

Estado Libre Asociado *Commonwealth (Associated Free State)*

de habla española *Spanish-speaking*

la mayoría se ha concentrado *the majority has concentrated* / **alrededores** *environs*

hispanos *persons of Spanish origin*

todo el mundo hispánico *the whole (all the) Hispanic world*

a partir de *beginning with*

En su mayoría *For the most part*

han logrado *they have succeeded in*

hoy día *nowadays, today*

71

Más de la mitad de los hispanoparlantes de nuestro país residen en los cinco estados del suroeste: California, Arizona, Nuevo México, Colorado y Texas. Hasta 1810 estas tierras formaban la frontera septentrional° del imperio español en América. Pertenecieron a México desde ese año hasta 1848, cuando, por el tratado de Guadalupe Hidalgo,[1] pasaron a ser° territorio de los Estados Unidos.

septentrional *northern*

pasaron a ser *they became*

Aunque las tierras del suroeste siempre han atraído inmigrantes de México, esta corriente ha aumentado considerablemente durante el siglo actual.° En California, por ejemplo, había menos de veinte mil personas de habla española en 1900. Hoy día se calcula que hay más de cinco millones de hispanoparlantes en el estado. La situación desfavorable en que se encuentran muchos de los inmigrantes recientes ha producido problemas graves, que sólo podrán resolverse eliminando° obstáculos y preparando el terreno° para una más efectiva cooperación y una más fecunda° coexistencia de las dos culturas.

actual *present*

eliminando *by eliminating*

preparando el terreno *(by) paving the way* / fecunda *fruitful*

PREGUNTAS

Para contestar en español en oraciones completas:

1. ¿Cuál es el tema de la Nota cultural de esta lección?　2. ¿Qué cambio de interés especial ha ocurrido en los Estados Unidos durante los últimos treinta años? 3. ¿Cuántos millones de personas en los Estados Unidos tienen el español como lengua materna?　4. ¿Qué naciones tienen un número mayor de personas de habla española que nuestro país?　5. ¿En qué zonas se ha concentrado la mayoría de las personas de habla española?

6. ¿De qué origen es la gran mayoría de los hispanos en Nueva York?　7. ¿En qué años se aceleró notablemente la inmigración de puertorriqueños?　8. ¿Qué otros grupos de hispanos se han establecido en Nueva York y sus alrededores?　9. ¿Cuántos hispanos se calcula que residen en Nueva York y sus alrededores?

10. ¿En qué zona de nuestro país es la población hispanoparlante predominantemente de origen cubano?　11. ¿Por qué han logrado los cubanos establecerse en nuestro país sin grandes dificultades?　12. ¿Cuántos hispanos se cree que residen en la Florida?　13. ¿En qué estados residen más de la mitad de los hispanoparlantes de nuestro país?　14. ¿Qué formaban esas tierras hasta 1810?　15. ¿A qué país pertenecieron desde ese año hasta 1848?

---

[1] Guadalupe Hidalgo is a town near Mexico City where the treaty of February 2, 1848, ceding California, Arizona, and New Mexico to the United States was signed.

16. ¿Cuándo pasaron esas tierras a ser territorio de los Estados Unidos?
17. ¿Cuántas personas de habla española había en California en 1900?   18. ¿Cuántos hispanoparlantes se cree que hay hoy día en el estado?   19. ¿Qué ha producido problemas graves?   20. ¿Cómo podrán resolverse estos problemas?

EJERCICIO ESCRITO

Traduzcan al español (*Translate into Spanish*) las frases siguientes:

1. Many changes have occurred in the United States during the last thirty years.
2. Today it is believed that some eighteen million persons in our country have Spanish as their mother tongue.   3. Most persons of Hispanic origin reside in Florida, the states of the Southwest, and New York and its environs.   4. In New York, the immigration of Puerto Ricans accelerated notably beginning with the second World War.   5. In more recent times, the great metropolis has attracted groups of Cubans, Colombians, and Mexicans.

6. During the last twenty years almost a million Cuban exiles have settled in Florida.   7. In the Southwest, the number of immigrants from Mexico has increased notably during the present century.   8. These lands belonged to Spain until 1810 and to Mexico until 1848.   9. The extraordinary increase in the (**del**) number of immigrants from Mexico has produced serious problems.   10. Many obstacles must be eliminated if we are to arrive at a more fruitful coexistence of the two cultures.

LECCIÓN SIETE

1 Uso del infinitivo después de una preposición

In Spanish the infinitive is used after a preposition; in English the present participle is often used:

> **Antes de entrar en el cuarto . . .**   Before entering the room . . .
> **Tomás salió sin decírmelo.**   Thomas left without telling me.

Al plus an infinitive in Spanish is the equivalent of *on* (*upon*) plus the present participle in English. Occasionally it may correspond to a clause beginning with *when*, which may be followed by any tense:

> **Al ver a Pepe . . .**   On (Upon) seeing Joe . . .   *or* When he (she) sees (saw) Joe   *or* When I (you, we, they) see (saw) Joe . . .

The Spanish infinitive may have a subject (which follows the infinitive), an object, or both:

> **Al saberlo yo, lo llamé.**   Upon finding it out (When I found it out), I called him.

2 Verbos seguidos del infinitivo sin preposición

A. Verbs that do not require a preposition before an infinitive

A few of the many verbs which do not require a preposition before an infinitive when there is no change in subject are: **deber, decidir, desear, esperar, necesitar, pensar (ie)** (when it means *to intend, plan*), **poder, preferir (ie, i), prometer, querer, saber, sentir (ie, i), temer:**

> **Juan habla de los deportes en que espera participar.**   John talks about the sports in which he hopes to participate.
> **Siento no poder ir contigo a la librería.**   I'm sorry I cannot go (I am sorry not to be able to go) with you to the bookstore.

The infinitive follows impersonal expressions without a preposition:

> **Es necesario escoger un asiento.**   It is necessary to choose a seat.

B. Some special uses of the infinitive

1. After **oír** and **ver,** the infinitive is regularly used in Spanish, while the present participle is often used in English. Note the word order in the first example:

Oímos cantar a Luisa.   We hear Louise sing (singing).
Yo la vi entrar.   I saw her enter (entering).

2. **Dejar, hacer, mandar,** and **permitir** are usually followed by an infinitive when the object of the main verb (which also serves as the subject of the following verb) is a pronoun (some exceptions to this usage will be discussed later):

Déjeme (Permítame) Ud. enviarlo.   Let me (Permit me to) send it.
Le mandé esperar un rato.   I ordered him to (had him) wait a while.

While usage varies, with **dejar** and **hacer** personal objects are usually direct; with other verbs they are usually indirect.

Often the infinitive has a passive meaning in Spanish, especially when its subject is not expressed and its object is a thing:

Ana mandó (hizo) poner los paquetes sobre la mesa.   Ann ordered *or*
    had the packages placed (put) on the table.
La mandó llamar la profesora.   The teacher had her called (sent for her).
Hicimos lavar el coche.   We had the car washed.

3 Verbos que necesitan preposición ante un infinitivo

A. Verbs which take **a** before an infinitive

All verbs expressing motion or movement to a place, the verbs meaning *to begin,* and certain others such as **atreverse,** *to dare,* **aprender,** *to learn,* **enseñar,** *to teach, show,* **ayudar,** *to help, aid,* and **obligar,** *to oblige,* require **a** before an infinitive. The verbs **enseñar, ayudar,** and **obligar** require personal objects as subjects of the following infinitive:

Fueron (Corrieron) a ver el avión.   They went (ran) to see the plane.
Yo aprendí (empecé) a jugar al tenis.   I learned (began) to play tennis.
Él me enseñó (ayudó) a preparar la solicitud.   He taught me to (helped me) prepare the application.

Volver a plus an infinitive means (to do something) *again:*

Ellos volvieron a llamarnos.   They called us again.

B. Verbs which take **de** before an infinitive

Three common verbs which require **de** are **acordarse (ue) (de),** *to remember (to),* **alegrarse (de),** *to be glad (to),* and **olvidarse (de),** *to forget (to):*

Pepe se olvidó de esperar a Lola.   Joe forgot to wait for Lola.

Remember that **olvidar** plus an infinitive also means *to forget to:* **Olvidé ir,** *I forgot to go.*

Dejar de plus an infinitive means *to stop, fail to.* **Tratar de** means *to try to,* and **tratarse de** means *to be a question of.* **Acabar de** in the present and imperfect tenses means *have just, had just* (done something), respectively:

> **Juan dejó de escuchar discos.**   John stopped listening to records.
> **No dejes de escribirme.**   Don't fail to write (to) me *or* Don't stop writing (to) me.
> **No se trata de hacer eso.**   It is not a question of doing that.
> **Roberto acaba (acababa) de salir.**   Robert has (had) just left.

Some verbs followed by an adjective or noun require **de** before an infinitive as well as before a noun or noun clause:

> **Estamos seguros de que Pablo puede venir.**   We are sure that Paul can come.
> **Estamos seguros de poder verlo.**   We are sure of being able to see him.
> **Los chicos están cansados de jugar.**   The boys are tired of playing.
> **Tenemos miedo de ir allá.**   We are afraid to go there.

C. Verbs which take **en** before an infinitive

Some common verbs that are followed by **en** before an infinitive are: **consentir (ie, i) en,** *to consent to, agree to,* **insistir en,** *to insist on,* **pensar (ie) en,** *to think of,* **tardar en,** *to delay in, take long to:*

> **Ellos insistieron en descansar un rato.**   They insisted on resting a while.

EJERCICIOS

A. Repitan la frase; luego, cámbienla a una forma de mandato con **Ud.** o **Uds.** como sujeto:

1. Margarita me enseña a preparar la solicitud.
2. Ana comienza a leer el cuento.
3. Luis lo ayuda a lavar el coche.
4. No dejan de practicar el tenis.
5. Laura aprende a tocar la canción mexicana.
6. No se olvidan de felicitarla.
7. No tratan de jugar al golf hoy.
8. No tardan mucho en vestirse.

B. Lean en español, supliendo la preposición correcta cuando sea necesario:

1. Los dos son aficionados _____ los deportes.   2. Pepe sabe _____ jugar bien al básquetbol.   3. Tardaron media hora _____ llegar al estadio.   4. ¿Te acuerdas _____ Miguel Sierra?   5. Acabamos _____ recibir una tarjeta de él.   6. No dejen Uds. _____ ir al gimnasio.   7. ¿Se olvidaron Uds. _____ comprar los boletos?   8. Clara insiste _____ quedarse aquí esta tarde.   9. Mi hermano no consentirá _____ asistir a la reunión.   10. Esperamos _____ divertirnos mucho.   11. Estamos seguros _____ que Luis puede _____ ir

también.   12. ¿Sabe Ud. si Tomás prefiere _____ tocar unos discos?   13. No se trata _____ pasar todo el día allí.   14. Felipe y Carlos piensan _____ salir a la calle.   15. Nos alegramos _____ saber eso.

4   Expresiones con **hacer, haber** y **tener**[1]

A. **Hacer** is used impersonally with certain nouns in Spanish to describe the weather and the temperature, while *to be* is used in English:

> **¿Qué tiempo hace hoy?**   What kind of weather is it (What is the weather like) today?
> **Hace buen (mal) tiempo.**   It is good (bad) weather.
> **Hizo (mucho) calor ayer.**   It was (very) warm yesterday.
> **Hará (mucho) fresco mañana.**   It will be (very) cool tomorrow.
> **Ha hecho (mucho) frío.**   It has been (very) cold.
> **Hacía (mucho) viento.**   It was (very) windy.
> **Hace mucho sol hoy.**   It is very sunny (The sun is shining brightly) today.

Since **calor, fresco, frío, viento, sol** are all nouns in these expressions, they are modified by the adjective **mucho,** not by the adverb **muy.**

B. **Haber** is also used impersonally to describe weather conditions that are seen:

> **Hay mucho sol.**   It is very sunny.
> **Hay luna esta noche.**   The moon is shining (There is moonlight) tonight.
> **Hay pocas nubes en el cielo.**   There are few clouds in the sky.
> **Había mucho polvo (lodo).**   It was very dusty (muddy).
> **Había niebla (neblina).**   It was foggy (misty).

C. In speaking of a person, or any living thing, **tener** is used with certain nouns to express how one feels:

> **Pepe tiene (mucho) calor.**   Joe is *or* feels (very) warm.
> **Tenemos (mucho) frío.**   We are (very) cold.

Compare the use of **estar** or **ser** with an adjective when referring to a changeable or inherent quality:

> **Está despejado (nublado).**   It is clear (cloudy).
> **El agua estaba muy fría.**   The water was very cold.
> **El hielo es frío.**   Ice is cold.

---

[1] New words and expressions used in this section are not repeated in the **Glosario.**

Other common idiomatic expressions with **tener** are:

tener cuidado   to be careful
tener éxito   to be successful
tener hambre   to be hungry
tener miedo   to be afraid, be frightened
tener prisa   to be in a hurry
tener razón   to be right
no tener razón   to be wrong
tener sed   to be thirsty
tener sueño   to be sleepy
tener suerte   to be lucky, fortunate
tener vergüenza   to be ashamed

With all the above nouns, **mucho, -a,** is expressed in English by *very, (very) much.*
Mucha is used with the feminine nouns **hambre, prisa, razón, sed, suerte, vergüenza.**

Examples of additional expressions with **tener** follow. Note the use of the plural adjectives **muchos** and **muchas** in the last two examples:

¿Cuántos años tienes (tiene Ud.)?   How old are you?
Tengo dieciséis años.   I am sixteen (years old).
¿Qué tiene Luis?   What's the matter with Louis?
Aquí tiene Ud. (el libro).   Here is (the book). (*Handing someone something.*)
José tenía la culpa.   Joseph was at fault (to blame).
Tenemos que darnos prisa.   We have to (must) hurry.
Ella tiene muchos deseos de cantar.   She is very eager (wishes very much)
   to sing.
Tienen muchas ganas de ir a casa.   They desire *or* wish very much *or* They
   are very eager to go home (They feel very much like going home).

NOTE: **Tener prisa** means *to be in a hurry,* while **darse prisa** means *to hurry (up).*

EJERCICIOS

A. Para contestar en español:

1. ¿Qué tiempo hace hoy?   2. ¿Qué tiempo hizo ayer?   3. ¿Qué tiempo ha hecho esta semana?   4. ¿En qué estación del año hace más calor?   5. ¿En cuál de las estaciones hace más frío?   6. ¿Qué tiempo hace en el otoño?   7. ¿Hace mucho frío aquí en la primavera?   8. ¿Qué tomamos cuando hace mucho calor?

9. ¿Hay sol hoy?   10. ¿Habrá luna esta noche?   11. ¿Hay mucho polvo ahora?   12. ¿Cuándo hay lodo?   13. ¿Hay niebla aquí a veces?

14. ¿Tienes (Tiene Ud.) frío en este momento?   15. ¿Qué haces (hace Ud.) cuando tienes (tiene) hambre?   16. ¿Qué tomas (toma Ud.) cuando tienes (tiene) mucha sed?   17. ¿Tienes (Tiene Ud.) sueño en clase a veces?   18. ¿Tienes (Tiene Ud.) muchas ganas de ir al cine esta noche?   19. ¿Siempre tienes (tiene Ud.) mucho cuidado con el coche?   20. ¿Cuántos años tienes (tiene Ud.)?

B. Para expresar en español:

1. They (*m.*) are not very cold.   2. The boys are hungry and thirsty.   3. What's the matter with Ann's sister?   4. How old is your (*fam. sing.*) brother?   5. The children are not afraid.   6. Here is the letter; take (*fam. sing.*) it.   7. It is good weather now.   8. It has not been very cool.   9. It is clear this morning. 10. There are no clouds in the sky.   11. It was very windy last week.   12. It is very sunny this afternoon.   13. Hurry up (*pl.*); it is late.   14. The water was very hot.   15. Be (*pl.*) very careful.   16. Are the boys sleepy?

5 Usos de las palabras indefinidas y negativas

Pronouns	
algo something, anything	**nada** nothing, (not) . . . anything
alguien someone, somebody, anyone, (anybody)	**nadie** no one, nobody, (not) . . . anyone (anybody)
Pronouns or Adjectives	
alguno, -a some, someone (of a group), any; *pl.* some, any, several	**ninguno, -a** no, no one, none, (not) . . . any (anybody)
cualquier(a) any *or* anyone (at all)	
Adverbs	
siempre always	**nunca**⎫ never, (not) . . . ever **jamás**⎭
también also, too	**tampoco** neither, (not *or* nor) . . . either
Conjunctions	
o or	**ni** nor, (not) . . . or
o . . . o either . . . or	**ni . . . ni** neither . . . nor, (not) . . . either . . . or

A. Simple negation is expressed by placing **no** immediately before the main verb (or the auxiliary verb in the compound tenses and in the progressive forms of the tenses).

If negatives such as **nada, nadie,** etc., follow the verb, **no** or some other negative word must precede the verb; if they precede the verb or stand alone, **no** is not used. If a negative precedes the verb, all the expressions in the Spanish sentence are negative, rather than indefinite as in English. After **que,** *than,* the negatives are used:

> **Tomás les dijo algo.**   Thomas told them something.
> **No tiene nada** *or* **Nada tiene.**   He has nothing (He doesn't have anything).
> **Él nunca (jamás) envió nada.**   He never sent anything.
> **Ana volvió sin traer nada.**   Ann returned without bringing anything.
> **Ella no lo hizo tampoco** *or* **Tampoco lo hizo ella.**   She didn't do it either (Neither did she do it).
> **—¿Qué sabes? —Nada.**   "What do you know?" "Nothing."
> **Laura lee más que nadie (nunca).**   Laura reads more than anyone (ever).
> **No me gusta ni el café ni el té.**   I don't like either coffee or tea (I like neither coffee nor tea).
> **Ni Pablo ni Luis pueden**[1] **cantar.**   Neither Paul nor Louis can sing.

If the verb is not expressed, **no** usually follows the word it negates: **Yo no,** *Not I;* **todavía no,** *not yet.*

B. The pronouns **alguien** and **nadie** refer only to persons, unknown or not mentioned before, and the personal **a** is required when they are used as objects of the verb:

> **¿Vio Ud. a alguien?**   Did you see anyone?
> **Nadie me llamó a mí, ni yo llamé a nadie.**   No one called me, nor did I call anybody.

C. **Alguno, -a** and **ninguno, -a,** used as adjectives or pronouns, refer to *someone* or *none* of a group of persons or things already thought of or mentioned. Before a masculine singular noun **alguno** is shortened to **algún,** and **ninguno** to **ningún.** The plural forms **algunos, -as** are used, but **ninguno, -a** is normally used only in the singular:

> **Alguno de ellos puede conducir el coche.**   Someone of them can drive the car.
> **Ninguna de ellas debe esperar.**   None of them (*f.*) should wait.
> **Pasarán por aquí algún día.**   They will stop (drop) by here some day.
> **Ningún hombre ha hecho eso.**   No man has done that.

The personal **a** is also used when the direct object is **alguno, -a** or **ninguno, -a** when referring to persons:

> **¿Conoces a algunas de las chicas?**   Do you know any (some) of the girls?
> **No conozco a ninguna de ellas.**   I don't know any(one) of them.

---

[1] Singular nouns connected by **o** or **ni** which precede the verb normally take a plural verb.

D. The plural **algunos, -as** means *some, any, several, a few*. **Unos, -as,** with the same meanings, is more indefinite and expresses indifference as to the exact number; before a **de**-phrase its place is taken by **algunos, -as** (fourth example, below). In some cases **unos, -as** corresponds to *a pair of, two*:

Hay algunas cintas sobre la mesa.   There are some tapes on the table.
Tengo que buscar algunos discos.   I have to look for some records.
Unos (Algunos) chicos están en el parque.   Some children are in the park.
Algunos de ellos quieren refrescos.   Some of them want refreshments.
Juan me dio unos guantes.   John gave me some (a pair of) gloves.

Remember that unemphatic *some* and *any* are not regularly expressed in Spanish:

¿Quieres huevos para el desayuno?   Do you want some (any) eggs for breakfast?

An emphatic way to express *any* (*at all*) is to place **alguno, -a** after the noun:

Sin duda alguna . . .   Without any doubt (at all) . . .

E. Both **nunca** and **jamás** mean *never*, but in a question **jamás** means *ever* and a negative answer is expected. When neither an affirmative nor a negative answer is implied, **alguna vez,** *ever, sometime,* (*at*) *any time,* is used:

Diana nunca (jamás) come mucho.   Diane never eats much.
—¿Has visto jamás tal cosa? —No, nunca.   "Have you ever seen such a thing?" "No, never."
¿Ha estado Ud. alguna vez en Puerto Rico?   Have you ever (at any time) been in Puerto Rico?

F. **Cualquiera** (*pl.* **cualesquiera**), which may drop the final **a** before a noun, means *any, anyone* in the sense of *any at all, just any*:

Cualquier(a) persona sabe eso.   Any person (at all) knows that.
Cualquiera de nosotros lo puede hacer.   Anyone of us can do it.

G. **Algo** and **nada** are sometimes used as adverbs, meaning *somewhat, rather,* and (*not*) *at all,* respectively:

A veces Pepe llega algo tarde.   At times Joe arrives rather late.
Ese libro no es nada interesante.   That book isn't at all interesting.

EJERCICIOS

A. Repitan la frase; luego, cámbienla a la forma negativa.

MODELO: Ramón tiene algo.   *Ramón tiene algo. Ramón no tiene nada.*

1. Juan le dio algo a Elena.   2. Alguien tiene que preparar la comida.   3. Veo

algo sobre la mesa.   4. Hemos visto a alguien en la sala.   5. Hay alguien en la cocina.   6. Alguno de los muchachos nos ha llamado.   7. Algún muchacho va a comprar los guantes.   8. Han invitado a alguno de los profesores.   9. ¿Viene alguna de tus amigas?   10. ¿Siempre dices algo a alguien?   11. Alguna de las niñas está gritando.   12. Han visto a Juan o a Pablo.   13. El cuento es algo largo.   14. Él lo hizo también.

B. Para contestar negativamente:

1. ¿Llamó alguien anoche?
2. ¿Se desayunó contigo alguno de los chicos?
3. ¿Va a ayudarnos algún joven?
4. ¿Han estado Uds. jamás en la ciudad de Mexico?
5. ¿Siempre tomas (toma Ud.) mucho para el almuerzo?
6. ¿Fueron Uds. al cine con alguien el sábado?
7. ¿Buscó él a alguna de las chicas?
8. ¿Crees (Cree Ud.) algo diferente?

C. Para completar empleando el equivalente de las palabras *some* o *any* cuando sea necesario:

1. _____ día pasaré por tu casa.   2. _____ estudiantes fueron al Café Español.   3. ¿Has comprado _____ zapatos en esta tienda?   4. Esta mañana queremos preparar _____ huevos fritos.   5. _____ de las jóvenes puede traer el postre.   6. Mi mamá va a servir _____ flan esta noche.   7. No conozco _____ orquesta más popular.   8. Mi hermano quiere poner _____ discos hispanoamericanos.

D. Para expresar en español:

1. Do you (*pl.*) know anyone here?   2. We do not know anyone.   3. We never buy anything in this store.   4. Helen has more friends than anyone.   5. Some boy brought the magazines.   6. Joe never gives anything to anyone.   7. Some of the girls are playing (*progressive*) in the patio.   8. Thomas hasn't done anything either.   9. None of the men saw us.   10. I invited some of the children.   11. Any woman can help us.   12. Did he buy some shoes this afternoon?

Glosario

la **ciudad de México**   Mexico City
en clase   in class
en este (ese) momento   at this (that) moment
pasar por   to drop by (in), stop by
poner   to put on (*record*)

por aquí   by (around) here, this way
ser aficionado, -a a   to be fond of
la **solicitud**   application
todo el día   all day, the whole (entire) day

LECCIÓN OCHO

El tiempo futuro de indicativo de los verbos regulares • El tiempo condicional de indicativo de los verbos regulares • Verbos que tienen formas irregulares en el futuro y en el condicional • Formación de dos tiempos compuestos, el futuro perfecto y el condicional perfecto • El futuro, el condicional, el futuro perfecto y el condicional perfecto para expresar probabilidad • Otros usos de **haber**

1 El tiempo futuro de indicativo de los verbos regulares

A. Forms of the future indicative tense

Future endings		*tomar*	
Singular	*Plural*	*Singular*	*Plural*
-é	**-emos**	tomaré	tomaremos
-ás	**-éis**	tomarás	tomaréis
-á	**-án**	tomará	tomarán

The future indicative tense is formed by adding the endings of the present indicative tense of **haber** to the infinitive. There is only one set of future endings for all verbs in Spanish. Observe that three of the endings begin with **e** or **é** and three with **-á,** and that all the endings except the first person plural have a written accent.

B. Meaning

In general, the future tense in Spanish corresponds to the future tense in English, expressed by *shall* or *will:*

Te llamaré uno de estos días para hacer una cita contigo.   I shall (I'll) call you one of these days to make a date with you.
Los jóvenes irán a la cancha (de tenis).   The young people will go to the tennis court.

C. Substitutes for the future

1. The present indicative tense is often substituted for the future (particularly if an expression of time is included) to make the statement more vivid, to imply greater certainty that the action will take place, and in questions, when immediate future time is involved:

El partido empezará a las dos.   The game will begin at two.
El partido empieza a las dos.   The game begins at two.
Vuelvo en seguida.   I'll return at once (be right back).
¿Escuchamos un disco ahora?   Shall we listen to a record now?

2. **Ir a** plus an infinitive is used in the present indicative tense to refer to the near future:

Van a regresar mañana.   They are going to return tomorrow.

The imperfect **iba a, ibas a,** etc., is similarly used to replace the conditional in indirect discourse, especially in Spanish America:

Pablo dijo que iba a venir.   Paul said that he would (was going to) come.

3. **Haber de** plus an infinitive, which denotes what *is,* or *is supposed, to* (happen), sometimes expresses a sense of obligation in the future:

He de ir a casa de Carolina.   I am to (am supposed to) go to Caroline's house.

4. In **si-**clauses the present indicative is normally used in Spanish, as in English, even though the action is to be completed in the future:

Si Roberto regresa mañana, me llamará.   If Robert returns tomorrow, he will call me.

NOTE: Do not confuse the use of **querer** plus an infinitive in asking a favor, which corresponds to English *will, be willing to,* with the true future. Similarly, **no querer** plus an infinitive may express *be unwilling to, will not:*

¿Quiere Ud. cerrar la puerta?   Will you close the door?
¿Quieres ir al concierto conmigo?   Will you (Are you willing to) go to the concert with me?
Ellos no quieren quedarse.   They won't (are unwilling to) stay.

The future must be used, however, in cases such as:

¿Estarás en casa esta noche?   Will you be at home tonight?

EJERCICIOS

A. Repitan la frase; luego, al oír un sujeto nuevo, substitúyanlo en la frase, cambiando la forma del verbo cuando sea necesario:

1. *Inés* los llevará a casa.
   (Yo, Tú, Mis hermanas, Carlos y yo, Mi amiga)
2. *Mis padres* no venderán el coche.
   (Mi tío, Juan y yo, Tú, Uds., Yo)
3. *Nosotros* no asistiremos a la fiesta.
   (Yo, Tú, Ud., Pepe y Ud., Tomás)

B. Repitan la frase; luego, repítanla, cambiando el verbo al futuro, según los modelos.

MODELOS: Ana ha de cantar hoy.   *Ana ha de cantar hoy.*   *Ana cantará hoy.*
           Van a salir mañana.   *Van a salir mañana.*   *Saldrán mañana.*

1. He de buscar unas noticias para el periódico.
2. Ana y yo hemos de escribir un artículo sobre la fiesta española.
3. Ha de aparecer mañana por la tarde.
4. ¿Qué han de preparar Felipe y Diana?

5. Va a ser mucho más cómodo trabajar en la oficina.
6. ¿Cuáles de las muchachas van a traer los refrescos?
7. ¿Van a asistir a la fiesta todos nuestros amigos?
8. Pepe y Juan no van a volver de la excursión hasta las ocho.

C. Para expresar en español:

1. The boys will arrive at three P.M.   2. Mary will go to the tennis court with me.
3. John's girlfriend will not return tonight.   4. If Joe pays me, I shall go to the
game.   5. Will you (*fam. sing.*) open the window, please?   6. Will you (*fam. sing.*) accompany me to the football game tomorrow afternoon?   7. Henry is to
buy the tickets this morning.   8. The students are to write a composition in
Spanish.   9. I am sure that the two girls will be at the party.   10. Shall we watch
television now?

2   El tiempo condicional de indicativo de los verbos regulares

A. Forms of the conditional indicative tense

Conditional endings		comer	
Singular	Plural	Singular	Plural
-ía	-íamos	comería	comeríamos
-ías	-íais	comerías	comeríais
-ía	-ían	comería	comerían

The conditional indicative tense is formed by adding the imperfect endings of
haber to the infinitive. There is only one set of conditional endings for all verbs
in Spanish. All six forms are accented.

B. Meaning

1. The conditional tense expresses a future action from the standpoint of the
past and is translated in English by *should* or *would*. (Its use in conditional
sentences will be discussed in Lección trece.)

   Luis dijo que jugaría mañana.   Louis said that he would play tomorrow.

2. Remember that when *would* (*used to*) in English expresses a repeated action in
the past, the imperfect indicative tense is used in Spanish, as explained in
Lección cuatro:

   A veces dábamos paseos por el campo.   At times we would take walks in
the country.

3. In the preterit tense, **no querer** plus an infinitive may express *would not* (*refused
to*), *was unwilling to*:

   Ricardo no quiso jugar más.   Richard would not (refused to) play more.

C. The conditional tense may be used to express a polite or softened future statement:

Me gustaría acompañarlos.   I should (would) like to accompany them.
Sería un gran placer ver a Elena.   It would be a great pleasure to see Helen.

EJERCICIOS

A. Repitan la frase; luego, al oír un sujeto nuevo, substitúyanlo en la frase, cambiando la forma del verbo cuando sea necesario:

1. *Ana* tomaría el desayuno a las ocho.
   (Mis amigos, Juan, Tomás y yo, Yo, Tú)
2. *Yo* no comería hasta las seis.
   (Nosotros, Marta, Diana y Luisa, Uds., Tú)
3. *Él* les escribiría mañana.
   (Yo, Nosotros, Juan y José, Tú, Ud.)

B. Para expresar en español:

1. Jane said that she would eat breakfast early.   2. Robert would not (refused to) go to the restaurant with them.   3. Wouldn't it be better to call Mary?   4. I should like to take a walk through the park.   5. Often we would take trips to the mountains.   6. I said that I would visit my cousin (*m.*) in January.

3   Verbos que tienen formas irregulares en el futuro y en el condicional

Verbs irregular in the future and conditional tenses are:

Infinitive	Future	Conditional
haber	**habré, -ás, -á**, etc.	**habría, -ías, -ía**, etc.
poder	**podré, -ás, -á**, etc.	**podría, -ías, -ía**, etc.
querer	**querré, -ás, -á**, etc.	**querría, -ías, -ía**, etc.
saber	**sabré, -ás, -á**, etc.	**sabría, -ías, -ía**, etc.
poner	**pondré, -ás, -á**, etc.	**pondría, -ías, -ía**, etc.
salir	**saldré, -ás, -á**, etc.	**saldría, -ías, -ía**, etc.
tener	**tendré, -ás, -á**, etc.	**tendría, -ías, -ía**, etc.
valer	**valdré, -ás, -á**, etc.	**valdría, -ías, -ía**, etc.
venir	**vendré, -ás, -á**, etc.	**vendría, -ías, -ía**, etc.
decir	**diré, -ás, -á**, etc.	**diría, -ías, -ía**, etc.
hacer	**haré, -ás, -á**, etc.	**haría, -ías, -ía**, etc.

The irregular verbs listed above have the same stem in the future and conditional tenses, and the endings are the same as for regular verbs. Note that the irregularity is in the infinitive stem used: in the first group the final vowel of the infinitive has been dropped, in the second the final vowel of the infinitive has been dropped and the letter **d** has been inserted to facilitate pronunciation, and in the third contracted stems are used.

APLICACIÓN: Pronuncien las formas siguientes; luego, den la forma correspondiente del tiempo condicional:

tomaré	pondrás	sabrán	irán	habremos
comeremos	saldrá	habrá	harás	dirás
vivirán	haré	irás	saldrás	querrá
podrá	vendrán	haremos	dirán	podré

EJERCICIO

Formen oraciones completas empleando las palabras **Tomás dice que** como elemento inicial y cambiando el infinitivo en cursiva a la forma correcta del futuro:

1. *tener* que trabajar el lunes.
2. *poder* ir a la librería.
3. *salir* de casa a las ocho.
4. *hacer* una excursión al parque el domingo.
5. *poner* las cosas en el coche en seguida.
6. *haber* mucha gente en el teatro.
7. *saber* la canción pronto.
8. no *venir* a vernos mañana.
9. no *querer* acompañarnos al cine.
10. *valer* más esperar hasta mañana por la noche.

Repitan el ejercicio, empleando las palabras **Tomás dijo que** como elemento inicial y cambiando el infinitivo en cursiva a la forma correcta del condicional.

4   Formación de dos tiempos compuestos, el futuro perfecto y el condicional perfecto

Future Perfect				Conditional Perfect			
Singular		Plural		Singular		Plural	
habré habrás habrá	} tomado	habremos habréis habrán	} tomado	habría habrías habría	} comido	habríamos habríais habrían	} comido

The future perfect and conditional perfect tenses, like the present perfect and pluperfect tenses, are formed by using the appropriate tense of the auxiliary verb

haber with the past participle. (See Lección cinco.) These two tenses are used as in English, and are expressed by *shall* or *will have taken,* and *should* or *would have taken,* respectively.

EJERCICIO

Repitan la frase; luego, repítanla dos veces más, cambiando la forma del verbo al futuro perfecto y al condicional perfecto de indicativo:

1. Yo le he devuelto el dinero.   2. Luisa no les ha dicho eso.   3. ¿Han vuelto ellos a casa?   4. ¿Quiénes los han visto?   5. ¿Adónde has ido?   6. Carlos nos lo ha traído.

5 El futuro, el condicional, el futuro perfecto y el condicional perfecto para expresar probabilidad

The future tense in Spanish is often used to indicate probability, supposition, or conjecture concerning an action or state in the present time:

> **¿Dónde estará Pablo?**   I wonder where Paul is. (Where do you suppose Paul is? Where can Paul be?)
> **Estará en casa.**   He is probably (must be) at home.
> **¿Qué hora será?**   What time can it be? (I wonder what time it is.)
> **Serán las diez.**   It must be (probably is) ten o'clock.

Similarly, the conditional tense indicates probability or conjecture with reference to the past:

> **¿Quién escribiría la carta?**   Who probably (do you suppose) wrote the letter?
> **¿Sería Lola?**   Do you suppose it was Lola? (I wonder if it was Lola.)
> **Serían las cinco cuando regresaron.**   It was probably five o'clock when they returned.

Probability or conjecture may also be expressed by the future perfect tense and occasionally by the conditional perfect tense:

> **¿Adónde habrá ido Ana?**   Where can Ann have gone? (Where has Ann probably gone? Where do you suppose Ann has gone?)
> **¿Habrá terminado él el trabajo?**   Do you suppose he has finished the work?
> **¿Qué habría hecho Pepe?**   What could Joe have done? (I wonder *or* was wondering what Joe had done.)

EJERCICIOS

A. Contesten cada pregunta, siguiendo los modelos.

MODELO: ¿Qué hora es? ¿Las ocho?   *Sí, serán las ocho.*

1. ¿Dónde está Marta? ¿En casa?
2. ¿Qué hora es? ¿La una?
3. ¿Cuándo vienen ellos? ¿Pronto?
4. ¿Adónde va Luis? ¿Al café?
5. ¿Cuándo sale Lola? ¿Mañana?
6. ¿Quién es? ¿Enrique?

MODELO: ¿Ha ido Jorge al centro?   *Sí, habrá ido al centro.*

7. ¿Ha llegado tu amiga?
8. ¿Ha sonado el timbre?
9. ¿Han vuelto los chicos?
10. ¿Ha puesto Elena la televisión?

MODELO: ¿Fue Ana al partido?   *Sí, iría al partido.*

11. ¿Jugó Miguel al golf?
12. ¿Compró Jaime una cámara?
13. ¿Fueron Luis y Laura al cine?
14. ¿Salió Felipe anoche?

B. Para expresar en español:

1. What time can it be?   2. Do you suppose Jane is ill?   3. I wonder who has the photos.   4. Joe probably has many friends in Mexico.   5. The students have probably written the news items.   6. Who do you suppose called Richard? 7. Charles has probably turned on the television.   8. Robert probably returned home early.

6 Otros usos de **haber**

A. In addition to its use as an auxiliary to form the compound or perfect tenses, **haber** is used impersonally, i.e., without a definite personal subject: **hay** (used for **ha**), *there is (are);* **había,** *there was (were);* **hubo** (*pret.*), *there was (were);* **habrá,** *there will be;* **habría,** *there would be;* **ha habido,** *there has been:*

Hay (Había, Ha habido, Habrá) mucha gente allí.   There are (were, have been, will be) many people there.
Hubo un concierto en el parque ayer.   There was (*occurred*) a concert in the park yesterday.

B. **Hay que** plus an infinitive means *It is necessary to* or *One, We, You, People,* etc. (indefinite subject) *must.* The imperfect **Había que,** and the preterit **Hubo que,** *It was necessary to,* are less common. **Es (Era, Fue) necesario** *or* **preciso** also means *It is (was) necessary (to).*

Hay que preparar la comida.   It is necessary to prepare the meal (food).
Había que practicar mucho.   It was necessary to practice a lot.

See section 1, C, 3, page 86, for the use of **haber de,** which always has a definite personal subject and expresses commitment or mild obligation.

Remember that when the subject is a definite person, **tener que** is used to express a strong obligation or necessity, and **deber** is used to express a moral obligation, duty, or customary action:

> **Mi mamá tuvo que ir al supermercado.**   My mother had to go to the supermarket.
>
> **Debo ayudar a mi hermana.**   I must (should, ought to) help my sister.

EJERCICIO

Para expresar en español:

1. There were many people in the park.   2. There have also been many cars in the streets today.   3. It is necessary (*two ways*) to take the bus.   4. We are to help Mr. Solís next week.   5. The girls had to go to the bookstore.   6. It was necessary to buy some pencils and paper.   7. Charles must write to his brother tonight.   8. We have had to work all day.

EJERCICIO DE REPASO

Repasen las formas de mandato y los pronombres personales, Lecciones dos y tres. Para contestar afirmativa y luego negativamente en español, cambiando el verbo a la forma de mandato correspondiente a **Ud.** y substituyendo el sustantivo en cursiva con el pronombre correspondiente.

MODELOS: ¿Hago *el trabajo* ahora?   *Sí, hágalo Ud. ahora. No, no lo haga Ud. ahora.*
¿Les doy *las fotos*?   *Sí, déselas Ud. No, no se las dé Ud.*

1. ¿Traigo *las cosas* hoy?
2. ¿Busco *a los chicos*?
3. ¿Pago *la cuenta* ahora?
4. ¿Cierro *las puertas*?
5. ¿Envuelvo *el paquete*?
6. ¿Pongo *la maleta* allí?

7. ¿Les llevo *el dinero*?
8. ¿Les escribo *la tarjeta*?
9. ¿Les leo *el cuento*?
10. ¿Les sirvo *los refrescos*?
11. ¿Les digo *la verdad*?
12. ¿Les envío *las rosas*?

Glosario

---

mañana por la tarde (noche) tomorrow afternoon (night *or* evening)
poner (la televisión)   to turn on (the television)

la (semana) que viene   next (week)
tomar el desayuno   to take (have, eat) breakfast
valer más   to be better

LECCIÓN NUEVE

Teoría del modo subjuntivo • Formas del presente de subjuntivo de los verbos regulares • Formas del presente de subjuntivo de los verbos irregulares • Formas del presente de subjuntivo de los verbos que cambian la vocal radical • Formas de otros tipos de verbos que tienen cambios en el presente de subjuntivo • El subjuntivo en cláusulas sustantivas • El subjuntivo en cláusulas sustantivas (continuación)

1 Teoría del modo (*mood*) subjuntivo

The word *subjunctive* means *subjoined,* and except for its use in main clauses to express commands, the subjunctive mood is regularly used in subordinate or dependent clauses. The indicative mood expresses *facts,* makes *assertions,* states *certainties,* or asks direct questions. In general, the subjunctive mood is dependent upon an *attitude,* a *wish,* a *feeling,* or some *uncertainty* in the mind of the speaker, expressed or implied in the main clause. The reference in the dependent clause is to an unaccomplished act or state.

In the case of a dependent clause, you must ask yourself two questions:

1. Is the verb in the main clause one that requires the subjunctive mood in the dependent clause in Spanish?

2. Is the subject of the main clause different from that of the dependent clause?

If the answers to both are yes, the subjunctive mood will be used.

NOTE: If the answer to the second question is no, the infinitive will be used.

The subjunctive mood is more widely used in English than many people realize because its forms differ from the indicative mood only in the third person singular and in some irregular verbs. In this and later lessons the subjunctive mood will be discussed according to its use in noun, adjective, and adverbial clauses. In the examples which follow, note, in the noun clauses, the various English equivalents of the Spanish subjunctive forms: English present tense, the future, use of the modal auxiliary *may,* and the infinitive:

> **Yo no creo que el hermano de Pepe esté aquí.**   I do not believe (that) Joe's brother is (will be) here.
> **Esperamos que Uds. lo hagan pronto.**   We hope (that) you may (will) do it soon.
> **Yo no quiero que Juan venga.**   I do not wish that John come (I don't want John to come).

2 Formas del presente de subjuntivo de los verbos regulares

In the present subjunctive tense the endings of **-ar** verbs begin with **e** and those of **-er** and **-ir** verbs begin with **a:**

tomar		comer		abrir	
Singular	*Plural*	*Singular*	*Plural*	*Singular*	*Plural*
tome	tomemos	coma	comamos	abra	abramos
tomes	toméis	comas	comáis	abras	abráis
tome	tomen	coma	coman	abra	abran

In Lección dos we have used the third person singular and plural and the second person singular forms of the present subjunctive tense in commands. The present subjunctive forms of all types of verbs are given in Appendix D, pages 224–234.

3 Formas del presente de subjuntivo de los verbos irregulares

In order to form the present subjunctive tense of all but six verbs in Spanish (**dar, estar, haber, ir, saber, ser**), drop the ending **-o** of the first person singular present indicative form and add to this stem the subjunctive endings for the corresponding conjugation:

Infinitive	*1st Sing. Pres. Ind.*	*Present Subjunctive*
caer	**caigo**	**caiga, caigas, caiga,** etc.
conocer	**conozco**	**conozca, conozcas, conozca,** etc.
decir	**digo**	**diga,** etc.
hacer	**hago**	**haga,** etc.
oír	**oigo**	**oiga,** etc.
poner	**pongo**	**ponga,** etc.
salir	**salgo**	**salga,** etc.
tener	**tengo**	**tenga,** etc.
traer	**traigo**	**traiga,** etc.
valer	**valgo**	**valga,** etc.
venir	**vengo**	**venga,** etc.
ver	**veo**	**vea,** etc.

dar		estar		haber	
Singular	*Plural*	*Singular*	*Plural*	*Singular*	*Plural*
dé	**demos**	**esté**	**estemos**	**haya**	**hayamos**
des	**deis**	**estés**	**estéis**	**hayas**	**hayáis**
dé	**den**	**esté**	**estén**	**haya**	**hayan**

ir		saber		ser	
vaya	**vayamos**	**sepa**	**sepamos**	**sea**	**seamos**
vayas	**vayáis**	**sepas**	**sepáis**	**seas**	**seáis**
vaya	**vayan**	**sepa**	**sepan**	**sea**	**sean**

APLICACIÓN: Formas de verbos en el presente de subjuntivo. Den la forma del verbo que corresponda a cada sujeto:

1. Que yo tomar, abrir, hacer, ver, conocer.
2. Que tú comer, decir, dar, estar, oír.
3. Que él salir, caer, ir, ser, terminar.
4. Que nosotros saber, tener, traer, venir, poner.

4 Formas del presente de subjuntivo de los verbos que cambian la vocal radical

Stem-changing verbs of Class I (ending in **-ar** and **-er**) have the same changes in the present subjunctive tense as in the present indicative, that is, throughout the singular and in the third person plural. This is also true of **poder** and **querer.**

cerrar	**cierre**	**cierres**	**cierre**	cerremos	cerréis	**cierren**
volver	**vuelva**	**vuelvas**	**vuelva**	volvamos	volváis	**vuelvan**
poder	**pueda**	**puedas**	**pueda**	podamos	podáis	**puedan**
querer	**quiera**	**quieras**	**quiera**	queramos	queráis	**quieran**

Stem-changing verbs of Class II and Class III (both of which end in **-ir**) have the same four changes in the present subjunctive tense which they have in the present indicative tense (throughout the singular and in the third person plural). In addition, Class II verbs change **e** to **i** and **o** to **u** in the first and second persons plural, and Class III verbs change **e** to **i** in these two forms also.

Class II				Class III	
sentir		*dormir*		*pedir*	
Singular	Plural	Singular	Plural	Singular	Plural
sienta	sintamos	duerma	durmamos	pida	pidamos
sientas	sintáis	duermas	durmáis	pidas	pidáis
sienta	sientan	duerma	duerman	pida	pidan

APLICACIÓN: Den la forma del verbo que corresponda a cada sujeto:

1. Que yo querer, envolver, pensar, perder, pedir.
2. Que tú encontrar, contar, preferir, dormir, servir.
3. Que Uds. pedir, consentir, sentarse, despertarse, divertirse.
4. Que nosotros poder, repetir, devolver, sentir, dormir.

5   Formas de otros tipos de verbos que tienen cambios en el presente de subjuntivo

A. Verbs ending in **-car, -gar,** and **-zar** have the following changes in all six forms of the present subjunctive tense: **c** to **qu, g** to **gu,** and **z** to **c,** respectively. Remember that these changes in spelling also occur in the first person singular of the preterit indicative tense. Note that **empezar** also has the stem change of **e** to **ie.**

buscar	**busque**	**busques**	**busque**	**busquemos**	**busquéis**	**busquen**
llegar	**llegue**	**llegues**	**llegue**	**lleguemos**	**lleguéis**	**lleguen**
empezar	**empiece**	**empieces**	**empiece**	**empecemos**	**empecéis**	**empiecen**

Other **-car** verbs used up to this point are: **acercarse, explicar, practicar, sacar, tocar;** other **-gar** verbs are: **colgar (ue), entregar, jugar (ue), obligar, pagar;** other **-zar** verbs are **almorzar (ue), comenzar (ie).**

B. Verbs ending in **-guir** drop the **u** after **g** before the endings **-o** and **-a,** that is, in the first person singular present indicative tense and in all six forms of the present subjunctive tense. The model verb for this change, **seguir,** *to follow, continue, go on,* is also a stem-changing verb, Class III, like **pedir.**

Pres. Part.	**siguiendo**					
Pres. Ind.	**sigo**	**sigues**	**sigue**	seguimos	seguís	**siguen**
Pres. Subj.	**siga**	**sigas**	**siga**	**sigamos**	**sigáis**	**sigan**
Preterit	seguí	seguiste	**siguió**	seguimos	seguisteis	**siguieron**
Sing. Imper.	**sigue**					

Seguir is followed by the present participle, like the English verb *to continue:* **Los chicos siguen charlando,** *The children continue chatting;* **Sigan Uds. leyendo,** *Continue reading.*

C. Verbs ending in **-ger** or **-gir** change **g** to **j** before **a,** as well as before **o** in the first person singular present indicative tense: **escoger,** *to choose;* **dirigir,** *to direct.*

Pres. Ind.	**escojo**	escoges	escoge	escogemos	escogéis	escogen
Pres. Subj.	**escoja**	**escojas**	**escoja**	**escojamos**	**escojáis**	**escojan**
Pres. Ind.	**dirijo**	diriges	dirige	dirigimos	dirigís	dirigen
Pres. Subj.	**dirija**	**dirijas**	**dirija**	**dirijamos**	**dirijáis**	**dirijan**

For the present subjunctive forms of a few other less common verbs, see Appendix D, pages 230–232.

EJERCICIOS

A. Para contestar afirmativamente, cambiando el verbo a la forma de mandato correspondiente a **Ud.** o **Uds.**, como en los modelos.

MODELOS: ¿Busco a Juan?   *Sí, busque Ud. a Juan.*
             ¿Le pedimos algo?   *Sí, pídanle Uds. algo.*

1. ¿Hago el trabajo?
2. ¿Toco un disco?
3. ¿Le entrego la cinta?
4. ¿Me acerco al coche?
5. ¿Almuerzo a las doce?
6. ¿Empezamos a las ocho?
7. ¿Le servimos refrescos?
8. ¿Nos sentamos a la derecha?
9. ¿Jugamos al tenis ahora?
10. ¿Vamos a la reunión?

B. Para contestar negativamente, cambiando el verbo a la forma de mandato correspondiente a **tú.**

MODELO: ¿Abro la ventana?   *No, no abras la ventana.*

1. ¿Salgo a la calle ahora?
2. ¿Pongo la televisión?
3. ¿Duermo la siesta esta tarde?
4. ¿Llego tarde a la fiesta?
5. ¿Sigo sonando el timbre?
6. ¿Busco al profesor?
7. ¿Le devuelvo el libro?
8. ¿Les pido un favor?
9. ¿Me siento cerca de Ana?
10. ¿Escojo un regalo para él?

6   El subjuntivo en cláusulas sustantivas

The subjunctive mood is regularly used in a noun clause (i.e., a clause used as the subject or object of a verb) when the verb in the main clause expresses or implies ideas of the speaker such as those of *wish, advice, request, command, permission, approval, cause, suggestion, preference, proposal, recommendation, insistence,* and the like, as well as their negatives.

Remember that in English the infinitive is most commonly used after such verbs, but in Spanish a noun clause, usually introduced by **que,** is regularly used if the subject of the dependent clause is *different* from that of the main clause. When there is no change in subject, or no subject is expressed for the English infinitive, the infinitive is also used in Spanish. Compare the following pairs of examples:

Lupe quiere salir.   Lupe wants to leave. *(Same subjects)*
Ella quiere que yo salga.   She wants me to leave. *(Different subjects)*

Ellos insisten en hacer la excursión.   They insist on taking the excursion.
   (Same subjects)
Ellos insisten en que se haga la excursión.   They insist that the excursion be taken. *(Different subjects)*

With certain verbs, e.g., **decir, pedir (i, i), aconsejar,** *to advise,* and others which require the indirect object of a person, the subject of the infinitive in English is expressed as the indirect object of the main verb and understood as the subject of the subjunctive verb in the dependent clause. In the case of a sentence such as *Ask him to go,* think of it as *Ask of (to) him that he go:*

> **Pídales Ud. a ellos que vayan a la playa.**   Ask them to go to the beach.
> **Alguien le aconseja a Ana que solicite la beca.**   Someone advises Ann to apply for the scholarship.
> **Les rogaré que no sirvan nada.**   I shall ask (beg) them not to serve anything.
> **El señor Solís les permitirá a los chicos que jueguen en el parque.**   Mr. Solís will permit the children to play (let the children play) in the park.
> **Le diré a Pepe que vuelva pronto.**   I shall tell Joe to return soon.

Decir is followed by the subjunctive mood when it is used to give an order (last example, above). Otherwise, the indicative mood is used, since the verb indicates a fact (unless the verb is used negatively, in which case it becomes a verb which expresses uncertainty; see Lección diez):

> **Pepe dice que volverá pronto.**   Joe says (that) he will return soon.
> *(Indirect discourse)*

In Lección siete we found that **dejar, hacer, mandar,** and **permitir** are usually followed by the infinitive when the subject of a dependent verb is a pronoun. The subjunctive mood may also be used after these verbs, particularly when the dependent verb has a noun subject (fourth example, above). One also says: **Permitiremos que ellos asistan a la reunión,** *We shall permit that they attend the meeting.*

EJERCICIOS

A. Repitan la oración; luego, al oír un sujeto nuevo, substitúyanlo en la oración, cambiando la forma del verbo cuando sea necesario:

  1. Desean que *Ud.* escoja una cámara.
     (yo, tú, nosotros, Ana y Carmen, Felipe)
  2. Ella prefiere que *yo* busque un radio.
     (Juan, los muchachos, mi hermano, Ana y yo, tú)
  3. El profesor quiere que *los estudiantes* lleguen a tiempo.
     (yo, Juan y yo, tú, Margarita, Pablo y Luis)

B. Repitan la oración; luego, al oír la frase con la conjunción (*conjunction*) **que,** formen una nueva oración, según el modelo.

  MODELO: Deseo comer un poco.   *Deseo comer un poco.*
       (que Ud.)   *Deseo que Ud. coma un poco.*

  1. Quiero hacer la excursión. (que Uds.)
  2. Prefieren jugar mañana por la mañana. (que yo)

3. José insiste en ir al centro. (que tú)
4. Marta no desea servir refrescos esta tarde. (que Lola)
5. ¿Prefieres sacar las fotos ahora? (que Carlota)
6. ¿Quieren Uds. seguir leyendo? (que Pepe y yo)
7. ¿Deseas empezar a cantar? (que nosotros)
8. Ellos no quieren sentarse en la primera fila. (que Carlos)

C. Después de oír una frase, oirán una oración incompleta; formen una nueva oración introducida por la oración incompleta, según el modelo.

MODELO: venir a las dos.   (Dígales Ud. que)   *Dígales Ud. que vengan a las dos.*

1. no salir de casa. (Le ruego a Ana que)
2. hacer el trabajo. (Pídale Ud. a José que)
3. levantarse en seguida. (Dígale Ud. a Pablo)
4. poner la televisión. (Les permito a los chicos que)
5. no olvidarse del programa. (Le aconsejamos a él que)
6. empezar a tocar. (Le dirán a Carmen que)
7. escoger un regalo para ella. (Preferimos que tú)
8. seguir practicando mucho. (La profesora quiere que ellos)

D. Para expresar en español:

1. He wants to leave early.   2. He wants me to leave early.   3. Helen and I want to meet her.   4. Helen wants me to meet her.   5. They prefer to continue reading.   6. They prefer that we continue listening to the tape.   7. Ask (*formal sing.*) him for the articles.   8. Ask (*formal sing.*) him to give you the articles. 9. Tell (*pl.*) them that we are going to return home.   10. Tell (*pl.*) them to return at once.

7   El subjuntivo en cláusulas sustantivas (continuación)

The subjunctive mood is used in noun clauses dependent upon verbs or expressions of emotion or feeling, such as *joy, sorrow, fear, hope, pity, surprise,* and the like, as well as their opposites, provided that the subject differs from that of the main verb. Some common expressions of emotion are:

alegrarse (de que)   to be glad
(that)
esperar   to hope
estar contento, -a (de que)   to be
happy (that)
sentir (ie, i)   to regret, be sorry

ser lástima   to be a pity
(too bad)
sorprender   to surprise
temer   to fear
tener miedo (de que)   to be
afraid (that)

Nos alegramos de estar aquí.   We are glad to be here. (*Same subject*)

¡Cuánto me alegro de que tú estés de vuelta!   How glad I am that you are back. (*Different subjects*)

Siento no poder quedarme.   I'm sorry I cannot (I'm sorry not to be able to) stay.

Sienten que yo no pueda esperar más.   They regret (that) I cannot wait longer.

¿Tienes miedo de que Pepe no llegue?   Are you afraid that Joe will not arrive?

¡Me sorprende (Es lástima) que haya[1] tanto tráfico ahora!   It surprises me (It is too bad) that there is so much traffic now!

EJERCICIOS

A. Repitan la oración; luego, al oír la frase con la conjunción **que,** úsenla para formar una nueva oración, siguiendo el modelo.

MODELO: Espero pagar la cuenta.   *Espero pagar la cuenta.*
           (que tú)   *Espero que tú pagues la cuenta.*

1. Se alegran de poder ir a la reunión contigo. (de que Elena)
2. Nos sorprende no verlos en la fiesta. (que tú)
3. ¿Temen Uds. llegar tarde? (que nosotros)
4. ¿Siente Luisa no conocer a Tomás? (que Uds.)
5. Es lástima no practicar más. (que los jóvenes)
6. Ellos esperan hacer un viaje a México. (que Juan y yo)
7. Estamos contentos de saber eso. (de que ella)
8. José no tiene miedo de ir en avión. (de que sus amigos)

B. Repitan la oración; luego, al oír la frase con la conjunción **que,** formen una nueva oración, según el modelo.

MODELO: Pepe irá a casa.   *Pepe irá a casa.*
           (Espero que)   *Espero que Pepe vaya a casa.*

1. Pablo pondrá un tocadiscos. (Queremos que)
2. Nosotros tendremos que esperar en el aeropuerto. (Ellos sienten que)
3. Mis padres buscarán una casa más grande. (Me alegro de que)
4. Marta no saldrá de casa temprano. (¿Tienes miedo de que . . . ?)
5. Nuestro amigo volverá la semana que viene. (¿Quieres que . . . ?)
6. Los chicos no se divertirán mucho allí. (Es lástima que)
7. Jorge seguirá tocando la guitarra. (Ellos prefieren que)
8. Carlota no quiere jugar al tenis hoy. (Nos sorprende que)

---

[1] Note that **haya** is the impersonal form of **haber** in the present subjunctive tense.

C. Para expresar en español:

1. They are glad that Jane will be back soon.   2. I am surprised (**Me sorprende**) that you (*fam. sing.*) do not play the guitar.   3. We are happy that our parents will arrive on time.   4. John is afraid that Lola will not return tomorrow morning. 5. It is too bad that there is so much traffic today.   6. Ann begs us to call her by telephone often.   7. They are sorry that Thomas and I cannot wait longer. 8. Do you (*fam. sing.*) hope to be able to help your cousin (*m.*)?

Glosario

a la derecha   on (to) the right
esperar más   to wait longer
estar de vuelta   to be back
la **fila**   row
llegar a tiempo   to arrive on time

mañana por la mañana   tomorrow morning
rogar (ue)   to ask, beg
el **tráfico**   traffic

Repaso tres

A. Lean en español, supliendo la preposición correcta cuando sea necesario:

1. No dejen Uds. _____ escribirnos.   2. Felipe no se atreve _____ acercarse.
3. Déjame tú _____ ayudarte.   4. Es difícil _____ aprender todas las expresiones.   5. ¿Qué piensas tú _____ hacer por la tarde?   6. Ellos insisten _____ terminar el trabajo hoy.   7. Juan se olvidó _____ llamar a Carlota.
8. No se trata _____ quedarse en casa.   9. Están seguros _____ poder _____ saber eso.   10. ¿Por qué tardó él tanto _____ volver a casa?

B. Para expresar en español:

1. The boys have just arrived.   2. Are you (pl.) tired of watching television?
3. The girls stopped playing tennis.   4. Mr. Solís had the letters written.
5. Did you (formal sing.) hear him play the guitar?   6. They decided not to wait longer.   7. I began to read the news.   8. We are glad to be able to attend the meeting.   9. Did you (fam. sing.) forget to call Lola?   10. Don't fail (fam. sing.) to practice tomorrow.

C. Para leer en español, supliendo la forma correcta de **estar, haber, hacer, ser o tener.** Usen el tiempo presente si no se indica otro tiempo:

1. ¿Qué tiempo _____ hoy?   2. _____ fresco y mucho viento.   3. Nosotros _____ mucho calor en este edificio.   4. No _____ (pres. perf.) mucho frío aquí este otoño.   5. A veces _____ mucho polvo.   6. No _____ luna esta noche.   7. _____ (fam. sing. command) mucho cuidado y no _____ miedo.
8. Ud. _____ razón; parece que él siempre _____ mucho frío.   9. _____ (imp.) niebla cuando salimos de casa.   10. El hielo _____ frío, pero a menudo el agua _____ caliente.

D. Lean en español; luego, cambien las oraciones a la forma negativa:

1. Tomás tiene algo en la mano.   2. Siempre les envío algo.   3. Alguien ha tratado de llamarnos.   4. Hay alguien en el coche.   5. Alguno de ellos puede traer los discos.   6. Algún muchacho puede hacer eso.   7. ¿Viste a alguien allí?
8. El cuento es algo interesante.   9. Conozco a alguno de los chicos.   10. Carlos fue al cine con alguien.

La Giralda, Sevilla, España.

E. Lean en español, cambiando el infinitivo entre paréntesis al tiempo indicado:

(Futuro)   1. El sábado por la noche Ana y yo (ir) al concierto.   2. Yo (comprar) los boletos mañana por la mañana.   3. Carlos y Marta no (poder) acompañarnos. 4. Carlos dice que (tener) que trabajar.   5. Nosotros (salir) de casa a las seis y (comer) en el restaurante.   6. Creo que varios amigos (estar) allí también. 7. Estoy seguro de que nosotros (divertirse) mucho.   8. Sin duda (haber) mucha gente en el concierto.

(Condicional)   9. Jorge me dijo que (venir) a mi cuarto mañana a la una. 10. Yo sabía que él (hacer) eso.   11. ¿Te (gustar) ir al partido de básquetbol con nosotros?   12. Jorge contestó que le (gustar) mucho ir.   13. Varias personas le dijeron anoche que (ser) un partido muy bueno.   14. Yo (decir) eso también.

(*Futuro perfecto*) 15. ¿Sabes si Carlos (volver) de San Antonio? 16. Jaime cree que él ya (llegar). 17. También cree que (ir) a trabajar temprano. 18. Sin duda alguna él (tomar) el autobús para ir al centro.

F. Para expresar en español:

1. We'll be back at once. 2. Shall we sit down now? 3. Will you (*fam. sing.*) close the door, please? 4. The girls will leave at two P.M. 5. My sister is to go to Argentina next week. 6. She would like to stay there for (**por**) two months. 7. It would be a great pleasure to meet her. 8. Mr. Sierra says that he will have to take a long trip soon. 9. He is probably in his office now. 10. What time can it be? 11. It must be nine o'clock. 12. I wonder where James has left the car. 13. The boys must (probably) have gone out into the street. 14. I am sure that there will be many people at (**en**) the meeting. 15. Jane must help her friend (*f.*) this afternoon. 16. It is necessary to practice a lot.

G. Para contestar afirmativa y luego negativamente en español, cambiando el verbo a la forma de mandato correspondiente a **Ud.** y substituyendo el sustantivo en cursiva con el pronombre correspondiente:

1. ¿Cierro *la ventana* ahora?
2. ¿Busco *a Carolina*?
3. ¿Pongo *las revistas* aquí?
4. ¿Pago *los libros*?

5. ¿Les repito *las palabras*?
6. ¿Les explico *la frase*?
7. ¿Les sirvo *el café*?
8. ¿Les pido *el favor*?

H. Lean en español; luego, formen una nueva frase con la conjunción **que:**

1. Nos alegramos de poder ir contigo. (de que Margarita)
2. Sentimos no conocer a María López. (que tú)
3. Esperamos tocar más discos esta noche. (que Uds. no)
4. Preferimos seguir escuchando la cinta. (que Juan no)
5. Mis padres quieren salir en seguida. (que mis hermanos)
6. Juanito insiste en jugar en el patio. (que sus amigos)
7. Es lástima no tener tiempo para eso. (que Uds.)
8. Queremos seguir escuchando discos. (que ella)

I. Para expresar en español:

1. They want me to turn on the television. 2. Ask (*formal sing.*) them to be here tomorrow morning. 3. They are glad that we are back. 4. I insist that you (*fam. sing.*) take breakfast with us. 5. We are sorry not to be able to attend the concert. 6. I advise you (*fam. sing.*) to apply for the scholarship. 7. Do you (*pl.*) want me to choose a camera? 8. We shall tell Louise to call us next week. 9. We are afraid to wait longer. 10. They will not permit the children to play in the street.

La Feria de Sevilla, Sevilla, España.

Notas culturales III

España: trescientos sesenta días de fiesta al año

Los únicos días «tristes» en España son el 12, 13 y 14 de enero, el 14 de abril y el 5 de diciembre—fechas todas ellas en que ninguna localidad española está de fiesta,° según el compendio° ofrecido en el Calendario Turístico. Por el contrario,° ni uno solo de los trescientos sesenta días restantes amanecerá° sin la alegre diana° de una feria, una romería,° una procesión o un festejo° localizado en alguna parte del país, ya sea° ciudad, villa,[1] pueblo, aldea,° o lugar.°

No menos de° 2,705 fiestas distintas se celebran al año.° Por lo que al verano se refiere,° durante sus noventa y dos días habrá un total mínimo de 1,160 festejos diferentes . . .

¿Cómo se divierte el pueblo durante sus fiestas? Principalmente bailando y yendo en romería. En 77 localidades del país, la base de la diversión se encuentra en sus típicas danzas; pero también, en otro aspecto, existen jornadas gastronómicas famosas,° como las fiestas de la lamprea° y del pulpo,° en Pontevedra;[2] de la sardina, en Padrón y Vigo; del langostino,° en Vinaroz, o de la manzana,° en Oviedo. La paella[3] es objeto de un concurso° nacional en Sueca (Valencia), y Castellón festeja° la uva de moscatel,° lo mismo que° Jerez y Valdepeñas hacen honores a° sus vinos. La fiesta del olivo, en Mora de Toledo, entre otras muchas,° completa el ciclo de fiestas que cantan los productos del campo español.

está de fiesta *has a holiday celebration*

compendio *summary*

Por el contrario *On the contrary*

amanecerá *will dawn* / **diana** *reveille (call, summons)* / **romería** *pilgrimage, excursion* / **festejo** *celebration* **ya sea** *whether it is (a)*

aldea *village* / **lugar** *hamlet, settlement*

No menos de *No fewer than*

al año *each year* / **Por lo que . . . se refiere** *Referring to the summer*

jornadas gastronómicas famosas *famous days devoted to good eating* / **lamprea** *eel* / **pulpo** *octopus* **langostino** *prawn*

manzana *apple*

concurso *competition* / **festeja** *celebrates* / **uva de moscatel** *muscatel grape* / **lo mismo que** *the same as* **hacer honores a** *to do (show) honors to*

otras muchas *many others*

---

[1] **villa,** *town* (= a town enjoying certain privileges by charter).
[2] For the location of the cities mentioned in this section, see the map of Spain, page 284.
[3] **La paella** is a rice dish containing meat, vegetables, and shellfish.

A los españoles les gusta combinar sus diversiones con la idea religiosa. En Galicia se celebran curiosas procesiones, en que, por ejemplo, los que se han hallado en grave peligro° de muerte transportan ataúdes° simbólicos. Las procesiones marítimas se multiplican en la época veraniega,° especialmente coincidiendo con la festividad de la Virgen del Carmen,[1] patrona del mar.

peligro *danger* / ataúdes *coffins*

época veraniega *summer season*

Los encierros taurinos° y corridas de toros° son plato fuerte° no sólo en Pamplona, sino en casi todas las poblaciones. A todo ello° se unen las fiestas de interés turístico, que juntan° las tradiciones y las costumbres de cientos de años con nuestros días° . . .

encierros taurinos *driving bulls into pen before fight* / corridas de toros *bullfights* / plato fuerte *the main course (i.e., the principal diversion)* / A todo ello *To all of it* / juntan *bring together*
con nuestros días *with today (the present)*

PREGUNTAS

Para contestar en español en oraciones completas:

1. ¿Cuántos días de fiesta se celebran al año en España?   2. ¿Por qué puede decirse que los cinco días restantes son tristes?   3. ¿Con qué amanecen los trescientos sesenta días de fiesta?   4. ¿Qué es una romería?   5. ¿Cuántas fiestas distintas se celebran al año en España?   6. ¿Cuántos festejos diferentes hay durante el verano?

7. ¿Cómo se divierte el pueblo español durante sus fiestas?   8. ¿En qué ciudades existen jornadas gastronómicas famosas?   9. ¿En qué región de España se hallan las ciudades de Pontevedra, Padrón y Vigo?   10. ¿En qué ciudad es la paella objeto de un concurso nacional?   11. ¿Qué ciudades hacen honores a sus vinos?   12. ¿En qué ciudad festejan el olivo?

13. ¿Con qué idea combinan los españoles sus diversiones?   14. ¿Qué curiosa procesión se celebra en Galicia?   15. ¿En qué época se multiplican las procesiones marítimas?   16. ¿Con qué coinciden las fiestas marítimas?

17. ¿En qué ciudad son famosos los encierros taurinos?   18. ¿En qué región de España se encuentra Pamplona?   19. ¿En qué ciudades de España se celebran corridas de toros?   20. ¿Qué juntan las fiestas de interés turístico?

EJERCICIO ESCRITO

Escriban un breve informe, de unas cien palabras, sobre uno de los temas siguientes:

1. El número de los días de fiesta en España, según el Calendario Turístico.
2. Las fiestas que cantan los productos del campo español.
3. La presencia de la idea religiosa en las diversiones de los españoles.

---

[1] The festival of **la Virgen del Carmen** (*Our Lady of Mount Carmel*) falls on July 16.

LECCIÓN DIEZ

1 El subjuntivo en cláusulas sustantivas (continuación)

The subjunctive mood is used in noun clauses after expressions of *doubt, uncertainty, belief expressed negatively,* and *denial.* Common verbs of this type are:

> **dudar**   to doubt
> **negar (ie)**   to deny
> **no creer**   not to believe
>
> **no estar seguro, -a de que**   not to be sure that

> **Creo (Estoy seguro de) que ellos están en casa.**   I believe *or* think (I am sure) that they are at home.   (*Certainty*)
> **No creemos que todos digan que sí.**   We don't believe (that) all will say yes.   (*Uncertainty*)
> **Dudan (No están seguros de) que Pepe llegue a tiempo.**   They doubt (They aren't sure) that Joe will arrive on time.
> **Carlos niega que haya mucha gente en el teatro.**   Charles denies that there are many people in the theater.

Creer and **estar seguro, -a de que** express certainty and are followed by the indicative mood in a clause, while **no creer que** and **no estar seguro, -a de que** express uncertainty or doubt and require the subjunctive mood in a dependent clause.

Note that **no dudar** and **no negar** express certainty and are followed by the indicative mood:

> **No dudo que los muchachos vendrán esta noche.**   I don't doubt that the boys will come tonight.   (*Certainty*)
> **No negamos que Juan lo ha hecho.**   We don't deny that John has done it.   (*Certainty*)

When **creer** is used in questions, the speaker may imply doubt of the action in the dependent clause, in which case the subjunctive mood is used. If no implication of doubt is made, the indicative mood is used. **No creer que** in a question implies certainty and is followed by the indicative:

> **¿Cree Ud. que haga buen tiempo mañana?**   Do you believe (that) it will be good (nice) weather tomorrow?   (*Doubt in the mind of the speaker*)
> **¿Crees que todos se divierten mucho?**   Do you believe (think) that all are having a very good time?   (*The speaker has no opinion*)
> **¿No crees que tendremos tiempo para eso?**   Don't you believe (that) we shall have time for that?   (*Certainty implied*)

EJERCICIO

Repitan la oración; luego, al oír el comienzo (*beginning*) de otra oración, complétenla, según los modelos.

MODELOS: José dirá que sí.   *José dirá que sí.*
             (Creo que)   *Creo que José dirá que sí.*
             (No creo que)   *No creo que José diga que sí.*

1. Ellos están jugando al tenis.   (Creemos que)
2. María va de compras esta tarde.   (Yo no creo que)
3. Miguel buscará otros discos.   (No estamos seguros de que)
4. Habrá luna esta noche.   (Dudamos que)
5. Todos asistirán a la reunión.   (¿No crees que . . . ?)
6. Los muchachos llegarán antes de la una.   (¿Dudas que . . . ?)
7. Juan volverá en seguida.   (Pablo niega que)
8. Lola preferirá esta pulsera.   (Estoy segura de que)

2   El subjuntivo en cláusulas sustantivas (fin)

A. The subjunctive is used after impersonal expressions (which usually begin with *it is*) of *possibility, necessity, uncertainty, probability, strangeness, doubt, pity,* and the like, provided that the verb of the dependent clause has a subject expressed. When no subject is expressed, the infinitive is used.

    Impersonal expressions of certainty, such as **Es cierto (verdad, evidente),** *It is certain (true, evident),* require the indicative mood in the dependent clause; however, when these expressions are negative, they imply *uncertainty* and require the subjunctive:

> **Será preciso (bueno) esperar aquí.**   It will be necessary (well) to wait here.
> **Es posible (probable) que ellos no se queden.**   It is possible (probable) that they will (may) not stay.
> **No es cierto (verdad) que él obtenga la beca.**   It is not certain (true) that he will get the scholarship.
> **Puede (ser) que Ana esté en el centro.**   It may be that Ann is (will *or* may be) downtown.

Some common impersonal expressions which often require the subjunctive are:

basta it is sufficient (enough)	**es fácil** it is easy
conviene it is fitting (advisable)	**es importante** it is important
es bueno it is well	**es imposible** it is impossible
es difícil it is difficult	**es lástima** it is a pity (too bad)
es dudoso it is doubtful	**es malo** it is bad
es extraño it is strange	**es mejor** it is better

es necesario it is necessary	**importa** it is important, it
es posible it is possible	matters
es preciso it is necessary	**más vale (vale más)** it is
es probable it is probable	better
es urgente it is urgent	**puede (ser)** it may be

These expressions really fall under sections 6 and 7, pages 98–101, and under section 1, above, but they are treated separately here for convenience and clarity.

B. The infinitive *may* be used after certain impersonal expressions if the subject of the dependent verb (expressed in English as the indirect object of the main verb) is a *personal pronoun,* not a noun. Some of the impersonal expressions used in this construction are: **conviene, es difícil, es fácil, es imposible, es mejor, es necesario, es preciso,** and **importa:**

Me (Te, Le, Nos, Les) conviene vender la casa.   It is advisable for me (you, him, her, us, them) to sell the house.

Me (Te, Le, Nos, Les) fue difícil terminar el trabajo.   It was difficult for me (you, etc.) to finish the work.

Me (Te, etc.) sería mejor salir ahora.   It would be better for me (you, etc.) to leave now.

BUT: **Es extraño que Pepe no tenga nada que hacer hoy.**   It is strange that Joe doesn't have anything to do today.

EJERCICIOS

A. Lean en español, supliendo la forma correcta del infinitivo entre paréntesis si se necesita un cambio:

1. Es preciso que nosotros (buscar) un lugar más hermoso.   2. ¿No será mejor (descansar) unos momentos?   3. Es cierto que todos (llegar) al poco rato.   4. Es lástima que (estar) nublado hoy.   5. Pero es probable que no (ir) a llover. 6. Importa que ellos (traer) los refrescos.   7. Es extraño que no (haber) más gente en el parque.   8. Será imposible (pasar) todo el día aquí.

B. Repitan la oración; luego, formen una nueva oración, siguiendo el modelo.

MODELO: Vale más que regresen hoy.   *Vale más que regresen hoy.*
                                        Vale más regresar hoy.

1. Importa que Uds. escriban el artículo.
2. Es urgente que lo preparen para mañana.
3. No será fácil que lo terminen pronto.
4. Pero importa que no tarden mucho en hacerlo.
5. No es necesario que llamen a Carmen.
6. ¿Será mejor que Luis compre otra bicicleta?
7. Es lástima que no tengan más tiempo.
8. Conviene que hagamos planes para mañana.

C. Para escribir en español:

1. It is possible that Inez will play the guitar.   2. We are not sure that Miss Flores will come to the meeting.   3. It is too bad that Caroline is ill today.   4. It is certain that most of the students are not very busy.   5. It is cloudy, and it is possible that it may rain.   6. Jane doesn't believe that Ann can accompany her. 7. It will be impossible for all to arrive on time.   8. We are surprised that John doesn't know anything about our plans.   9. It is true that we like Spanish music very much.   10. Don't you (*fam. sing.*) believe that the boys will have a good time?

3   Otras formas de mandato

A. The first person plural of the present subjunctive tense, and also **vamos a** plus the infinitive, express commands equal to *let's* or *let us* plus a verb. **A ver** is regularly used for *Let's see*.

Remember that object pronouns are attached to affirmative commands and to infinitives, but they precede the verb in negative commands:

Llamemos a Carlota.   Let's call Charlotte.
Cerrémosla.
Vamos a cerrarla. } Let's close it.
No los dejemos allí.   Let's not leave them there.

NOTE: **Vamos** is used for the affirmative *Let's (Let us) go*. The subjunctive **No vayamos** must be used for *Let's not go:* **No vayamos todavía,** *Let's not go yet.* **No vamos a casa** can only mean *We are not going home.*

When the reflexive pronoun **nos** is added to this command form, the final **-s** is dropped from the verb:

Vámonos.   Let's be going (Let's go).
Quedémonos (Vamos a quedarnos) un rato.   Let's stay a while.
No nos levantemos.   Let's not get up.

B. **Que,** equivalent to *have, let, may, I wish,* or *I hope* in English, introduces indirect commands in the second and third persons. In such cases object pronouns precede the verb, and if a subject is expressed, it usually follows the verb. This construction is really a clause dependent upon a verb of *wishing, hoping, permitting,* etc., with the main verb understood but not expressed:

Que lo traiga Tomás.   Have (Let, May) Thomas bring it.
Que estén ellos aquí a las seis.   Let them be here at six.
Que descanses bien.   May (I hope) you rest well.
¡Que te diviertas mucho!   May you (I want you to, I hope you) have a very good time!

Remember that when *let* means *allow* or *permit*, it is translated by **dejar** or **permitir**: **Déjele (Permítale) usted a Pablo que vaya a la reunión,** *Let Paul (Allow or Permit Paul to) go to the meeting.*

EJERCICIOS

A. Para contestar dos veces, primero afirmativa, y luego negativamente, según los modelos.

MODELO: ¿Escribimos la frase?   *Sí, escribámosla. No, no la escribamos.*

1. ¿Llevamos los boletos?
2. ¿Seguimos la carretera?
3. ¿Entregamos el paquete?

4. ¿Buscamos a Margarita?
5. ¿Devolvemos las bicicletas?
6. ¿Traemos los refrescos?

MODELO: ¿Nos acostamos?   *Sí, acostémonos. No, no nos acostemos.*

7. ¿Nos levantamos?
8. ¿Nos sentamos?

9. ¿Nos vamos?
10. ¿Nos vestimos?

B. Después de oír un mandato, formen otra frase de mandato precedida de la frase **Yo no puedo** o **Nosotros no podemos,** siguiendo los modelos.

MODELOS: Lleve Ud. el paraguas.   *Yo no puedo, que lo lleve él.*
             Toquen Uds. los discos.   *Nosotros no podemos, que los toquen ellos.*

1. Traiga Ud. los periódicos.
2. Sirva Ud. el café.
3. Pague Ud. la cuenta.
4. Siéntese Ud.

5. Escojan Uds. la cámara.
6. Saquen Uds. las fotos.
7. Váyanse Uds.
8. Acérquense Uds.

C. Para expresar en español:

1. Let's open them (*f.*) (*two ways*).   2. Let's sit down (*two ways*).   3. Let's not get up.   4. Let's go downtown.   5. Let's not go to the bookstore yet.   6. Have Lola play the tape.   7. May Louise bring them (*m.*) to them.   8. Have George take it (*f.*) to her.   9. May you (*pl.*) be happy!   10. May you (*fam. sing.*) have a good time tonight!

4   Resumen de los usos de **para** y **por**

A. **Para** is used:

1. To express the purpose, use, person, or destination for which something is intended:

¿Tienes planes para el futuro?   Do you have (any) plans for the future?
Ya han partido (salido) para España.   They have already left for Spain.
Este cinturón es para Pepe, ¿verdad?   This belt is for Joe, isn't it?

2. To express *by* or *for*, referring to a certain time in the future:

El programa es para pasado mañana.   The program is for day after tomorrow.
Que estés aquí para las seis.   May you be here by six o'clock.

3. With an infinitive to express purpose, meaning *to, in order to:*

Ana tiene una cita con la profesora para hablar de sus vacaciones.   Ann has an appointment with the teacher to talk about her vacation.

4. To express disposition or readiness after **estar,** meaning (to be) *about to* or *on the point of:*

Estamos para terminar el semestre.   We are about to finish (on the point of finishing) the semester.

5. To express *for* in a comparison that may be understood or stated:

Juanito habla bien para un niño.   Johnny talks well for a child.
Para Uds., esto no será difícil.   For you, this will not be difficult.

B. **Por** is used:

1. To express *for* in the sense of *because of, on account of, for the sake of, on behalf of, in exchange for, about,* as:

Por falta de dinero él no pudo ir.   For lack of money he couldn't go.
Te doy las gracias por todo lo que has hecho por mí.   I thank you for all that you have done for me.
Pagué veinte dólares por la camisa.   I paid twenty dollars for the shirt.
Lo tomaron por español.   They took him for (as) a Spaniard.

2. To express the space of time during which an action continues (*for, during*):

Estarán en México por quince días.   They will be in Mexico for fifteen days (two weeks).
Saldré mañana por la noche.   I shall leave tomorrow night (evening).

3. To show *by what* or *by whom* something is done:

Juan habló con Lola por teléfono.   John talked with Lola by telephone.
Luis fue recomendado por el señor Sierra.   Louis was recommended by Mr. Sierra.

4. To indicate the object of an errand or search, *for,* after verbs such as **ir, enviar, mandar, preguntar, venir:**

Han enviado (venido, ido) por Marta.   They have sent (come, gone) for Martha.
Pregunten Uds. por Rita.   Ask for (about) Rita.

5. To express *through, along, around:*

Dimos una vuelta por las calles.   We took a walk through the streets.
Ellos viven por aquí.   They live around here.

6. With an infinitive to express uncertain outcome (often to denote striving for something), or something yet to be done:

Jaime trabajaba mucho por ganar una beca.   James was working hard to earn a scholarship.
La carta está (queda) todavía por escribir.   The letter is still to be written.

7. To form certain idiomatic expressions (some of which could be placed under the above headings):

por allí around (along) there	**por fin** finally, at last
por aquí around (by) here, this way	**por lo general** in
por cierto certainly, for sure	general, generally
por completo completely	**por lo menos** at least
por desgracia unfortunately	**por lo tanto** therefore
¡por Dios! heavens!	**por medio de** by means of
por ejemplo for example	**por primera vez** for the first
por eso because of that, therefore,	time
that's why	**por supuesto** of course,
por falta de for lack of	certainly
por favor please	**por último** finally, ultimately

NOTE: **¿Por qué?** means *Why? For what reason?*, while **¿para qué?** means *why? for what purpose?*

EJERCICIOS

A. Para leer en español, supliendo **para** o **por**:

1. ¿Cuándo partirán _____ la Argentina?   2. ¿Tiene Ud. muchos planes _____ las vacaciones?   3. Le damos a Ud. las gracias _____ todo.   4. Ana me dijo que vendría _____ mí a las cuatro.   5. ¿Por qué preguntaste _____ Ricardo?   6. La mamá de Isabel hizo el vestido _____ ella (i.e., *for her use*). 7. —¿_____ quién es este boleto? —Es _____ mí.   8. Es _____ el concierto que van a presentar el sábado _____ la noche.   9. Estoy seguro de que está _____ llover.   10. Tráeme tú una taza _____ té, _____ favor.   11. Los muchachos jugaron _____ dos horas.   12. Pasaron despacio _____ la calle. 13. Escoja Ud. una tarjeta _____ Diana.   14. ¿Cuánto pagaste _____ ese libro?   15. Parece que todos trabajan _____ ganar más dinero.   16. ¿Es verdad que comemos _____ vivir?   17. ¿Crees que lo tomaron _____ argentino? 18. _____ fin podemos hacer planes _____ la reunión.   19. Tendremos que darnos prisa _____ llegar a tiempo.   20. Voy a enviar _____ Felipe _____ entregarle estas cartas.   21. Que vuelvan ellos _____ el almuerzo.   22. Este artículo, que fue escrito _____ Luis, es _____ el periódico de hoy.   23. Lupe volvió tarde; _____ eso no la vimos.   24. Tomaron un autobús _____ ir al parque.   25. Piensan viajar _____ México durante el verano.

B. Para escribir en español:

1. I bought some gloves for my brother.   2. The girls left for the concert.
3. We took a walk through the country.   4. Finally John called me on the (by)
telephone.   5. The two were downtown for an hour and a half.   6. Henry
bought two tickets for Saturday.   7. George will come for us at seven o'clock.
8. Mary thanked us for the bracelet.   9. They had to go for Johnny.   10. The
children came by here in order to play with him.   11. George brought this
magazine for Ann.   12. Heavens! Why are you (*fam. sing.*) running along the
street?   13. These articles were written by Paul for our newspaper, weren't they?
14. Mrs. Solís made this blouse for Caroline.   15. We saw her yesterday for the
first time.   16. It seems that they don't have anything to do.

Glosario

el **cinturón** (*pl.* **cinturones**)   belt
dar las gracias a   to thank
decir que sí   to say yes
¿no es verdad? *or* **¿verdad?**   isn't it?
  weren't they? etc.
no tener nada que hacer   not to
  have anything to do

obtener (*like* **tener**)   to obtain, get
pasado mañana   day after tomorrow
el **periódico de hoy**   today's newspaper
  quince días   two weeks, fifteen days
el **sábado por la noche**   Saturday night
  (evening)
trabajar mucho   to work hard

LECCIÓN ONCE

El pretérito perfecto de subjuntivo • Las cláusulas adjetivas y los pronombres
relativos • El subjuntivo en cláusulas adjetivas • La construcción reflexiva
para traducir *each other, one another* • Usos especiales del objeto indirecto

1 El pretérito perfecto (*present perfect*) de subjuntivo

The present perfect subjunctive tense is formed by the present subjunctive tense
of **haber** with the past participle. If the verb in the main clause requires the subjunctive mood in the dependent clause, the present perfect subjunctive tense is used in
Spanish in the dependent clause to express *have* (*has*) plus the past participle.

	Present Perfect Subjunctive		
Singular		*Plural*	
haya ⎫		hayamos ⎫	
hayas ⎬ tomado, comido, vivido		hayáis ⎬ tomado, comido, vivido	
haya ⎭		hayan ⎭	

Dudo que ellos hayan dicho eso.   I doubt that they have said that.
Esperemos que Luis no se haya roto el brazo.   Let's hope that Louis hasn't
  broken his arm.
Es posible que Lupe haya tenido dolor de cabeza.   It is possible that Lupe
  has had a headache.

EJERCICIOS

A. Repitan cada oración; luego, al oír el comienzo de otra oración, completen la
  nueva oración, según los modelos.

MODELOS: Rita está aquí.   *Rita está aquí.*
         Dudo que   *Dudo que Rita esté aquí.*

         Rita estuvo aquí.   *Rita estuvo aquí.*
         Dudo que   *Dudo que Rita haya estado aquí.*

1. Felipe no se siente bien. Es lástima que
   Felipe no se sentía bien. Es lástima que
2. Ellos pueden ir a las montañas. No estamos seguros de que
   Ellos pudieron ir a las montañas. No estamos seguros de que
3. Ella tiene que esperar más. Tengo miedo de que
   Ella tuvo que esperar más. Tengo miedo de que

4. Ramón no quiere seguir jugando. Es extraño que
Ramón no quiso seguir jugando. Es extraño que
5. Tú siempre llegas a tiempo. Nos alegramos de que
Tú siempre llegabas a tiempo. Nos alegramos de que
6. Uds. conocen a la señora López. Vicente duda que
Uds. conocieron a la señora López. Vicente duda que

B. Para expresar en español:

1. We do not believe that John has returned home from California.
2. I am sorry that you (*fam. sing.*) have had a headache this afternoon.
3. It is too bad that Robert has broken his arm.
4. Richard is glad that we finally have said yes.
5. It may be that Rita hasn't seen her friend Joe today.
6. Do you (*pl.*) doubt that Charles has not returned the package?
7. I am not surprised that he has put on that suit.
8. The children are happy that their parents have left for Spain.

2   Las cláusulas adjetivas y los pronombres relativos

An adjective clause modifies a noun or pronoun and is introduced by a relative pronoun. In the sentence *I know a boy who can help us,* the adjective clause *who can help us* modifies *boy. Who* is a relative pronoun, and *boy* is the antecedent of the adjective clause.

A. Simple relative pronouns

1. **Que,** *that, which, who,* and *whom,* when used as the direct object of a verb, is invariable and refers to persons or things. When used as the object of a preposition, **que** normally refers to things and only occasionally to persons. The relative pronoun is sometimes omitted in English when used as the object of a verb, but not in Spanish:

   la casa de campo que él compró   the country house (that) he bought
   los amigos que se acercan   the friends who are approaching
   la conferencia de que hablan   the lecture of (about) which they are talking
   los jóvenes que vimos   the young people (whom) we saw

2. **Quien** (*pl.* **quienes**), *who, whom,* refers only to persons. It is used mainly as the object of a preposition, always meaning *whom,* and sometimes instead of **que** when the relative pronoun *who* is separated from the antecedent by a comma. The personal **a** is required when **quien(es)** is the direct object of a verb:

   la secretaria con quien hablé   the secretary with whom I talked

el señor Solís, quien me llamó ayer, quiere . . .   Mr. Solís, who called
me yesterday, wishes . . .

las muchachas a quienes saludamos   the girls (whom) we greeted

In the last sentence **que** may replace **a quienes,** and in conversation it is more
widely used.

3. **El cual (la cual, los cuales, las cuales),** *that, which, who, whom,* is used to clarify
which one of two possible antecedents the clause modifies, and also after
prepositions such as **sin, por,** and those of more than one syllable. Be sure
that the long relative agrees with its antecedent. (These long relatives are
much more widely used in literary style than in everyday conversation.)

La hermana de Roberto, la cual nos saludó . . .   Robert's sister, who said
hello to us, . . .

. . . el coche cerca del cual (del que) están charlando . . .   . . . the car
near which they are chatting . . .

Los abuelos de Pepe, los cuales viven en . . .   Joe's grandparents, who
live in . . .

El que (la que, los que, las que) may be substituted for forms of **el cual,**
particularly after prepositions, as in the second example, above.

4. **Lo cual** (sometimes **lo que**), *which (fact),* a neuter form, is used to refer back
to an idea, statement, or situation, but not to a specific noun:

Miguel no está contento, lo cual me parece extraño.   Michael isn't
happy, which (fact) seems strange to me.

B. Compound relative pronouns

1. **El (la) que,** *he (she) who, the one who (that, which),* and **los (las) que,** *those or the ones
who (that, which),* may refer to persons or things. These forms are often called
compound relatives because the definite article (which originated from the
Latin demonstrative) serves as the antecedent of the **que**-clause. (Do *not* use
forms of **el cual** in this construction.)

Juan pregunta por el que no está aquí.   John asks about the one who
is not here.

Estas muchachas y las que están en la acera . . .   These girls and the
ones (those) who are on the sidewalk . . .

Los que se reúnen[1] aquí . . .   Those who meet here . . .

Quien (*pl.* **quienes),** which refers only to persons, sometimes means *he (those)
who, the one(s) who,* particularly in proverbs:

Quien mucho duerme, poco aprende.   He who sleeps much, learns little.

---

[1] See page 231, footnote 1, for accented forms of **reunir(se),** *to gather, meet.*

2. **Lo que,** *what, that which,* a neuter form, refers only to an idea or statement:

¿No te han dicho lo que ha pasado?   Haven't they told you what has happened?

Tú sabes lo que él quiere hacer.   You know what he wants to do.

3. **Cuyo, -a, -os, -as,** *whose, of whom, of which,* is a relative possessive adjective. It agrees in gender and number with the noun it modifies:

el edificio en cuyo piso bajo   the building on the first floor of which (on whose first floor)

la mujer cuyos hijos   the woman whose children (the children of whom)

Remember that **¿De quién(es)?** expresses *Whose?* in a question: **¿De quién es esta casa?** *Whose house is this?* (lit., *Of whom is this house?*)

EJERCICIOS

A. Después de oír las dos oraciones, combínenlas, usando el pronombre relativo **que,** según el modelo.

MODELO: Ella tenía un libro. Era nuevo.   *El libro que ella tenía era nuevo.*

1. Ana compró un vestido. Es muy bonito.
2. Juanita sirvió unos refrescos. Eran excelentes.
3. Vimos a la estudiante. Estaba sentada a la derecha.
4. Conocimos al hombre ayer. Es ingeniero.
5. Invité a varios jóvenes. Son estudiantes.

Combinen las dos oraciones de dos maneras, usando el pronombre relativo **quien (quienes),** según el modelo.

MODELO: Vimos al joven. Es mexicano.   *Vimos al joven, quien es mexicano.*
                                         El joven a quien vimos es mexicano.

6. Saludé a la artista. Es peruana.
7. Charlamos con la muchacha. Es estudiante de la universidad.
8. Hablamos con aquellos señores. Trabajan en esta tienda.
9. Llamé a aquella niña. Está jugando en el patio.
10. Anoche conocimos a aquella señorita. Es profesora de inglés.

Combinen las dos oraciones, usando **el cual** o una de sus formas, según el modelo.

MODELO: La madre de Carlos vive en   *La madre de Carlos, la cual vive en*
                 Los Ángeles. Vendrá a   *Los Ángeles, vendrá a visitarlo*
                 visitarlo pronto.   *pronto.*

11. Los amigos de Marta estudian en sus cuartos. Tienen un examen mañana.
12. La hermana de Miguel viaja por España. Me ha enviado una tarjeta.
13. La tía de Inés ha escrito libros sobre México. Vive en San Antonio.
14. Las hijas de la señora Díaz corren hacia el parque. Son muy simpáticas.

B. Lean en español, supliendo el pronombre relativo:

1. La casa de campo _____ compraron es hermosa. 2. La residencia en _____ vivo es nueva. 3. El niño _____ (*two ways*) vieron Uds. es mi hermanito. 4. El señor Navarro, _____ (*two ways*) es argentino, dio la conferencia. 5. El edificio de _____ hablan es muy grande. 6. Las señoras con _____ charla mi mamá son mexicanas. 7. Me gusta la casa cerca de _____ juegan los muchachos. 8. Los amigos de Juan, _____ se reúnen aquí, son estudiantes de la universidad. 9. ¿Hiciste _____ te dijo la profesora? 10. Los jóvenes no han vuelto, _____ nos parece extraño. 11. Estos cuadros y _____ vimos ayer son muy bonitos. 12. Esta tarjeta y _____ recibí la semana pasada son de mis padres. 13. El señor Pidal compró este edificio y _____ está en la esquina. 14. _____ busca, halla.

3   El subjuntivo en cláusulas adjetivas

When the antecedent of an adjective clause is *indefinite* or *negative,* that is, when the adjective clause refers back to someone or something that is uncertain, unknown, indefinite, or nonexistent, the subjunctive mood is used in it. In general, if *any, whatever,* or *whoever* can be applied to the antecedent, the subjunctive mood is required. The idea of futurity is often involved.

The indicative mood is used, however, when the antecedent refers back to someone or something that is certain or definite. This includes an action that occurs as a general rule:

¿Hay alguien que pueda ayudarme?   Is there anyone who can help me?

Necesitan una casa que sea más grande.   They need a (any) house that is larger.

¿Tienes un amigo que haya estado en Chile?   Do you have a friend who has been in Chile?

Habrá que hacer lo que diga el médico.   It will be necessary to do what(ever) the doctor says (may say).

No hay nadie que haya jugado mejor.   There is no one who has played better.

Marta no ve nada que le guste.   Martha doesn't see anything (sees nothing) that she likes.

BUT: **Marta ha encontrado algo que le gusta mucho.**   Martha has found something that she likes a great deal.

Yo siempre hago lo que me piden.   I always do what (that which) they ask of me.

Carlos tiene un abuelo rico que vive en San Francisco.   Charles has a rich grandfather who lives in San Francisco.

In adjective clauses the personal **a** is omitted when a noun does not refer to a specific person (first example, below). It is used, however, before the pronouns **alguien** and **nadie,** and before forms of **alguno** and **ninguno** when the latter refer to a person and are used as direct objects:

> **Necesito un muchacho que me ayude mañana.**   I need a boy who will (may) help me tomorrow.
>
> **¿Has visto a alguien que quiera comprar tu coche?**   Have you seen anyone who will (may) buy your car?
>
> **No conocemos a nadie que recomiende eso.**   We do not know anyone who may (will) recommend that.
>
> **¿Conoces a algún abogado que hable español?**   Do you know a (any) lawyer who speaks Spanish?

EJERCICIOS

A. Repitan cada oración; luego, al oír el comienzo de otra oración, completen la nueva oración, según el modelo.

> MODELO: Tengo un traje que me gusta.   *Tengo un traje que me gusta.*
>   (Quiero un traje)   *Quiero un traje que me guste.*

1. Buscamos al joven que habla bien el español.   (Buscamos un joven)
2. Viven en una casa que tiene ocho cuartos.   (Necesitan una casa)
3. Cerca de aquí hay un lugar que es más hermoso.   (Cerca de aquí no hay ningún lugar)
4. Deseamos reunirnos en el café donde sirven comidas mexicanas.   (Deseamos reunirnos en algún café)
5. Quiero encontrar a la señorita que ha vivido en México.   (Quiero encontrar una señorita)
6. Espero ver al estudiante que ha estado en la clínica.   (Espero ver un estudiante)

B. Para expresar en español:

1. We see some of the young people who meet here every day.   2. Philip is ill; is there anyone who can take him to the clinic?   3. We are looking for a student who doesn't have a class at this hour.   4. Do you (*formal sing.*) know a doctor who speaks Spanish well?   5. Philip knows that it will be necessary to do whatever the doctor may say.   6. Is there any boy who wants to go there, too?   7. We do not see anyone who has time (in order) to do it at this moment.   8. Mr. Martínez needs a woman who can work in his new store.   9. He prefers a person who has worked in the United States.   10. We are not sure that he will find anyone very soon.   11. Do you know anyone who likes this picture better?   12. George says that he has nothing to do today, doesn't he?

4 La construcción reflexiva para traducir (*translate*) *each other, one another*

The plural reflexive pronouns **nos, os, se** may express a mutual or reciprocal action (one subject acting upon another):

Debemos felicitarnos. We must congratulate each other (one another) *or* We must congratulate ourselves.

Nos vemos en las reuniones. We see (We'll see, We'll be seeing) each other (one another) at the meetings.

Nos escribíamos a menudo. We wrote to each other (one another) often.

Se saludan todos los días. They greet each other (one another) every day.

The redundant construction **uno (-a) a otro (-a), el uno al otro, unos a otros (unas a otras)**, etc., may be added for clarity or emphasis. With prepositions other than **a,** the redundant form is added regularly:

Se burlan uno de otro. They make fun of each other (one another).

Ellos se gritaron el uno al otro. They shouted to each other (one another).

EJERCICIO

Para contestar afirmativamente en español:

1. ¿Se escriben Uds. a menudo?
2. ¿Se miraron ellos en clase?
3. ¿Van a ayudarse uno a otro?
4. ¿Se verán Uds. mañana?
5. ¿Se quejaban uno de otro?
6. ¿Se saludaron Ana y Pablo?

5 Usos especiales del objeto indirecto

A. If an action is performed on one person by another, the corresponding indirect object pronoun is used with the verb. This construction most often involves parts of the body, articles of clothing, or things closely related to the person. Note that the definite article replaces the possessive adjective:

Le tomé a él la temperatura. I took his temperature (lit., I took to him the temperature).

La madre les lavó las manos. The mother washed their hands.

Remember that the reflexive pronoun is used when the subject acts upon itself:

Mi madre se tomó la temperatura. My mother took her (*own*) temperature.

Juanito se lavó las manos. Johnny washed his hands.

B. The verb **doler (ue)**, *to ache, hurt,* has as its subject a noun expressing a part of the body, and the person is the indirect object:

> **Me (Le) duele la cabeza.**   My (Her, His) head aches (I have [She, He has] a headache).
>
> **A ella le duele (Le duele a ella) la garganta.**   Her throat aches (hurts).
>
> **¿Te duele mucho el pie (la pierna)?**   Does your foot (leg) hurt much?

NOTE: **Tengo dolor de cabeza** has the same meaning as **Me duele la cabeza,** *I have a headache.* One would also say **Él tiene el dedo roto,** *His finger is broken, He has a broken finger.*

EJERCICIO

A. Repitan la oración; luego, al oír un nuevo sujeto, formen otra oración, según el modelo.

> MODELO: Ana se tomó la temperatura.   *Ana se tomó la temperatura.*
> (Mi hermana)   *Mi hermana le tomó la temperatura a Ana.*

1. Juanito se lavó las manos.   (Yo)
2. Pablo se quitó los zapatos.   (Ellos)
3. Ana se compró un reloj.   (Su papá)
4. Marta se puso la ropa.   (Lola)
5. José se sirvió café.   (Carolina)
6. Luisa se cortó el dedo.   (Yo no)

B. Para expresar en español:

1. Her arm hurts.   2. My head aches (*two ways*).   3. Does your (*formal sing.*) head ache?   4. The children washed their hands.   5. Their mother washed their hands.   6. Does your (*fam. sing.*) leg hurt?   7. She took her (*own*) temperature. 8. John has cut his foot.   9. Have you (*formal sing.*) broken your finger?   10. He did not cut his hand.

GLOSARIO

la **acera**   sidewalk
la **casa de campo**   country house
la **clínica**   clinic, hospital
la **conferencia**   lecture
el **dolor de cabeza**   headache

la **garganta**   throat
el **hermanito**   little brother
el **piso bajo**   lower (first) floor
   sentirse (ie, i) bien   to feel well

LECCIÓN DOCE

Formas del imperfecto de subjuntivo • El pluscuamperfecto de subjuntivo •
Usos de los tiempos del subjuntivo • El subjuntivo en cláusulas adverbiales •
Repaso de los adjetivos y pronombres demostrativos

1   Formas del imperfecto de subjuntivo

A. Forms of regular verbs

The imperfect subjunctive tense in Spanish has two sets of endings, often referred to as the **-ra** and **-se** forms; both sets of endings are used for the three conjugations. To form the imperfect subjunctive tense of *all* verbs, regular and irregular, drop **-ron** from the third person plural preterit indicative tense and add **-ra, -ras, -ra, -ramos, -rais, -ran** or **-se, -ses, -se, -semos, -seis, -sen.**

-ra forms		**-se** forms	
Singular	*Plural*	*Singular*	*Plural*
-ra	-ramos	-se	-semos
-ras	-rais	-ses	-seis
-ra	-ran	-se	-sen

Only the first person plural form has a written accent. Remember that the **-er** and **-ir** verbs have the same endings in all tenses except in the present indicative tense. The two imperfect subjunctive tenses are interchangeable in Spanish, except in conditional sentences and in softened statements (Lección trece).

Imperfect Subjunctive			
tomar		**comer, vivir**	
Singular		*Singular*	
tomara	tomase	comiera	viviese
tomaras	tomases	comieras	vivieses
tomara	tomase	comiera	viviese
Plural		*Plural*	
tomáramos	tomásemos	comiéramos	viviésemos
tomarais	tomaseis	comierais	vivieseis
tomaran	tomasen	comieran	viviesen

Just as the present subjunctive tense is often expressed with *may* as part of its meaning, so the imperfect subjunctive tense is expressed with *might*: **que él tomara (tomase)**, *that he might take*; **que ellos comieran (comiesen)**, *that they might eat.*

B. Forms of some irregular verbs

For easy reference, the infinitive, the third person plural preterit indicative, and the first person singular imperfect subjunctive forms of some common irregular verbs are listed in the table below. See Appendix D, pages 225–234, for the imperfect subjunctive forms of other irregular verbs of varied types.

Inf.	3rd Pl. Pret.	Imp. Subj.	Inf.	3rd Pl. Pret.	Imp. Subj.
andar	anduvieron	anduviera, -se	ir	fueron	fuera, -se
caer	cayeron	cayera, -se	oír	oyeron	oyera, -se
conducir	condujeron	condujera, -se	poder	pudieron	pudiera, -se
construir	construyeron	construyera, -se	poner	pusieron	pusiera, -se
creer	creyeron	creyera, -se	querer	quisieron	quisiera, -se
dar	dieron	diera, -se	saber	supieron	supiera, -se
decir	dijeron	dijera, -se	ser	fueron	fuera, -se
estar	estuvieron	estuviera, -se	tener	tuvieron	tuviera, -se
haber	hubieron[1]	hubiera, -se	traer	trajeron	trajera, -se
hacer	hicieron	hiciera, -se	ver	vieron	viera, -se

C. Forms of stem-changing verbs

Stem-changing verbs, Class I (which end in **-ar** and **-er**), have no stem change in the imperfect subjunctive tense:

cerrar	cerrara, cerraras, etc.	cerrase, cerrases, etc.
volver	volviera, volvieras, etc.	volviese, volvieses, etc.

In Class II verbs (**sentir, dormir**), the stem vowel **e** becomes **i**, and **o** becomes **u**, in the third person singular and plural of the preterit indicative tense and in the entire imperfect subjunctive tense. In Class III verbs (**pedir**), the stem vowel **e** becomes **i** in the same forms:

Inf.	3rd Pl. Pret.	Imperfect Subjunctive	
sentir	sintieron	sintiera, -ras, etc.	sintiese, -ses, etc.
dormir	durmieron	durmiera, -ras, etc.	durmiese, -ses, etc.
pedir	pidieron	pidiera, -ras, etc.	pidiese, -ses, etc.

APLICACIÓN: Formas de verbos en el imperfecto de subjuntivo. Den las formas del verbo que correspondan a cada sujeto:

1. Que yo vivir, tomar, estar, tener, ir, sentir.
2. Que tú comer, dar, poder, saber, venir, pedir.
3. Que nosotros ser, ver, decir, creer, andar, haber.

---

[1] See page 167 for the preterit forms of **haber.**

4. Que Uds. traer, querer, poner, dormir, volver, construir.
5. Que ella caer, oír, cerrar, hacer, seguir, preferir.

2 El pluscuamperfecto de subjuntivo

The pluperfect subjunctive tense is formed by the **-ra** or **-se** imperfect subjunctive

	Pluperfect Subjunctive	
hubiera	hubiese	
hubieras	hubieses	
hubiera	hubiese	tomado, comido, vivido
hubiéramos	hubiésemos	
hubierais	hubieseis	
hubieran	hubiesen	

3 Usos de los tiempos del subjuntivo

Main Clause		*Dependent Clause*	
Present			
Future	Indicative	Present	Subjunctive
Present Perfect		Present Perfect	
Command			
Preterit			
Imperfect	Indicative	Imperfect	Subjunctive
Conditional		Pluperfect	
Pluperfect			

A. When the main verb in a sentence which requires the subjunctive mood in a dependent clause is in the present, future, or present perfect tense, or is a command, the verb in the dependent clause is regularly in the <u>present</u> or <u>present perfect</u> subjunctive tense:

Ellos quieren que nos quedemos aquí.   They want us to stay here.
Les diré (he dicho) a ellos que esperen.   I shall tell (have told) them to wait.
Pídale Ud. a ella que vuelva pronto.   Ask her to return soon.
Es posible que ya hayan partido.   It is possible that they have already left.

B. When the main verb is in the preterit, imperfect, conditional, or pluperfect tense, the verb in the dependent clause is usually in the <u>imperfect</u> subjunctive tense, unless the past perfect tense is used in the dependent in English, in which case the pluperfect subjunctive tense is used in Spanish:

> **Les pedí (pedía) a ellos que fueran (fuesen) a la conferencia.**   I asked (was asking) them to go to the lecture.
>
> **Yo no creí que Juan trajera (trajese) las cosas.**   I didn't believe that John would bring the things.
>
> **No había nadie que pudiera (pudiese) venir temprano.**   There was no one who could come early.
>
> **Yo sentía mucho que él ya hubiera (hubiese) comido.**   I was very sorry that he had already eaten.
>
> **Yo dudaría que Ana hubiera (hubiese) ido a la reunión.**   I would doubt that Ann had gone to the meeting.

The imperfect subjunctive tense may also follow the present, future, or present perfect tense when the action of the dependent clause took place in the past:

> **Es lástima que comenzáramos (comenzásemos) el concierto tan tarde.**   It is too bad we began the concert so late.
>
> **Me alegro de que ellos anduvieran (anduviesen) por el parque ayer.**   I am glad that they walked through the park yesterday.

EJERCICIOS

A. Lean en español, supliendo la forma correcta del verbo entre paréntesis; cuando sea necesario el imperfecto de subjuntivo, usen las dos formas:

1. Rita insiste en que yo (jugar) al tenis con ella.   2. Carlos insistió en que nosotros (reunirse) en el café.   3. Quiero que Ud. les (explicar) algunas de las expresiones.   4. Diana quería que yo (traer) unos refrescos.   5. Sienten mucho que Juan no (haber) devuelto el diccionario.   6. Siempre le aconsejaban que (acostarse) más temprano.   7. No creemos que todo el mundo (saber) hacer eso.   8. Queríamos encontrar alguna cosa que le (gustar) a Luis.

B. Repitan cada oración; luego, al oír una nueva frase inicial, completen la oración, haciendo los cambios necesarios:

1. Marta no quiere que Jorge lea el artículo.   (Pepe no quería)
2. Les pediré que lo traigan mañana.   (Yo les pediría)
3. Será posible que ella compre otra blusa.   (Sería posible)
4. No hay nadie que tenga mejores ideas que Lupe.   (No había nadie)
5. ¿Busca Ud. a alguien que escoja un regalo?   (¿Buscaba Ud. a alguien . . . ?)
6. Quieren que nos encontremos en la esquina.   (Querían)
7. Es posible que Diana escriba un anuncio.   (Era posible)
8. No creemos que ellos hagan la excursión.   (No creímos)

4   El subjuntivo en cláusulas adverbiales

An adverbial clause, which modifies a verb and indicates *time, purpose, concession, condition, result, negative result,* and the like, is introduced by a conjunction, often a compound with **que** as the last element. If the action has taken place or is an accepted fact, the indicative mood is used; if the action may take place but has not actually been accomplished, the subjunctive mood is normally used in the dependent clause.

A. Time clauses

The subjunctive mood is used after conjunctions of time if the action in the dependent clause has not been completed at the time indicated by the main clause, that is, when the time referred to in the dependent clause is indefinite and future, and therefore uncertain, from the standpoint of the time expressed in the main clause. **Antes (de) que,** *before,* always requires the subjunctive mood, since the action indicated in the time clause cannot have taken place.

When the time clause expresses an accomplished fact in the present or past, or a customary occurrence, the indicative mood is used.

Some common conjunctions which introduce time clauses are:

antes (de) que before	**en cuanto** as soon as
cuando when	**hasta que** until
después (de) que after	**mientras (que)** while, as long as

Yo esperé hasta que regresó Miguel.   I waited until Michael returned.
Yo esperaré hasta que regrese Miguel.   I shall wait until Michael returns.
Cuando yo veo a Juan, lo saludo.   When I see John, I greet him.
En cuanto yo lo vea, lo saludaré.   As soon as I see him, I shall greet him.
Antes de que vengas, Pablo te llamará.   Before you come, Paul will call you.
Antes de que vinieras, Pablo te llamó.   Before you came, Paul called you.
Podré devolver el artículo mañana cuando vaya a clase.   I shall be able to return the article tomorrow when I go to class.
Ana quería continuar leyendo hasta que Diana volviera.   Ann wanted to continue reading until Diane returned (should return).

B. Concessive and result clauses

1. **Aunque,** *although, even though, even if,* is followed by the subjunctive mood unless the speaker wishes to express a statement as a certainty or is indicating an accomplished fact, in both of which cases the indicative mood is used:

Aunque sea tarde, he venido a la reunión.   Even though it may be late, I have come to the meeting.
Aunque es tarde, he venido a la reunión.   Although it is late, I have come to the meeting.   (*Certainty implied*)
Aunque yo estaba cansado, seguí andando.   Although I was tired, I continued walking.

2. Two other conjunctions, **de manera que** and **de modo que,** both meaning *so that,* may express result, in which case they are followed by the indicative mood. They may also express desired, unaccomplished result, in which case the subjunctive mood is used. Compare the following sentences (also see C, which follows):

Juan habló de manera (modo) que lo entendimos.   John spoke so that (in such a way that) we understood (did understand) him.

Juan, hable Ud. de manera (modo) que lo entendamos.   John, speak so that we may understand you.   (*No certainty that we will*)

C. Purpose, proviso, conditional, and negative result clauses

Certain conjunctions denoting *purpose, proviso, condition, negative result,* and the like, always require the subjunctive mood because they cannot introduce a statement of fact. By their very meaning, they indicate that the action in the clause is uncertain, or that the action may not, or did not, actually take place. In addition to **de manera que** and **de modo que,** *so that* (see B, above), some other conjunctions of these types are:

a fin de que in order that	**para que** in order that
a menos que unless	**siempre que** provided that
con tal (de) que provided that	**sin que** without

¿Por qué no me llamaste para que yo te ayudara (ayudase)?   Why didn't you call me in order that I might help you?

Prometo acompañarte con tal que yo consiga el dinero.   I promise to go with you provided that I get (obtain) the money.

Los muchachos salieron sin que yo los oyera (oyese).   The boys went out without my hearing them.

EJERCICIOS

A. Para leer en español, supliendo la forma correcta del verbo entre paréntesis:

1. Siempre empieza la clase en cuanto (entrar) el profesor.
2. Eran las once de la noche cuando Ricardo (regresar) del aeropuerto.
3. Voy a enseñarles la composición en cuanto (llegar) ellos.
4. Compré el tocadiscos aunque me (costar) demasiado.
5. Aunque (llover) esta noche, tendremos que ir al teatro.
6. Dijeron que se irían mañana aunque (hacer) mal tiempo.
7. Quédense Uds. en casa hasta que (volver) yo de la tienda.
8. Ellos no llegarán a tiempo a menos que (darse) prisa.
9. Hable Ud. de modo que lo (oír) bien todo el mundo.
10. Traeré las cintas para que tú las (escuchar).
11. Jorge me las trajo para que yo te las (entregar).
12. Tráeme tú café con tal que (estar) caliente.
13. Ya habíamos cenado antes de que ellos (haber) vuelto del centro.

14. Inés no podrá ir con Uds. sin que yo le (dar) el dinero.

15. Marta no ganará mucho mientras que (trabajar) en esta tienda.

B. Repitan cada pregunta; luego, contéstenla afirmativamente, agregando (*adding*) una cláusula introducida por la frase **aunque Luis,** según el modelo.

MODELO: ¿Harás el viaje?   *¿Harás el viaje? Sí, aunque Luis lo haga también.*

1. ¿Escogerá Ud. la maleta?   4. ¿Mirarás la televisión?
2. ¿Buscará Ud. la revista?   5. ¿Irás al parque?
3. ¿Pedirá Ud. la beca?   6. ¿Seguirás andando un rato?

C. Para expresar en español:

1. We were at the café when they arrived.   2. Will you (*fam. sing.*) be here when Henry arrives?   3. He bought the suit after his father gave him the money.   4. I shall buy something for Jane as soon as I have time.   5. We went to see Jane as soon as it was possible.   6. They will go to see her before her parents come.   7. I received the check, so that I was able to pay Charles.   8. We shall give him a check in order that he can cash it.   9. We did not leave the airport until the plane left.   10. John said that he would not leave the airport until the plane should leave (left).   11. Although it is cool and windy, we shall try to play tennis.   12. James left for Los Angeles without his roommate knowing it.

5   Repaso de los adjetivos y pronombres demostrativos

A. A demonstrative adjective agrees in gender and number with the noun it modifies, and, in Spanish, is repeated before nouns in a series. **Este** points out persons or things near the speaker; **ese,** persons or things near to, or associated with, the person addressed; **aquel,** persons or things distant from the speaker or person addressed, or unrelated to either. (Do not confuse the demonstrative, which points out the noun to which it refers, with the relative pronoun **que,** *that, which, who, whom.*)

| *Singular* | | | *Plural* | | |
Masculine	*Feminine*		*Masculine*	*Feminine*	
este	**esta**	this	**estos**	**estas**	these
ese	**esa**	that (*nearby*)	**esos**	**esas**	those (*nearby*)
aquel	**aquella**	that (*distant*)	**aquellos**	**aquellas**	those (*distant*)

este hombre y esta mujer   this man and woman
esos chicos que están cerca de ti   those little boys who are near you
aquella joven que está allí   that young lady who is there (*distant*)

B. 1. The demonstrative pronouns are formed by placing an accent mark on the stressed syllable of the adjectives: **éste, ése, aquél,** etc. The use of the pronouns corresponds to that of the adjectives, except that singular forms often mean *this (one), that (one)*. They may be used as subject or object of the verb, or they may stand alone:

> **Me gustan ese radio y éste.**   I like that (*nearby*) radio and this one.
> **¿Quieres que yo ponga éste o ése?**   Do you want me to turn on this one or that one (*nearby*)?
> **Este modelo y aquéllos son nuevos.**   This model and those (*distant*) are new.
> **¿Cuál de las marcas prefieres? ¿Ésta?**   Which one of the brands do you prefer? This one?

2. There are three neuter pronouns (**esto,** *this,* **eso,** *that,* **aquello,** *that*) which are used when the antecendent is a statement, a general idea, or something which has not been identified. Since there are no neuter adjectives, an accent mark is not required on these three forms:

> **¿Qué es esto?**   What is this?
> **Eso no es fácil.**   That isn't (That's not) easy.

C. The demonstrative pronoun **éste** is used to indicate *the latter* (that is, *the nearer*), and **aquél,** *the former.* Contrary to English usage, in Spanish, when both are used, *the latter* always comes first:

> **Ana y Marta no vienen porque ésta no se siente bien.**   Ann and Martha aren't coming because the latter doesn't feel well.
> **Pepe y su hermana van de compras; ésta busca un vestido y aquél, un traje.**   Joe and his sister are going shopping; the former is looking for a suit and the latter, a dress.

D. We found in Lección once, page 121, that the definite article in Spanish replaces the demonstrative pronoun before **que.** Similarly, it replaces the demonstrative pronoun before **de. El (la, los, las) de** mean *that (those) of, the one(s) of (with, in)*; sometimes this construction is expressed by a possessive in English (first two examples):

> **mi coche y el de Juan**   my car and John's (that of John)
> **estos discos y los de Ana**   these records and Ann's (those of Ann)
> **las del pelo rubio**   the ones (girls) with (the) blond hair
> **la del sombrero rojo**   the one (girl) with (in) the red hat

The neuter article **lo** followed by **de** means *that (matter, affair) of*:

> **Lo de su amigo me sorprende.**   That (affair) of your friend surprises me.
> **Hablamos con Juan sobre lo de las becas.**   We talked with John about that (matter) of the scholarships.

EJERCICIOS

A. Para contestar afirmativamente, empleando el pronombre demostrativo correspondiente.

MODELOS: ¿Quieres este radio?   *Sí, quiero ése.*
            ¿Es buena esa marca?   *Sí, ésta es buena.*

1. ¿Te gusta esta camisa?
2. ¿Quieres este traje?
3. ¿Vas a comprar estos guantes?
4. ¿Llevas esta maleta?

5. ¿Son buenas estas cámaras?
6. ¿Prefieres oír aquel tocadiscos?
7. ¿Escogerá Ud. este paraguas?
8. ¿Le gustan a Ud. esas fotos?

B. Para expresar en español:

1. This record and that one (*distant*) are new, aren't they?   2. We prefer this blouse to that one (*nearby*).   3. Which one of the dresses do you (*fam. sing.*) want to put on? This one?   4. That (*distant*) girl and the one in the white hat are cousins of Jane.   5. Which one of the purses do you (*pl.*) like better? This one?   6. Mary's dress and Helen's are very pretty.   7. Who is that (*distant*) boy, the one with red hair?   8. Shall I buy these gloves or those (*distant*)?   9. Martha and Louise are here; the latter doesn't feel well.   10. It is said that Paul bought a new car. Do you (*fam. sing.*) believe that?

Glosario

conseguir (i, i) (*like* **seguir**)   to get, obtain
entender (ie)   to understand

la marca   brand, make, kind
todo el mundo   everybody, the whole (entire) world

Repaso cuatro

A. Lean en español, supliendo la forma correcta del infinitivo entre paréntesis si se necesita un cambio:

1. Es cierto que los estudiantes (estar) en sus cuartos. 2. Es dudoso que (haber) mucha gente en el concierto. 3. Será imposible (esperar) todo el día. 4. Creemos que las muchachas (estar) jugando al tenis. 5. Será probable que (hacer) mal tiempo mañana. 6. Niego que Juanita (haber) tenido mucho frío. 7. No estamos seguros de que ellos (divertirse) en la fiesta. 8. Es importante que ella (escoger) un regalo esta tarde. 9. No es cierto que Carlos (haber) comprado rosas para Lola. 10. Les es necesario (quedarse) allí varios días.

B. Para contestar en español, primero afirmativa y luego negativamente, según los modelos.

MODELO: ¿Dejamos *las cosas?* *Sí, dejémoslas. No, no las dejemos.*

1. ¿Abrimos *la puerta?*
2. ¿Cerramos *los libros?*
3. ¿Servimos *el café?*
4. ¿Sacamos *las fotos?*
5. ¿Seguimos *el coche?*
6. ¿Envolvemos *el paquete?*

MODELO: ¿Nos despedimos? *Sí, despidámonos. No, no nos despidamos.*

7. ¿Nos levantamos ahora?
8. ¿Nos sentamos a la derecha?
9. ¿Nos lavamos las manos?
10. ¿Nos vamos?

Vuelvan a contestar todas las preguntas afirmativamente, empezando con **Vamos a.**

MODELO: ¿Dejamos las cosas? *Sí, vamos a dejarlas.*

C. Para expresar en español:

1. Let's look for John (*two ways*). 2. Let's not wait for her. 3. Let's go to the airport. 4. Let's not go downtown. 5. Let's sit down here. 6. Let's not put on our shoes. 7. Have Mary bring the refreshments. 8. Have Joe take them to Louise.

D. Para leer en español, supliendo **para** o **por**:

1. Yo compré los guantes _____ Isabel. 2. Juan quiere dos boletos _____
el sábado. 3. ¿Cuánto tuviste que pagar _____ el sombrero? 4. Tomaron un
autobús _____ ir al parque. 5. Ella ha solicitado una beca _____ estudiar
arte. 6. Él lo hizo _____ mí (*for my sake*). 7. Han enviado _____ Pablo.
8. _____ último han terminado el trabajo. 9. Repítanlo Uds., _____ favor.
10. Tienes que estar allí _____ las siete. 11. Cuando conocí a Miguel Torres,
lo tomé _____ español. 12. Lola ha vuelto tarde; _____ eso no la vimos.

E. Para escribir en español:

1. We are glad that our friends have already left for Mexico. 2. I am sure that
they have decided to stay there for two weeks. 3. Don't you (*fam. sing.*) believe
that they will have an interesting trip? 4. I am sorry that James and I have not
been able to travel in (through) Mexico. 5. It is possible that we shall take a trip
there next summer. 6. I shall ask Robert to bring me a book that he has been
reading about that (**ese**) country. 7. We must practice every day in order to
talk Spanish there. 8. It is certain that we have enough time to learn a great deal.

F. Repitan cada oración; luego, al oír el comienzo de otra oración, completen la nueva
oración:

1. Roberto tiene un puesto que le gusta. (Roberto quiere un puesto)
2. Hay algo en este artículo que es interesante. (No hay nada)
3. Hay alguien aquí que puede recomendar a Pablo. (¿Hay alguien . . . ?)
4. Busco al joven que ha vivido en Puerto Rico. (Busco un joven)
5. Conozco a una secretaria que ha aprendido bien el español. (Necesitamos
una secretaria)
6. ¿Hay alguien que haya jugado mejor que Juan? (No hay nadie)
7. Saludo a Felipe cuando pasa por aquí. (Saludaré a Felipe)
8. Vuelven a casa en cuanto yo los llamo. (Volverán)
9. Tenemos que irnos aunque está lloviendo. (Tendremos que irnos esta
noche)
10. Creemos que todo el mundo sabe eso. (No creemos)
11. Él dice que saldrá cuando vengan ellos. (Él dijo que saldría)
12. Pídale Ud. a Jorge que vaya a la librería. (Le pedí a Jorge)

G. Lean en español, supliendo el pronombre relativo:

1. El señor López, con _____ trabaja mi padre, es de Colombia. 2. Mi abuelo,
_____ vive en California, es abogado. 3. El tío de aquella mujer, _____ es
amigo de mi mamá, vive en esta ciudad. 4. La casa del señor Solís, _____ es
de estilo español, es muy hermosa. 5. Los jóvenes a _____ vemos son mexicanos. 6. La hermana de Pepe, _____ viaja por México, le ha enviado una
tarjeta. 7. Los artículos de _____ hablaban son muy buenos. 8. Aquellos
jóvenes _____ andan por la calle son estudiantes extranjeros, ¿verdad?

H. Lean en español, supliendo la forma correcta del infinitivo entre paréntesis:

1. Siempre tomamos el autobús cuando (ir) al centro.
2. Aunque Miguel todavía (estar) en la clínica, se siente mejor.
3. Los señores Sierra harán el viaje en cuanto (ser) posible.
4. No les diré nada, a menos que tú (obtener) el puesto.
5. Iremos a la conferencia con tal que Pepe (llegar) a tiempo.
6. Es lástima que los muchachos no (divertirse) mucho en la fiesta.
7. Las muchachas no saldrán del cuarto sin que yo los (oír).
8. Tráeme tú la cámara para que yo se la (dar) a Carlos.
9. Enrique pasó por aquí antes (de) que tú (volver) del aeropuerto.
10. No había nadie que (poder) jugar al tenis con nosotros.
11. Mi padre me aconsejó que (traer) el paraguas.
12. Sentíamos mucho que Lola se (haber) roto el brazo.
13. El profesor hablará de modo que nosotros lo (entender) bien.
14. Te di el cheque para que lo (cobrar) esta mañana.

I. Para expresar en español:

1. I asked several friends to drop by our room tonight.   2. John gave me the article in order that I might read it.   3. We doubted that everybody would attend the lecture.   4. They were sorry that we had already left for the concert.   5. John's father advised us to take a camera.   6. There was no one who understood what the man said.   7. Our Spanish teacher was looking for a house which was near the school.   8. I am sorry that they have not done anything this afternoon.

9. His head aches.   10. Have you (*fam. sing.*) broken your foot?   11. Who is the one (*f.*) with red hair?   12. Which one of the purses does she want? This one?   13. We are not sure of that.   14. Who are the ones (*m.*) who are in the street?   15. He who seeks (looks for), finds.   16. Do you (*pl.*) like this brand or that one (*nearby*)?   17. Do you (*formal sing.*) believe what they said?   18. We shall see each other day after tomorrow.

Restaurante "El Refugio", Ciudad de México, México.

Notas culturales IV

Observaciones sobre las comidas hispanoamericanas

Las comidas hispanoamericanas reflejan, en general, los cultivos° y las condiciones de vida° de las diversas regiones. En México y en la América Central, por ejemplo, el maíz[1] ha sido durante siglos la base de la alimentación. No es sorprendente, por lo tanto, encontrar que de harina de maíz se hacen las tortillas mexicanas, que se necesitan para preparar las enchiladas, tostadas y tacos tan conocidos en el suroeste de nuestro país.

    La enchilada es una tortilla de harina de maíz enrollada,° que se rellena de queso o carne y se cuece en el horno. La tostada es una tortilla tostada que se cubre de frijoles refritos y se adereza con lechuga, tomate, cebolla y queso. Se prepara el taco doblando° la tortilla tostada y rellenándola de carne picada; se cuece en el horno y al servirse se cubre de lechuga, tomate y queso rallado. Como condimento no falta° la salsa de chile (un pimiento, o ají, como se llama en América, muy picante).

    Otros platos típicos de las mismas regiones son el tamal, los chiles rellenos y el mole de guajolote (el nombre que dan al pavo en México). El tamal cambia con las localidades. En México es una especie° de empanada de harina de maíz que se rellena de pescado o carne y se envuelve en hojas de plátano o de la mazorca del maíz; se cuece al vapor o en el horno. La hayaca de Venezuela y la humita del Perú, Chile y la Argentina son variedades del tamal, con ingredientes diferentes. Los chiles rellenos contienen carne picada de vaca o de cerdo, aderezada con almendras, pasas y un poco de chocolate.

cultivos *crops* / de vida *living*

enrollada *rolled*

doblando *by folding*

no falta *there is not lacking (missing)*

especie *kind*

---

[1] To facilitate preparation of this selection, see the glossary on pages 143–144 for meanings of words and expressions used here and in the *Preguntas,* and, with a few exceptions, not elsewhere in the text. The words listed in the glossary are not repeated in the end vocabulary.

El mole es la salsa con que se preparan en México los guisados de carne, como el guajolote, por ejemplo. Es famoso el mole poblano. Se prepara con tomate, cebolla, canela, chile y chocolate, entre otros ingredientes.

En las regiones marítimas de Hispanoamérica, los pescados y los mariscos son una parte importante de las comidas. Un plato muy popular es el escabeche. Se prepara macerando° el pescado frito en una salsa de vinagre, aceite, ají, cebolla y pimienta; se sirve frío. Entre los mariscos son corrientes los cangrejos, langostas, langostinos, calamares, almejas y ostiones (el nombre que se da en América a las ostras).

macerando *by steeping (soaking)*

En los países en que abunda el ganado vacuno,° como en la Argentina y el Uruguay, la carne asada es el plato favorito. Los biftecs de estas regiones, asados al horno o en parrillas, como en el caso de la famosa parrillada argentina, son de primera calidad.

ganado vacuno *cattle*

Otros platos hispanoamericanos, como el arroz con pollo y la paella, son de origen español. Suelen variar° un poco según la localidad.

Suelen variar *They are accustomed to vary (i.e., They generally vary)*

PREGUNTAS

Para contestar en español en oraciones completas:

1. ¿Qué reflejan, en general, las comidas hispanoamericanas?   2. ¿Cuál es la base de la alimentación en México y en la América Central?   3. ¿De qué se hacen las tortillas mexicanas?   4. ¿Qué es una enchilada?   5. ¿Qué es una tostada?   6. ¿Cómo se prepara el taco?   7. ¿Qué se usa como condimento?

8. ¿Cuáles son otros platos típicos de las mismas regiones?   9. ¿Cómo se prepara el tamal en México?   10. ¿Qué nombre dan al tamal en Venezuela?   11. ¿Cómo se llama el tamal en el Perú, Chile y la Argentina?

12. ¿Qué contienen los chiles rellenos?   13. ¿Con qué se aderezan los chiles rellenos?   14. ¿Cómo se llama la salsa con que se preparan en México los guisados de carne?   15. ¿Con qué ingredientes se prepara el mole poblano?

16. ¿En qué regiones son los pescados y los mariscos una parte importante de las comidas?   17. ¿Cómo se prepara el escabeche?   18. ¿Cuáles son los mariscos más corrientes?   19. ¿En qué países es la carne asada el plato favorito?   20. ¿De qué origen son el arroz con pollo y la paella?

EJERCICIO ESCRITO

Traduzcan al español las frases siguientes:

1. We would need many pages to describe the typical foods of all the Spanish-American countries.   2. Persons who live in the Southwest are well acquainted with many Mexican dishes, such as the enchilada, the taco, and the tostada.   3. The enchilada is a rolled corn cake which contains meat or cheese; as seasoning, chili sauce is used.

4. There are different types of tamales according to the ingredients they contain.   5. In Mexico, the tamale is a kind of small pie which is filled with fish or meat, and is wrapped in corn husks.   6. Stuffed peppers are prepared with ground pork or beef, garnished with almonds, raisins, and chocolate.

7. In the maritime regions many kinds of fish and shellfish are served; stuffed crab is a very popular dish.   8. To prepare pickled fish one steeps fried fish in a sauce made of vinegar, olive oil, chili, onion, and (black) pepper.   9. In countries in which cattle abound, roast meat is the favorite food, as in the case of the Argentine *parrillada*. 10. Rice with chicken and paella, which are of Spanish origin, are also popular in Spanish America.

Glosario

el **aceite**   olive oil
  aderezar   to garnish
el **ají**   chili, pepper (*vegetable*) (*Mex.*)
la **alimentación**   nutrition, diet, food
la **almeja**   clam
la **almendra**   almond
el **arroz (con leche)**   rice (pudding)
  arroz con pollo   rice with chicken
  asado, -a   roast(ed)
el **biftec**   (beef)steak
el **calamar**   squid
la **canela**   cinnamon
el **cangrejo**   crab
la **carne**   meat
  carne asada   roast, roasted meat
  carne de cerdo   pork
  carne de vaca   beef
  carne picada   ground meat
la **cebolla**   onion
  cocer (ue)   to cook
el **condimento**   condiment, seasoning
el **chile**   chili, pepper
  salsa de chile   chili sauce
la **empanada**   *small meat (or fish) pie*

la **enchilada**   *corn cake with chili, meat, or cheese*
el **escabeche**   pickled fish
los **frijoles (refritos)**   (refried) kidney beans
  frito, -a   fried
el **guajolote**   turkey (*Mex.*)
el **guisado**   stew
la **harina**   flour
  harina de maíz   cornmeal
la **hayaca**   tamale (*Venezuela*)
el **horno**   oven
  al horno   in an oven
la **humita**   tamale (*South America*)
el **ingrediente**   ingredient
la **langosta**   lobster
el **langostino**   prawn, crawfish
la **lechuga**   lettuce
el **maíz**   maize, corn
el **marisco**   shellfish; *pl.* seafood, shellfish
la **mazorca**   ear (*of corn*)
  hojas de la mazorca del maíz   corn husks

el **mole**   *a sauce*
   mole poblano   *sauce in the style of Puebla (Mexico)*
el **ostión** (*pl.* **ostiones**)   oyster
la **ostra**   oyster
la **parrilla**   grill
la **parrillada**   barbecued beef
la **pasa**   raisin
el **pavo**   turkey (*Spain*)
el **pescado**   fish
   picado, -a   minced, chopped, ground
   picante   hot, highly seasoned, spicy
la **pimienta**   black pepper
el **pimiento**   pepper (*vegetable*)

el **plátano**   plantain, banana
   hojas de plátano   banana leaves
el **queso**   cheese
   rallado, -a   grated
   rellenar (de)   to fill *or* stuff (with)
   relleno, -a   stuffed, filled
la **salsa**   sauce
el **taco**   *a folded corn cake*
el **tamal**   tamale
el **tomate**   tomato
la **tortilla**   corn pancake (*Mex.*)
la **tostada**   toasted corn cake
   tostar (ue)   to toast
el **vapor**   steam
   al vapor   in steam, steamed
el **vinagre**   vinegar

LECCIÓN TRECE

1 El subjuntivo en frases condicionales

A. In earlier lessons we have used simple conditions in which the present indicative tense is used in the English *if*-clause and the same tense in the Spanish **si**-clause (see Lección ocho, page 86):

> **Si Lola está en su cuarto,**   **está escuchando la radio.**
> If Lola is in her room,   she is listening to the radio.
> **Si ellos tienen dinero,**   **comprarán el coche.**
> If they have (the) money,   they will buy the car.

Simple conditions are also expressed in past time:

> **Si Luis recibió (ha recibido) el cheque,**   **lo cobró.**
> If Louis received (has received) the check,   he cashed it.

B. In a **si**-clause which implies that a statement is contrary to fact (i.e., not true) in the present, the imperfect subjunctive tense (either form) is used in Spanish; in the main clause or conclusion, the conditional tense is used as in English.

    When a contrary-to-fact sentence is expressed in the past, the pluperfect subjunctive tense is used in the **si**-clause, and the conditional perfect tense is used in the main clause (see the second example, below). (In reading you will also find the **-ra** form of the imperfect or pluperfect subjunctive tense in the main, or result, clause; in the exercises of this text, only the conditional or conditional perfect tense will be used.)

> **Si yo tuviera (tuviese) dinero,**   **compraría el coche.**
> If I had (the) money (*but I don't*),   I would buy the car.
> **Si Rita hubiese (hubiera) vuelto,**   **me habría llamado.**
> If Rita had returned (*but she didn't*),   she would have called me.

C. **Como si,** *as if,* also expresses a contrary-to-fact condition, in which case the conclusion, or main clause, is understood, and therefore must be followed by the imperfect or pluperfect subjunctive tense:

> **Están charlando como si no tuvieran nada que hacer.**   They are chatting as if they had nothing to do.

D. Similarly, either form of the imperfect subjunctive tense is used in the **si**-clause to express a condition that <u>may</u> (<u>might</u>) not be fulfilled in the future. Whenever the English sentence has *should* or *were to* in the *if*-clause, the imperfect subjunctive tense is used in Spanish:

Si fuésemos (fuéramos) allá,   **podríamos verlos.**
   If we should (were to) go there,   we could see them.
Si vinieran (viniesen) mañana,   **asistirían a la reunión.**
   If they should (were to) come tomorrow,   they would attend the
                                     meeting.

NOTE: The future and conditional indicative and the present subjunctive tenses are not used after **si** meaning *if*. When **si** means *whether*, the indicative mood must be used: **No sé si ellos podrán venir,** *I do not know whether they will be able to come.*

EJERCICIOS

A. Repitan cada oración; luego, al oír otra cláusula con **si,** completen la oración:

   1. Si Juan tiene dinero, comprará un reloj.
      Si Juan tuviera dinero,
      Si Juan hubiera tenido dinero,
   2. Si Marta ve a Diana, le dará el boleto.
      Si Marta viese a Diana,
      Si Marta hubiese visto a Diana,
   3. Si vamos a la fiesta, nos divertiremos.
      Si fuéramos a la fiesta,
      Si hubiéramos ido a la fiesta,

B. Repitan la oración; luego, cambien la forma de los verbos, según el modelo.

   MODELO: Si tengo tiempo, iré al café.   *Si tengo tiempo, iré al café.*
                                        Si yo tuviera tiempo, iría al café.

   1. Si Pablo vuelve del centro, nos llamará.
   2. Si Laura está en su cuarto, estará estudiando.
   3. Si vamos a México, sacaremos muchas fotografías.
   4. Si no es tarde, charlaré con Uds. unos momentos.

   MODELO: Si vienen, los veré.   *Si vienen, los veré.*
                                  Si viniesen, yo los vería.

   5. Si tenemos tiempo, hablaremos con el señor Solís.
   6. Si ellos están aquí, podrán oír la conferencia.
   7. Si Pepe trae los boletos, se los daremos a los otros muchachos.
   8. Si él recibe el cheque, comprará una bicicleta.

   MODELO: Si han venido, lo habrán visto.   *Si han venido, lo habrán visto.*
                                      Si hubieran venido, lo habrían visto.

   9. Si han leído el periódico, habrán visto el anuncio.
  10. Si ella ha escrito la tarjeta, se la habrá enviado a Carlos.

C. Para expresar en español:

1. If my friend is in Mexico, he will send me a card.   2. If my friend were in Mexico, he would send me a card.   3. If my uncle comes tonight, he will bring me a Spanish newspaper.   4. If my uncle should come tonight, he would bring me something.   5. If Charles had found my watch, he would have brought it to me.   6. That young man talks as if he were from Peru.

2   Otros usos del subjuntivo

Uses of the subjunctive mood in the main verb of a sentence, other than in formal commands, in negative familiar commands (see Lección dos, pages 12–14), and in commands equal to *let us* (*let's*) plus a verb (see Lección diez, page 113), are:

A. After **tal vez** and **quizá(s),** and less commonly **acaso,** all meaning *perhaps,* when doubt or uncertainty is implied:

> **Quizás él ha venido.**   Perhaps he has come. (*Certainty implied*)
> **Tal vez tengas razón.**   Perhaps you may be right. (*Uncertainty implied*)

B. To make a statement or question milder or more polite (sometimes called a softened statement or question), the **-ra** imperfect subjunctive forms of **deber, querer,** and sometimes **poder,** are used:

> **Debo ayudar a mi papá.**   I must (ought to) help my father. (*Strong obligation*)
> **Yo debiera ayudarlo.**   I should help him. (*Milder obligation*)
> **Quiero ir al centro.**   I want to go downtown. (*Strong wish*)
> **Yo quisiera ir contigo.**   I should (would) like to go with you. (*More polite*)
> **¿Pudieras esperar un momento?**   Could you wait a moment? (*Polite question*)

NOTE: Remember that the conditional tense of **gustar** also means *should* (*would*) *like* and may be used instead of **quisiera,** etc.: **Nos (Me) gustaría sentarnos (sentarme) ahora,** *We (I) should (would) like to sit down now.*

C. After **¡Ojalá!,** with or without **que,** *Would that! I wish that!* the present subjunctive tense is used in an exclamatory wish which refers to something which may happen in the future. The imperfect subjunctive tense is used to express a wish concerning something that is contrary to fact in the present, and the pluperfect subjunctive tense to express a wish concerning something that was contrary to fact in the past:

> **¡Ojalá (que) él obtenga el puesto!**   Would that he get the position!
> **¡Ojalá que supiesen eso!**   Would that they knew that!
> **¡Ojalá hubieran llegado antes!**   (How) I wish they had arrived before!

When used alone, ¡Ojalá! means *God grant it! I hope so!*

—¿**Viene Ana mañana?** —¡**Ojalá!**   "Is Ann coming tomorrow?" "I hope so!"

EJERCICIOS

A. Para contestar negativamente, agregando una frase introducida por **pero quisiera,** y substituyendo el objeto del verbo con el pronombre correspondiente.

MODELO: ¿Has leído el libro?   *No, pero quisiera leerlo.*

1. ¿Has llamado a tu hermana?
2. ¿Has comprado la cámara?
3. ¿Has hecho la excursión?
4. ¿Has obtenido el puesto?

B. Para cambiar al imperfecto de subjuntivo, según los modelos.

MODELOS: Quiero poner el radio.   *Yo quisiera poner el radio.*
         Quiero que tú saques la foto.   *Yo quisiera que tú sacaras la foto.*
         Debo saludar a María.   *Yo debiera saludar a María.*

1. Quiero usar el coche.
2. Queremos llamar a Diana.
3. Quieren seguir andando.
4. ¿Quieres que yo ponga éste?
5. Queremos que Uds. oigan aquél.
6. Debo hablar con mi mamá.
7. Debemos ayudar a Jaime.
8. No deben esperar más.

C. Para contestar con una oración introducida por **tal vez (quizás).**

MODELO: ¿Vendrán ellos esta noche?   *Tal vez (Quizás) vengan esta noche.*

1. ¿Saldrá Elena mañana?
2. ¿Obtendrá él el puesto?
3. ¿Escogerán otra marca?
4. ¿Buscará ella otra cámara?

D. Para cambiar al presente de subjuntivo después de ¡**Ojalá que!**

MODELO: ¿Leerán el cuento?   *¡Ojalá que lean el cuento!*

1. ¿Cantará Ana esta noche?
2. ¿Podrá él visitarnos?
3. ¿Se divertirán en la fiesta?
4. ¿Les gustará la película?

E. Para cambiar al imperfecto y al pluscuamperfecto de subjuntivo después de ¡**Ojalá que!,** siguiendo los modelos.

MODELOS: No creen lo que él dijo.   *¡Ojalá que creyeran lo que él dijo!*
         No han llegado a tiempo.   *¡Ojalá que hubieran llegado a tiempo!*

1. Ellos no están en casa.
2. Ella no sabe la canción.
3. No pueden pasar por aquí.
4. No van a San Antonio.
5. No han vuelto del viaje.
6. Él no ha felicitado a Carlota.

3 Los adjetivos posesivos

Possessive adjectives agree in gender and number with the thing possessed (that is, with the noun modified), not with the possessor, as in English. The short, or unstressed, forms precede the nouns, and they are repeated before nouns in a series in Spanish:

Singular	Plural	
mi	mis	my
tu	tus	your (*fam.*)
su	sus	his, her, its, your (*formal*)
nuestro, nuestra	nuestros, nuestras	our
vuestro, vuestra	vuestros, vuestras	your (*fam. pl.*)
su	sus	their, your (*pl.*)

The long, or stressed, forms follow the noun. They are used for clearness and emphasis, after the verb **ser**, to translate *of mine, of his*, etc., in direct address, and in a few set phrases. These forms are:

Singular	Plural	
mío, mía	míos, mías	my, (of) mine
tuyo, tuya	tuyos, tuyas	your (*fam.*), (of) yours
suyo, suya	suyos, suyas	his, her, your (*formal*), its, (of) his, (of) hers, (of) yours, (of) its
nuestro, nuestra	nuestros, nuestras	our, (of) ours
vuestro, vuestra	vuestros, vuestras	your (*fam. pl.*), (of) yours
suyo, suya	suyos, suyas	their, your (*pl.*), (of) theirs, (of) yours

¿Traes tu cámara?   Are you bringing your camera?

Ramón, ¿son suyas estas cosas?   Raymond, are these things yours?

Estos lápices son míos y ésos son tuyos.   These pencils are mine and those are yours.

Inés tiene dos cintas mías.   Inez has two tapes of mine.

Ana y una amiga suya vienen pronto.   Ann and a friend of hers are coming soon.

Los dos jóvenes son buenos amigos míos (nuestros).   The two young men are good friends of mine (ours).

Querida (amiga) mía: My dear (friend):

¡Dios mío!   Heavens!

Since **su(s)** and **suyo (-a, -os, -as)** have several meanings, the forms **de él, de ella,** etc., may be substituted to make the meaning clear. (The prepositional form is not used for any long possessive other than **suyo, -a, -os, -as.**)

Me gusta su casa nueva.   I like (his, her, your, their) new house.
Me gusta la casa de él (de ella, de usted).   I like his (her, your) house.
—¿Es de ellos este coche? —No, es de él.   "Is this car theirs?" "No, it is his."

EJERCICIOS

A. Repitan cada frase; luego, repítanla otra vez empleando una frase con una forma de **suyo,** según el modelo.

MODELO: Jaime y una amiga *de él*   *Jaime y una amiga de él*
Jaime y una amiga suya

1. este sombrero *de él*
2. ese radio *de ella*
3. aquellas cintas *de ellos*
4. esos discos *de usted*

5. aquel tocadiscos *de ellos*
6. esta cámara *de él*
7. esas maletas *de ustedes*
8. varias fotos *de ella*

B. Para contestar afirmativamente, según los modelos.

MODELOS: ¿Es nuestra esta cámara?   *Sí, es nuestra* (or *es suya*).
¿Son míos esos libros?   *Sí, son suyos* (or *son tuyos*).
¿Son suyas esas compras?   *Sí, son mías* (or *son nuestras*).

1. ¿Es nuestro aquel disco?
2. ¿Son míos estos dos lápices?
3. ¿Son suyas estas fotos?
4. ¿Es suya esta bicicleta?

5. ¿Es nuestra aquella guitarra?
6. ¿Son nuestros aquellos cuadros?
7. ¿Es tuyo ese cinturón?
8. ¿Son mías esas revistas?

4 Los pronombres posesivos

The possessive pronouns are formed by using the definite article with the long forms of the possessive adjectives. Remember that after **ser** the article is usually omitted.

| Singular | | Plural | | |
Masculine	Feminine	Masculine	Feminine	
el mío	la mía	los míos	las mías	mine
el tuyo	la tuya	los tuyos	las tuyas	yours (*fam.*)
el suyo	la suya	los suyos	las suyas	his, hers, its, yours (*formal*)
el nuestro	la nuestra	los nuestros	las nuestras	ours
el vuestro	la vuestra	los vuestros	las vuestras	yours (*fam. pl.*)
el suyo	la suya	los suyos	las suyas	theirs, yours (*pl.*)

mi coche, nuestro coche; el mío, el nuestro   my car, our car; mine, ours
nuestra casa, mi casa; la nuestra, la mía   our house, my house; ours, mine
Ana, yo tengo los libros míos y los tuyos.   Ann, I have *my* books and yours.
Señor Solís, ¿tiene Ud. los suyos?   Mr. Solís, do you have yours?
Este paquete es mío (nuestro).   This package is mine (ours).

Since **el suyo (la suya, los suyos, las suyas)** may mean *his, hers, its, yours* (formal), *theirs*, these pronouns may be clarified by using **el (la) de él, el (la) de ella,** etc. The article agrees with the thing possessed:

Pablo vende el suyo.   Paul is selling his (hers, yours, theirs).
El coche de ellos y el de ustedes están aquí.   Their car and yours are here.
Nuestros padres y los de ella vienen.   Our parents and hers are coming.

EJERCICIOS

A. Repitan cada oración; luego, repítanla otra vez, substituyendo el sustantivo en cursiva con el pronombre posesivo, o con la frase **el (la) de él (de ella,** etc.).

MODELOS: Él trae *su maleta.*   Él trae su maleta. Él trae la suya.
Tengo *el reloj de Juan.*   Tengo el reloj de Juan. Tengo el de él.

1. La hermana de Ana tiene *su blusa.*
2. Tomás y yo vamos a *nuestra casa.*
3. ¿Tiene ella *su pulsera?*
4. Miguel lleva *mis cámaras.*

5. *El jardín de mi mamá* es bonito.
6. *Las flores de Inés* son hermosas.
7. ¿Quieres ver *nuestras rosas?*
8. Juan, no conduzcas *tu coche* hoy.

B. Para contestar afirmativamente, según los modelos.

MODELOS: ¿Tienes *tu cámara?*   Sí, tengo la mía.
¿Quieren ellos *sus fotos?*   Sí, quieren las suyas.

1. ¿Ve Ud. *su coche?*
2. ¿Escuchan Uds. *su tocadiscos?*
3. ¿Traen Uds. *sus composiciones?*
4. ¿Buscas *tus guantes?*

5. ¿Mira Clara *su vestido?*
6. ¿Tiene Carlos *sus compras?*
7. ¿Desean ellos *sus regalos?*
8. ¿Lleva él *su maleta?*

C. Para expresar en español:

1. I want you (*formal sing.*) to bring your camera and mine.   2. Tell (*formal sing.*) them to take their photos and yours to the meeting.   3. Joe doubts that his sister and mine will go to the movie.   4. Wait (*fam. sing.*) a moment in order that I may give you her composition and his.   5. Let (*formal sing.*) me bring my small radio and hers tomorrow.   6. Whose records are these? Do you (*fam. sing.*) have theirs?

5 Usos de los adjetivos como sustantivos

Many adjectives may be used with the definite article, demonstratives, numerals, and other limiting adjectives to form nouns. In this case the adjective agrees in gender and number with the noun understood. The word *one(s)* is often included in the English meaning. Remember that adjectives of nationality are also used as nouns: **Luis es mexicano,** *Louis is (a) Mexican.*

> **Este último me parece el mejor.**   This last one seems to me (to be) the best (one) (*m.*).
>
> **Nos trajeron el más pequeño.**   They brought us the smaller (smallest) one (*m.*).
>
> **No me gusta tanto como el otro.**   I don't like it so much as the other one (*m.*).
>
> **Una joven compró las blancas.**   A young lady bought the white ones (*f.*).

EJERCICIO

Repitan cada oración; luego, repítanla otra vez, empleando el adjetivo como sustantivo.

MODELO: ¿Te gusta la blusa roja?   *¿Te gusta la blusa roja? ¿Te gusta la roja?*

1. La casa amarilla es del señor Díaz.   2. Me gusta este cartel grande.
3. Quieren buscar una casa más grande.   4. Prefiero ver unos zapatos negros.
5. Esta última camisa es muy bonita.   6. ¿Les gusta a ellos la música popular?
7. ¿Cuánto cuesta la otra marca?   8. Miramos varios radios nuevos.   9. Yo quisiera escuchar algunos discos españoles.   10. ¿Qué les parece a Uds. este radio pequeño?

6 Los diminutivos

In Spanish, diminutive endings are often used to express not only small size, but also affection, pity, scorn, ridicule, and the like. The most common endings are: **-ito, -a; -illo, -a; -(e)cito, -a; -(e)cillo, -a.** Frequently, the use of these suffixes with nouns precludes the need for adjectives. For the choice of ending, rely on observation. A final vowel is often dropped before adding the ending:

hermana	sister	**hermanita**	little sister
hermano	brother	**hermanito**	little brother
Juan	John	**Juanito**	Johnny

pueblo town	**pueblecito** small town, village
señora lady, woman	**señorita** young lady (woman)
ventana window	**ventanilla** ticket window

Applied to first names, these endings indicate affection, with no implication of size: **Juanita,** *Jane;* **Anita,**[1] *Annie;* **Tomasito,** *Tommy.* Sometimes a change in spelling is necessary to preserve the sound of a consonant when a final vowel is dropped: **Diego,** *James,* and **Dieguito,** *Jimmie.* Similarly, note the change in spelling in the adverb **poco,** *little* (quantity), and **poquito,** *very little;* also, in the noun **taza,** *cup,* and **tacita,** *small (tiny) cup.*

EJERCICIO

Give the base word to which each diminutive suffix has been added:

casita small house, cottage	**momentito** (short) moment
cosilla small thing, trifle	**mujercita** pleasant little woman
florecita small (tiny) flower	
golpecito slight blow, tap	**piedrecita** small stone, pebble
hombrecito nice little man	**pobrecito** poor boy (man, thing)
jovencito nice young fellow	
mesita small table, stand	**regalito** small gift

---

[1] The diminutives given in the rest of this section are not listed in the end vocabulary unless they are used elsewhere in this text. Watch for similar and other uses of diminutives in reading.

LECCIÓN CATORCE

1 Comparación de los adjetivos y de los adverbios

A. Comparison of adjectives

When one makes comparisons in English, one says, for example, *tall, taller, tallest; expensive, more (less) expensive, most (least) expensive.*

To form the comparative of adjectives in Spanish, place **más,** *more,* or **menos,** *less,* before the adjective: **alto, -a,** *tall;* **más alto, -a,** *taller,* **menos alto, -a,** *less tall.*

To form the superlative, place the definite article before the comparative form: **el más alto, la más alta, los más altos, las más altas,** *the tallest,* **el menos alto, la menos alta,** etc., *the least tall.* The article, however, is not repeated when the superlative adjective follows the noun it modifies: **el camino más corto,** *the shortest road.* Sometimes the possessive adjective (**mi, tu,** etc.) replaces the definite article: **mi vestido más bonito,** *my prettiest dress.* As the examples cited below show, the adjective must agree in gender and number with the noun it modifies:

> **Este árbol es el más alto de todos.**   This tree is the tallest of all.
> **Éste es el edificio más grande.**   This is the larger (largest) building.
> **Aquel coche es el menos caro.**   That car is the less (least) expensive.

Note that the distinction that is made in English between the comparative and the superlative degree when two or more than two persons or objects are compared is not made in Spanish. One can usually tell from the context, however, when an adjective in Spanish has comparative or superlative force, that is, whether **más** means *more* or *most,* and whether **menos** means *less* or *least.* Compare, for example, the two following sentences:

> **Elena es la más lista (menos lista) de las dos.**   Helen is the cleverer *or* more clever (less clever) of the two.
> **Elena es la más lista (menos lista) de todas.**   Helen is the cleverest *or* most clever (least clever) of all.

After a superlative, the preposition *in* is translated by **de:**

> **El señor Martinez es el abogado más rico de la ciudad.**   Mr. Martinez is the richest lawyer in the city.

Even though an adjective modified by **más** or **menos** usually follows the noun, in reading you will note exceptions to this practice (see, also, Lección seis, pages 62–63).

B. Translation of *than*

Than is translated by **que** before a noun or pronoun. After **que,** *than,* the negatives **nadie, nunca, nada, ninguno, -a,** replace **alguien, siempre, algo, alguno, -a,** respectively:

> **Este vestido es más lindo que ése.**   This dress is prettier than that one.
> **Esa pulsera es menos cara que ésta.**   That bracelet is less expensive than this one.
> **Ella toca más que nadie (nunca).**   She plays more than anyone (ever).

Than is translated by **de** before a numeral or numerical expression in an affirmative sentence; if the sentence is negative, either **que** or **de** may be used, the preference being for **que.** Theoretically, **no . . . más que** means *only,* and **no . . . más de** means *not . . . more than:*

> **Él trabajó más de ocho horas.**   He worked more than eight hours.
> **No necesito más que diez dólares.**   I need only ten dollars.
> **No necesito más de diez dólares.**   I do not need more than ten dollars.

When *than* is followed by a conjugated verb form and what is compared is a noun which is the object of the first verb and is elliptically omitted in the second part of the sentence, it is expressed by **de** + the definite article + **que,** that is, by **del que, de la que, de los que, de las que,** meaning *than the one(s) who (which, that):*

> **Él tiene más flores de las que vende.**   He has more flowers than he sells.
> **Hace más frío hoy del que hizo ayer.**   It is colder today than it was yesterday.

When *than* is followed by a conjugated verb form, but the second member is elliptical in such a way that the verb of the first member must be repeated in order to complete the idea, **que** is replaced by **de lo que** (in such sentences the verb which follows **de lo que** often expresses a mental state):

> **Diana es más bonita de lo que crees.**   Diane is prettier than (what) you believe (she is).
> **Hemos tardado menos (tiempo) de lo que yo pensaba (creía).**   We have taken less time than I thought *or* believed (we would take).
> **La novela es más interesante de lo que yo esperaba.**   The novel is more interesting than I expected (it to be).

C. Comparison of adverbs

The comparative of adverbs is also regularly formed by placing **más** or **menos** before the adverb. The definite article is not used in the superlative, except that the neuter form **lo** is used when an expression of possibility follows:

> **Los autobuses pasan más rápidamente que nunca.**   The buses pass more rapidly (faster) than ever.
> **Tienen que salir lo más pronto posible.**   They must (have to) leave as soon as possible (the soonest possible).

D. Six adjectives and four adverbs, most of which have already been used in this text, are compared irregularly:

Adjectives		
bueno good	**(el) mejor** (the) better, best	
malo bad	**(el) peor** (the) worse, worst	
grande large	{**(el) más grande** (the) larger, largest {**(el) mayor** (the) greater, older, greatest, oldest	
pequeño small	{**(el) más pequeño** (the) smaller, smallest {**(el) menor** (the) smaller, younger, smallest, youngest	
mucho(s) much (many)	**más** more, most	
poco(s) little (few)	**menos** less, fewer	

Mejor and **peor** precede the noun, just as **bueno, -a** and **malo, -a** regularly precede it, except when emphasized. Used with the definite article, the forms are:

el mejor (peor)   **los mejores (peores)**
la mejor (peor)   **las mejores (peores)**

Ella tiene las mejores ideas de todos.   She has the best ideas of all.
Habrá menos interés en la exposición.   There will be (probably is) less interest in the exhibition.

Grande and **pequeño, -a** have regular forms which refer to size, while the irregular forms **mayor** (*m.* and *f.*) and **menor** (*m.* and *f.*) usually refer to persons and mean *older* and *younger,* respectively:

Estas pinturas son más grandes que ésas.   These paintings are larger than those.
Mi hermano mayor ha conseguido un buen puesto.   My older brother has obtained a good position.

Most (of), The greater part of, is expressed by **La mayor parte de.** The verb normally agrees with the noun following this expression: **La mayor parte de los estudiantes van a los conciertos,** *Most (of the) students go to (the) concerts.*

Adverbs			
bien well	**mejor** better, best	**mucho** much	**más** more, most
mal bad, badly	**peor** worse, worst	**poco** little	**menos** less, least

La exposición ha sido menos interesante este año.   The exhibition has been less interesting this year.
¿No se verían mejor en esta pared del salón?   Wouldn't they be seen better on this wall of the salon?

E. The absolute superlative (a high degree of quality without any element of comparison) is expressed by the use of **muy** before the adjective or adverb, or by adding the ending **-ísimo, -a (-os, -as)** to the adjective. When **-ísimo** is added, a final vowel is dropped. **Muchísimo, -a (-os, -as)** is used for the adjective *very much* (*many*), and **muchísimo** for the adverb *very much:*

> **Lucía es muy hermosa (hermosísima).**   Lucy is very pretty.
> **Éste es un lugar lindísimo.**   This is a very pretty place.
> **Me gusta muchísimo la música clásica.**   I like classical music very much.

EJERCICIOS

A. Completen las oraciones con la forma comparativa del adjetivo o del adverbio.

> MODELO: Esta novela es buena, pero   *Esta novela es buena, pero la otra*
> la otra es _____.   *es mejor.*

1. Esta calle es larga, pero aquélla es _____.   2. Este edificio es grande, pero aquél es _____.   3. Esta música popular es buena, pero la clásica es _____.
4. Aquella casa blanca es pequeña, pero la amarilla es _____.   5. Esos artículos son cortos, pero éste es _____.   6. Yo estoy cansado, pero mi hermana está _____.   7. Ramón tiene dos años más que Pepe; éste es el _____ de los dos.   8. María tiene un año menos que Ana; aquélla es la _____ de las dos.
9. Margarita toca bien, pero su amiga toca _____.   10. Jorge juega mal, pero Carlos juega _____.   11. A mí me gusta mucho la pintura, pero a él le gusta _____.   12. Ellos tienen poco tiempo, pero yo tengo _____.

B. Para contestar afirmativamente, siguiendo los modelos.

> MODELOS: ¿Es grande el parque?   *Sí, es más grande que éste.*
> ¿Son difíciles las frases?   *Sí, son más difíciles que éstas.*

1. ¿Está contenta la muchacha?   4. ¿Es popular la música?
2. ¿Es larga la carretera?   5. ¿Es mala la novela?
3. ¿Son hermosas las flores?   6. ¿Es buena la pintura?

> MODELO: ¿Es bonita la casa?   *Sí, es la más bonita de todas.*

7. ¿Es grande el cuadro?   9. ¿Es famoso el hombre?
8. ¿Es simpática la muchacha?   10. ¿Es interesante el libro?

> MODELO: ¿Es hermosa Inés?   *Sí, es muy hermosa; es hermosísima.*

11. ¿Es guapo su novio?   13. ¿Son famosas las pinturas?
12. ¿Son altos los árboles?   14. ¿Es caro el traje?

C. Lean en español, supliendo la palabra o frase equivalente a *than:*

1. Creo que hay más _____ mil estudiantes en el teatro.   2. Este concierto es mejor _____ el último.   3. Hay más parques en California _____ tenemos en este estado.   4. Jaime tiene más amigos en la ciudad _____ tú crees.
5. María ha escrito más composiciones _____ yo creía.   6. Hoy ella tocará

más números _____ tocó la semana pasada.   7. Esta música es más popular _____ yo esperaba.   8. No te olvides de que esta novela es más larga _____ la otra.

D. Para expresar en español:

1. This song is less popular than that one (*nearby*).   2. Mary sings better than her sister.   3. These flowers are prettier than those (*nearby*).   4. This is the shortest street of all.   5. Charles is the best player of the team.   6. Jane is younger than Martha.   7. The city is larger than you (*pl.*) believe.   8. I have less than twenty dollars.   9. This car is older than John's.   10. That tree is very tall (*two ways*).   11. I like this painting very much.   12. Most of the boys have gone home.

2   Comparaciones de igualdad (*equality*)

Tan + an adjective or adverb + **como** means *as (so) . . . as.* **Tan** used without **como** means *so,* sometimes *as:*

> **Este cuadro no es tan lindo como ése.**   This picture is not as (so) pretty as that one.
> **¿Por qué están ellas tan contentas?**   Why are they so happy?

Before an adjective **tan** is used instead of **tal** to mean *such (a):*

> **¡Es una obra tan excelente!**   It is such an excellent work!
> **Nunca he colgado pinturas tan interesantes.**   I have never hung such interesting pictures.
>
> BUT: **¿Has visto jamás tal cosa?**   Have you ever seen such a thing?

Tanto, -a (-os, -as) + a noun + **como** means *as (so) much (many) . . . as.* **Tanto** is also used as a pronoun or adverb, with or without **como,** meaning *as (so) much (many) (. . . as):*

> **No hay tantas exposiciones como antes.**   There aren't so many exhibitions as before.
> **Nunca hemos visto tantos coches.**   We have never seen so many cars.
> **Dígale Ud. a Marta que no estudie tanto.**   Tell Martha not to study so much.
> **Nos gusta esta pintura tanto como la otra.**   We like this picture as much as the other one.

EJERCICIOS

A. Repitan cada oración; luego, al oír un sustantivo o un adjetivo, substitúyanlo en la oración original, haciendo los cambios necesarios:

1. Esta casa no es tan *nueva* como aquélla.   (viejo, grande, cómodo, pequeño)
2. Este año no hay tantas *exposiciones* como antes.   (cuadros, pinturas, obras, estudiantes)
3. Ella recibe muchos *regalos,* pero yo no recibo tantos.   (cartas, dinero, revistas, periódicos)

B. Oirán una oración y luego una o más palabras. Formen una oración nueva empleando **tan ... como,** según el modelo.

MODELO: Luis está cansado.   (Carlos)   *Luis está tan cansado como Carlos.*

1. Las estudiantes estaban contentas.   (la profesora)
2. Esta exposición es grande.   (la primera)
3. El jardín es muy hermoso.   (el de mi mamá)
4. Las pinturas son excelentes.   (las que vimos en Los Ángeles)
5. La composición es buena.   (la de Luisa)

Formen oraciones nuevas empleando **no ... tanto, -a (-os, -as) ... como,** según el modelo.

MODELO: Él escribe muchas cartas.   *Él no escribe tantas cartas como Ana.*

6. Ella toca muchos discos.
7. Ramón cuelga muchas pinturas.
8. Nosotros hemos asistido a varias exposiciones.
9. Carmen pasa mucho tiempo preparando la comida.
10. Juan ha traído varias obras para la exposición.

C. Para expresar en español:

1. This house is not as large as his.   2. Their car is not as small as ours.
3. That (*nearby*) picture is as pretty as this one.   4. I have never seen such an interesting work.   5. They do not work so much as we.   6. Tell (*formal sing.*) him not to run so rapidly.   7. Joe has several magazines, but Thomas doesn't have so many.   8. I have never seen such a thing.

3 La formación de los adverbios

In Spanish, adverbs of manner are formed by adding **-mente** (compare the English suffix *-ly*) to the feminine singular of adjectives. Adverbs may also be formed by using **con** plus a noun:

claro	clear	**claramente**	clearly	**con cuidado**	carefully
fácil	easy	**fácilmente**	easily	**con éxito**	successfully

When two or more adverbs are used in a series, **-mente** is added only to the last one:

Ana habla rápida y correctamente.   Ann speaks rapidly and correctly.

Occasionally, adjectives are used in Spanish as adverbs, particularly in the spoken language and regularly in poetry, with no change in form other than the usual agreement:

Ellos vivían felices.   They were living happily.
Todas iban muy contentas.   All (*f.*) were going very contentedly.

EJERCICIO

Den los adverbios que correspondan a los adjetivos siguientes:

1. general 2. triste 3. cortés 4. solo 5. último 6. feliz 7. rico 8. personal
9. urgente   10. evidente   11. correcto y rápido   12. afirmativo y negativo

4 **Hacer** en expresiones de tiempo

A. In Spanish, **hace** followed by a period of time (**minuto, hora, día, mes, año,** etc.) plus **que** and a verb in the present tense, or a present tense plus **desde hace** followed by a period of time, indicates that an action began in the past and that it is still going on in the present. When **desde hace** is used, the word order in Spanish is the same as in English. Note that in English the present perfect progressive tense is frequently used:

Hace una hora que estoy aquí *or* **Estoy aquí desde hace una hora.**   I have been here for an hour (lit., It makes an hour that I am here).
¿Cuánto tiempo hace que viven ellas aquí?   How long have they been living (lit., How long does it make that they live) here?
Hace varios días que Pepe busca un coche.   Joe has been looking for a car for several days (For several days Joe has been looking for a car).
¿Hace tiempo que nos esperan Uds.?   Have you been waiting for us long (a long time)?
Hace mucho tiempo que no te veo.   I haven't seen you for a long time (It is a long time since I have seen you).

Hacía followed by a period of time plus **que** and a verb in the imperfect tense, or the imperfect tense plus **desde hacía** followed by a period of time, indicates that an action had been going on for a certain length of time and was still continuing when something else happened. The pluperfect or pluperfect progressive tense is used in English:

Hacía un mes que yo vivía allí cuando la conocí *or* **Yo vivía allí desde hacía un mes cuando la conocí.**   I had been living there (for) a month when I met her (lit., It made a month that I was living there . . .).
Hacía tiempo que yo no los veía.   I had not seen you (them) for a long time.

NOTE: If the verb of the main clause is negative, the present perfect and pluperfect tenses may be used, as in English. The following alternate constructions, then, are often used: **Hace tiempo que no te he visto, Hacía tiempo que yo no los había visto.**

B. When **hace** is followed by a period of time after a verb in a past tense, it regularly means *ago, since.* If the **hace**-clause comes first in the sentence, **que** usually (although not always) introduces the main clause:

> **Llegaron hace media hora** *or* **Hace media hora que llegaron.**   They arrived a half hour ago *or* It is a half hour since they arrived.
> **Nos vimos hace quince días.**   We saw each other two weeks ago.

EJERCICIOS

A. Después de oír una oración, oirán una expresión de tiempo; combinen los dos elementos en una nueva oración, siguiendo el modelo.

MODELO: Miro la televisión.   (Hace una hora)   *Hace una hora que miro la televisión.*

1. Estudian español.   (Hace más de un año)
2. Estamos en el salón.   (Hace una hora y media)
3. Están en México.   (Hace tres semanas)
4. No te veo en el centro.   (Hace tiempo) (*two ways*)
5. No vamos al cine.   (Hace un mes) (*two ways*)
6. Estamos esperando a María.   (Hace quince minutos)

B. Después de oír una pregunta, oirán una expresión de tiempo; úsenla para contestar la pregunta, según los modelos.

MODELO: ¿Cuánto tiempo hace que lees?   (una hora)   *Leo desde hace una hora.*

1. ¿Cuánto tiempo hace que tocas la guitarra?   (tres años)
2. ¿Cuánto tiempo hace que ella habla por teléfono?   (veinte minutos)
3. ¿Cuánto tiempo hace que vives aquí?   (seis meses)
4. ¿Cuánto tiempo hace que conoce Ud. a Marta?   (un mes y medio)

MODELO: ¿Cuándo salió él?   (hace una hora)   *Él salió hace una hora.*
Hace una hora que él salió.

5. ¿Cuándo escogieron ellos el cuadro?   (hace tiempo)
6. ¿Cuándo fueron Uds. a la exposición?   (hace treinta minutos)
7. ¿Cuándo colgaron Uds. las pinturas?   (hace varios días)
8. ¿Cuándo llegaste al salón?   (hace media hora)
9. ¿Cuándo viste a Carolina?   (hace una semana)
10. ¿Cuándo volvieron ellos de México?   (hace un mes)

C. Para expresar en español:

1. John has been working in this store for six months.   2. We have known Miss Flores for about two years.   3. How long have you (*fam. sing.*) been playing tennis?   4. How long have you (*pl.*) been in the salon?   5. Philip has been watching television for a half hour.   6. We haven't seen her for a long time. 7. John had been looking for a position for several weeks.   8. Our friends made a trip to Mexico a year ago.   9. It is two days since my father returned from Los Angeles.   10. John began to play the guitar twenty minutes ago.

Glosario

¿cuánto tiempo?   how long?
la **exposición** (*pl.* **exposiciones**)
    exposition, exhibition

lindo, -a   pretty, beautiful
la **obra**   work (*art, music, literature*)
el **salón** (*pl.* **salones**)   salon, (large) hall

LECCIÓN QUINCE

Usos del participio pasado · El pretérito anterior de indicativo · Usos del participio presente · La traducción de *must* · Verbos auxiliares para expresar el modo · El artículo neutro **lo** · El pronombre neutro **lo** · Las conjunciones **e** y **u** · Usos de **pero, sino** y **sino que** · Formas de mandato correspondientes a **vosotros, -as**

1 Usos del participio pasado

A. The past participle is used:

1. With the appropriate tense of **haber** to form the perfect or compound tenses. In this case the participle always ends in **-o**:

   Hemos estudiado la lección.   We have studied the lesson.
   ¿Has envuelto el paquete para Margarita?   Have you wrapped up the package for Margaret?

2. Frequently as an adjective, including its use with **estar** and similar verbs to express a state or condition that results from a previous action (see Lección cinco, page 50):

   La puerta estaba (se encontraba) cerrada.   The door was closed.
   Las ventanas del edificio todavía estaban (se hallaban) abiertas.   The windows of the building were still open.

3. With **ser** to form the passive voice (see Lección cinco, pages 51–52). In this and the previous construction, the participle agrees in gender and number with the noun or pronoun it modifies:

   Las tazas fueron rotas por Juanito.   The cups were broken by Johnny.
   Los artículos para el periódico fueron escritos ayer por la tarde.   The articles for the newspaper were written yesterday afternoon.

   NOTE: **De** often replaces **por** with verbs other than **estar** or **ser** to introduce an agent dependent upon a past participle: **Parto para Buenos Aires, acompañado de mi hermano Juan,** *I am leaving (I'll leave) for Buenos Aires, accompanied by my brother John.*

B. The past participle also may be used independently with a noun or pronoun to express *time, manner, means,* and the like. (This is sometimes called the absolute use of the past participle.) Used thus, the participle precedes the noun or pronoun it modifies, and agrees with it in gender and number. The translation depends on the context:

   Salido el avión, cenamos en el aeropuerto.   After the plane had left (The plane having left), we ate supper in the airport.
   Hechos los planes, volvimos a nuestros cuartos.   The plans made (After the plans were made), we returned to our rooms.

EJERCICIO

Escuchen la oración; luego, cámbienla, usando el participio pasado, según el modelo.

MODELO: Al escribir la tarjeta, Ana se la   *Escrita la tarjeta, Ana se la*
            envió a su amiga.   *envió a su amiga.*

1. Al cerrar la puerta, la profesora empezó a leer los exámenes.
2. Después de envolver las cosas, Pablo se las llevó a María.
3. Al comprar los boletos, Ricardo se los dio a sus amigos.
4. Después de entregar los artículos, Carmen fue a la biblioteca.

2   El pretérito anterior (*preterit perfect*) de indicativo

The preterit perfect tense is formed with the preterit tense of **haber** and the past participle. It is translated like the English past perfect tense, but is used only after conjunctions such as **cuando, en cuanto, después que, apenas** (*scarcely, hardly*). In the case of **apenas,** the word *when* is carried over to the following clause in English; it is not expressed in Spanish:

Preterit Perfect		
Singular		*Plural*
hube		**hubimos**
hubiste } tomado, comido, vivido		**hubisteis** } tomado, comido, vivido
hubo		**hubieron**

En cuanto (Cuando) ellos hubieron colgado las pinturas, salieron del salón.
   As soon as (When) they had hung the paintings, they left the salon.
Apenas él hubo vuelto, me llamó.   Scarcely had he returned, when he
   called me.

In spoken Spanish, the simple preterit often replaces the preterit perfect tense.

3   Usos del participio presente

The present participle, also called the gerund, has a number of important functions.

A. **Estar** is used with the present participle to express the progressive forms of the tenses, that is, to express the action of the verb as continuing at a given moment (see Lección cinco, page 50):

   Los niños están (estaban) gritando.   The children are (were) shouting.
   ¿Qué estás haciendo?   What are you doing?

B. Verbs of motion, particularly **ir, andar, venir,** are used with the present participle to give a more graphic representation of an action in progress. These verbs normally retain something of their literal meaning. **Seguir (i, i)** and **continuar,** *to continue, keep on,* are followed by the present participle. (The progressive forms of **ir, salir, venir** are seldom used.)

> **Ella iba (venía) cantando.**   She was (went along, came) singing.
> **Sigue (Continúa) tú tocando.**   Continue *or* Keep on playing.

Ir + a present participle is also equivalent to the English *to go on* or *keep on* + present participle, or *to do something gradually* (*slowly, more and more*):

> **Va terminando el segundo semestre.**   The second semester is gradually ending.

C. Referring to the subject expressed or understood, the present participle may be used to convey a variety of adverbial relationships:

> **Pasan mucho tiempo leyendo.**   They spend much time reading.
> **Andando rápidamente, llegué a tiempo.**   By walking rapidly, I arrived on time.

EJERCICIO

Repitan la oración; luego, al oír un verbo, substituyan la forma correcta del verbo seguida del participio presente, según los modelos.

MODELOS: Ana mira un mapa. (estar)   *Ana mira un mapa. Ana está mirando un mapa.*

Andaban despacio. (ir)   *Andaban despacio. Iban andando despacio.*

1. Miguel visita a sus primos.   (estar)
2. Carlos hacía un viaje por México.   (estar)
3. Los chicos corren hacia nosotros.   (venir)
4. Nosotros aprendemos a hablar español.   (ir)
5. Juan anda rápidamente por la calle.   (venir)
6. José solicita una beca para el año que viene.   (estar)
7. Ellos se acercaban al patio.   (ir)
8. Lea Ud. hasta las cuatro de la tarde.   (seguir)

4   La traducción de *must*

A. When *must* means *have to,* expressing a strong obligation or necessity, **tener que** + an infinitive is used:

> **Los muchachos tienen que esperar.**   The boys have to wait.

The impersonal form is **hay** (**ha habido, había, hubo, habrá,** etc.) **que** + an infinitive:

Hay que practicar.   One must (It is necessary to) practice.

B. When *must* means *is (was) to, is (was) supposed to,* expressing a mild obligation or commitment, **haber de** + an infinitive is used:

Han de reunirse esta noche.   They must (are to) meet tonight.
Él había de salir a las tres.   He was (supposed) to leave at three.

C. For a moral obligation, duty, customary action, etc., **deber** is used:

Yo debo llamar a Carlos.   I must (ought to) call Charles.

D. When *must* expresses probability in the present (or present perfect), it is indicated by the future (or future perfect) tense of the verb (see Lección ocho, page 90), or by **deber (de)** + an infinitive:

Estarán *or* **Deben de estar en el salón.**   They must be (probably are) in the salon.
¿Qué les habrá pasado? *or* **¿Qué debe de haberles pasado?**[1]   What can have happened to them?
Deben de ser *or* **Serán las siete y cuarto.**   It must be (probably is) a quarter after seven.
Diana debe de haber salido[1] *or* **Diana habrá salido.**   Diane must have left.

EJERCICIO

Después de oír una pregunta, oirán un verbo o una frase; contesten afirmativamente, usando la forma correcta del verbo correspondiente.

MODELO: *¿Son* las nueve?   (deber de)   *Sí, deben de ser las nueve.*
           ¿Has de irte ahora?   (tener que)   *Sí, tengo que irme ahora.*

1. ¿*Han de* pagar la cuenta ahora?   (tener que)
2. ¿*Está* ella en la biblioteca?   (deber de)
3. ¿*Va* Juan *a* tocar la guitarra?   (haber de)
4. ¿*Iban a* reunirse temprano?   (haber de)
5. ¿*Es necesario* acercarse despacio?   (haber que)
6. ¿*Será preciso* colgar las pinturas en la pared?   (haber que)
7. ¿*Debemos* ir al concierto esta noche?   (tener que)
8. ¿Creían que *podían* esperar aquí?   (deber)

---

[1] Note the perfect infinitive forms, **haber pasado,** (*to*) *have happened,* and **haber salido,** (*to*) *have left* (see Appendix D, page 222, under The Compound Tenses).

5   Verbos auxiliares para expresar el modo (*modal auxiliaries*)

A. Translation of *can* and *may*

1. If *can* expresses physical ability, the present tense of **poder** is used; if it indicates mental ability, **saber** is used:

   Él no puede jugar porque está enfermo.   He cannot play because he is ill.
   ¿Sabes tocar la guitarra?   Can you (Do you know how to) play the guitar?

2. Some of the ways in which *may* is expressed are:

   Puedes sentarte si quieres.   You may sit down if you wish.
   Es posible que no contesten.   They may (It is possible that they may) not reply.
   Puede (ser) que se vayan hoy.   They may (It may be that they will) leave today.
   Aunque él venga, no se lo daré.   Even though he may come, I won't give it to him.
   ¡Que sean Uds. felices!   May you be happy!
   ¿Se puede entrar?   May I (we, one) come in?

B. Translation of *could* and *might*

Could, meaning *would be able to, might,* is expressed in Spanish by the imperfect, preterit, or conditional indicative tense, or by the imperfect subjunctive tense of **poder:**

   Carmen podía cantar bien.   Carmen could (was able to) sing well.
   Pepe no pudo terminar la composición.   Joe couldn't finish the composition.
   ¿Podrías ayudarme?   Could you (Would you be able to) help me?
   Ana dijo que podría esperar un rato.   Ann said she could (would *or* might be able to) wait a while.
   Era posible que se fueran.   It was possible that they might leave (go away).

C. Translation of *should (ought to), should like*

Deber may be used in all tenses to express various degrees of obligation. When *should* indicates a mild obligation (not so strong as that expressed by the present tense of **deber**), the **-ra** form of the imperfect subjunctive tense, the imperfect indicative, or the conditional indicative tense of **deber** is used:

   Debieras ir a verla.   You should (ought to) go (to) see her.
   Yo sabía que debía terminarlo.   I knew that I should finish it.
   Yo creía que Lola debía (debiera, debería) llamar.   I thought (that) Lola should call.

In a sentence that expresses a contrary-to-fact condition, or an improbable condition in the future (see Lección trece, pages 146–147), *should* is translated by the conditional tense in the main clause, and by the imperfect subjunctive tense in the **si-**clause:

> **Si yo tuviera (tuviese) tiempo, lo haría.**   If I had (should have) time, I should (would) do it.

Should (*would*) *like* may be translated by the **-ra** forms of the imperfect subjunctive tense of **querer,** or by the conditional tense of **gustar:**

> **Yo quisiera (Me gustaría) ir con él.**   I should like to go with him.

EJERCICIO

Para expresar en español:

1. Thomas can play tennis well, but he cannot play today because he doesn't feel well.   2. Can't you (*fam. sing.*) chat with me a while?   3. You (*pl.*) may sit down here if you wish.   4. I should like (*two ways*) to take an excursion to the mountains. 5. Caroline knows that she must attend the lecture.   6. May you (*pl.*) have a good time tonight!   7. You (*fam. sing.*) should (*mild obligation*) look at the Mexican paintings if you should go to the exhibition.   8. The employee said that he could do the work next week.   9. Where can Paul have gone?   10. It may be that he has gone to class.   11. If I were John, I would try to get a scholarship.

6   El artículo neutro **lo**

A. The neuter article **lo** is used with masculine singular adjectives, with adverbs, and with past participles used as adjectives, to form an expression almost equivalent to an abstract noun. The translation of this abstract idea or concept varies according to the context:

> **Lo bueno es que Pepe está aquí.**   What is good (The good part *or* thing) is that Joe is here.
> **Lean Uds. lo escrito.**   Read what is (has been) written.

B. The neuter article **lo** used with an adjective or adverb followed by **que** is the equivalent of *how* in English:

> **Tú no sabes lo interesante que es.**   You don't know how interesting it is.

C. Remember the uses of the neuter article **lo** explained earlier: **lo que** meaning *what, that which;* **lo de** meaning *that* (*matter, affair*) *of* (see Lección doce, page 135); **de lo que,** *than,* in certain comparisons; and **lo más pronto posible,** *as soon as possible* (*the soonest possible*) (see Lección catorce, page 157).

EJERCICIO

Después de oír una oración, oirán una frase; substituyan la frase en la oración, según el modelo.

MODELO: *Lo bueno* es que ya han vuelto.   (Lo mejor)   *Lo mejor es que ya han vuelto.*

1. *Lo importante* es que Pepe ganó la beca.   (Lo necesario)
2. *Lo malo* es que no están en casa.   (Lo peor)
3. *Lo difícil* es hablar correctamente.   (Lo preciso)
4. Hay que recordar *lo dicho.*   (lo hecho)
5. No traten Uds. de hacer *lo imposible.*   (lo dudoso)
6. No te olvides de *lo nuestro.*   (lo tuyo)
7. Siempre andan *lo más rápidamente* posible.   (lo más despacio)
8. Sabemos *lo tristes que* están ellos.   (lo contentos que)
9. Parece que saldrán *lo más pronto* posible.   (lo más tarde)
10. No sabes *lo largas que* son las lecciones.   (lo difíciles que)

7   El pronombre neutro **lo**

In addition to its use as a pronoun object meaning *it* (**No lo creo,** *I don't believe it*), the neuter pronoun **lo** is used:

A. To complete the sentence when no direct object is expressed, with verbs such as **decir, pedir (i, i), preguntar, saber,** and the like (see Lección cuatro, page 45):

Como Uds. no lo saben, yo se lo diré.   Since you don't know it, I'll tell you.
—¿Podrías salir? —No lo sé. Pregúntaselo a ellos.   "Could you leave?"
"I don't know. Ask them."

B. With certain verbs such as **ser** and **parecer,** in answer to a question or to refer back to a noun, adjective, or whole idea, sometimes with the meaning of *so:*

—¿Eres tú estudiante? —Sí, lo soy.   "Are you a student?" "Yes, I am."
Ella estará cansada, pero no lo parece.   She must be tired, but she doesn't
seem so.

EJERCICIOS

A. Para contestar afirmativamente, usando el pronombre neutro **lo.**

MODELO: ¿Es escritora la señora Gómez?   *Sí, lo es.*

1. ¿Es abogado el señor Sierra?
2. ¿Son mexicanos los padres de él?
3. ¿Son Uds. estudiantes?

4. ¿Soy yo profesor (profesora)?
5. ¿Parece ella estar contenta?
6. ¿Parece ser difícil el examen?

B. Para expresar en español:

1. The good thing is that James knows the city well.   2. The important thing is that he speaks correctly.   3. John always reads as fast as (the fastest) possible. 4. Most persons do not know how happy (contented) she is.   5. It is necessary to remember what is said.   6. "Is Mrs. Solís a teacher?" "Yes, she is."   7. "Can John go with us?" "I don't know. Ask (*fam. sing.*) him."   8. They are probably busy, but they don't seem so.

8   Las conjunciones **e** y **u**

In Spanish, the conjunction **y,** *and,* becomes **e** before words beginning with **i-** or **hi-** (but not **hie-**); the conjunction **o,** *or,* becomes **u** before **o-** or **ho-:**

Hablamos español e inglés.   We speak Spanish and English.
Juanita hizo eso siete u ocho veces.   Jane did that seven or eight times.

BUT: **nieve y hielo**   snow and ice

9   Usos de **pero, sino** y **sino que**

The English conjunction *but* is usually expressed by **pero** in Spanish. However, when *but* means *on the contrary, but instead,* **sino** is used in an affirmative statement which contradicts a preceding negative statement. Usually no verb form—other than an infinitive—may be used after **sino:**

Me puse el traje, pero no lo compré.   I put on the suit, but I did not buy it.
No fueron en avión, sino en autobús.   They didn't go by plane, but by bus.
Él no quiere trabajar, sino descansar.   He doesn't want to work, but to rest.

If the sentence contains contradictory clauses, **sino que** is used:

Ellos no leían, sino que miraban la televisión.   They weren't reading, but they were watching television.

EJERCICIO

Para leer en español, supliendo la conjunción **pero, sino** o **sino que:**

1. Traté de hablar con Pepe, _____ no pude encontrarlo.   2. A Carmen le gusta la pintura mexicana, _____ a mí no.   3. No van al centro, _____ a la librería.   4. Los muchachos no fueron en coche, _____ en autobús.   5. Los niños no corrían rápidamente, _____ andaban despacio.   6. Mis tíos van a México, _____ no pueden visitar a Guadalajara.   7. Laura dice que no quiere estudiar, _____ dormir la siesta.   8. Roberto solicitó una beca, _____ no la consiguió.

10   Formas de mandato correspondientes a **vosotros, -as**

You have probably observed that in this text we have used the formal **ustedes** with the third person plural form of the present subjunctive tense to express both formal and familiar plural commands. This practice is common in Spanish America, but not in Spain. The familiar plural forms will now be introduced, since you may encounter these forms in reading. (For commands with **usted, ustedes,** and **tú,** see Lección dos, pages 12–14.)

To form the affirmative familiar plural command (the plural imperative) of all verbs, drop **-r** of the infinitive and add **-d.** For the negative familiar plural command, use the second person plural of the present subjunctive tense. The subject **vosotros, -as,** is usually omitted. (See Appendix D, page 222, for the familiar plural command forms of all types of verbs.)

Infinitive	Affirmative	Negative
tomar	tomad	no toméis
comer	comed	no comáis
abrir	abrid	no abráis
hacer	haced	no **hagáis**
salir	salid	no **salgáis**
tener	tened	no **tengáis**
buscar	buscad	no **busquéis**
cerrar	cerrad	no cerréis
contar	contad	no contéis
volver	volved	no volváis
colgar	colgad	no **colguéis**
sentir	sentid	no **sintáis**
dormir	dormid	no **durmáis**
pedir	pedid	no **pidáis**

To form the familiar plural commands of reflexive verbs, drop final **-d** before adding the reflexive pronoun **-os,** except for **idos** (**irse**). All **-ir** reflexive verbs except **irse** require an accent mark on the **i** of the stem of the verb: **vestíos.**

Infinitive	Affirmative	Negative
levantarse	levantaos	no os levantéis
sentarse	sentaos	no os sentéis
ponerse	poneos	no os **pongáis**
vestirse	vestíos	no os **vistáis**
irse	idos	no os **vayáis**

EJERCICIO

Cambien el infinitivo a la forma de mandato correspondiente a **vosotros, -as;** luego, expresen el mandato negativamente:

1. Hablar más despacio.   2. Comer antes de las seis.   3. Escribir las cartas hoy.
4. Venir a vernos mañana.   5. Ponerse los guantes.   6. Acercarse al coche.
7. Vestirse pronto.   8. Irse en seguida.

Repaso cinco

A. Usos del subjuntivo en frases condicionales. Lean en español, supliendo la forma correcta del infinitivo entre paréntesis:

1. Si Laura (volver) esta tarde, yo podré hablar con ella.
2. Si Pablo (quedarse) en casa, no se sentía bien.
3. Si Luis (estar) en San Francisco, me enviaría una tarjeta.
4. Si los muchachos (venir) esta noche, yo los vería.
5. Ellos andaban por la calle como si (tener) mucha prisa.
6. Yo le habría dado el dinero a Ana si la (haber) visto.
7. Si Carlos (llega) antes de las seis, iremos a cenar en el centro.
8. Si no (ser) tan tarde, podríamos charlar un rato.
9. Si yo (tener) tiempo, iría al parque con ellos.
10. Si ella (poder) venir, nos traería las cosas.

B. Para escribir en español:

1. If I have time this afternoon, I shall go to Mr. Lopez's office.
2. If our friends should (were to) go to Mexico, they would take many photographs.
3. If my brother were to come today, he would bring me two tickets for the game.
4. If we had gone to the exhibition, we would have seen Caroline.
5. Would that Carlos Gómez arrives today! I should like to meet him.
6. Perhaps Joseph will get the job in Mexico, but I doubt it.
7. Diane wanted us to bring some refreshments for the party.
8. I was glad that you (*fam. sing.*) called before Joe left for San Antonio.

C. Los adjetivos y los pronombres posesivos. Para expresar en español:

1. Our car and his are new. 2. Their house and yours (*formal sing.*) are on another street. 3. John has my camera and his. 4. Her roses and ours are very pretty. 5. Some friends of theirs are coming to visit them. 6. Are these things yours (*fam. sing.*) or hers? 7. My watch and his are (of) gold. 8. This package is ours. Where is yours (*formal sing.*)?

D. Repitan cada oración; luego, formen otra oración, empleando **no ... tan ... como,** siguiendo el modelo.

MODELO: Lola es más alta que Lupe.   *Lola es más alta que Lupe.*
Lupe no es tan alta como Lola.

1. Marta lee más despacio que yo.
2. Él corre más rápidamente que Ud.
3. Esta música es más clásica que ésa.
4. Yo me levanté más tarde que él.

Usen **no ... tanto, -a (-os, -as) ... como,** siguiendo el modelo.

MODELO: Yo tengo más cosas que ella.   *Yo tengo más cosas que ella.*
Ella no tiene tantas cosas como yo.

5. Pepe toca más obras que Luis.
6. Ana recibe más cartas que Inés.
7. Hay más flores allí que aquí.
8. Elena lleva más paquetes que Pablo.

E. Usos de las formas comparativas de los adjetivos y de los adverbios. Para expresar en español:

1. This house is large; it is larger than that one (*distant*); it is the largest one in the city.   2. This picture is small; it is smaller than the one which is on the wall; it is the smallest one in the salon.   3. We saw George's younger brother and Martha's older sister at the exhibition yesterday afternoon.   4. There are more than one hundred foreign students here; there are more than I thought.   5. Thomas says that he has already written more compositions this semester than he wrote last year.   6. Most of the students in (of) our class speak Spanish better than you (*pl.*) believe.

F. Para traducir *must, to have to, to be to,* etc. Para expresar en español:

1. They must be (*two ways*) at the exhibition.   2. Jane and Paul must have arrived late.   3. My roommate (*m.*) had to write a long composition last night.   4. One must remember that Mr. Ortiz is a great teacher.   5. Don't forget (*fam. sing.*) that the concert is to begin at eight o'clock.   6. Robert was to play the guitar at the party; he plays better than I.

G. Escuchen el modelo; luego, formen dos oraciones nuevas, una empleando la voz pasiva, y la otra empleando **estar** con el participio pasado, según el modelo.

MODELO: Todos aceptaron el plan.   *El plan fue aceptado por todos.*
El plan está aceptado.

1. Una amiga mía hizo la blusa.
2. Laura vendió la bicicleta.
3. Pablo abrió las ventanas.
4. María escribió la tarjeta.
5. Carlos cerró las puertas.
6. El profesor preparó el examen.

Vista general de Bogotá, Colombia.

H. Usos del participio pasado, del participio presente y del pretérito anterior de indicativo. Para expresar en español:

1. Continue (*pl.*) playing in the patio until I call you.   2. The students are (gradually) learning some Spanish songs.   3. Richard was walking (*progressive*) rapidly toward Jane's house.   4. As soon as they had returned, they sent for us. 5. By working six or eight hours, I can finish this composition.   6. The article written, I shall hand it to the teacher (*m.*).   7. Someone forgot to open the door; therefore, it was still closed.   8. Robert, accompanied by some friends of his, was making (*progressive*) plans for his (the) vacation (*pl.*) in Mexico.

I. Usos del artículo y del pronombre neutro **lo.** Para expresar en español:

1. The best thing is to apply for the scholarship.   2. That matter of Michael seems strange to us.   3. Come (*formal pl.*) to see us as soon as possible.   4. That is what Charles and I intend to do.   5. "Is Mr. Gómez a lawyer?" "Yes, he is." 6. "Is Laura's sister a teacher?" "No, she isn't."   7. "Can you (*fam. sing.*) tell them that?" "Yes, I shall tell them (it)."   8. "Did he read the composition?" "I did not ask him (it)."

J. Para contestar afirmativamente en español:

1. ¿Sabes jugar al tenis?   2. ¿Puedes jugar conmigo hoy?   3. ¿Podrías llevarle a Ana el paquete?   4. ¿Deben Uds. escribirles a sus padres?   5. ¿Debieran Uds. visitar a sus tíos?   6. ¿Quisieran Uds. ir a México este verano?   7. ¿Es posible que tu padre te dé el dinero para ir allá?   8. ¿Sería posible que él te lo diera? 9. ¿Puede ser que tú consigas el puesto que deseas?   10. ¿Podría ser que tú lo consiguieras?   11. ¿Irá Ud. a la playa si alguien lo (la) invita?   12. ¿Iría Ud. a México si alguien lo (la) invitara?

K. Para expresar en español, empleando la forma de mandato correspondiente a **vosotros, -as:**

1. Say the sentence in Spanish.   2. Do that tomorrow morning.   3. Don't leave the room.   4. Don't look for him.   5. Sit down near the window.   6. Don't get up so early.   7. Go away soon.   8. Don't go away yet.

Mercado al aire libre en Otavalo, al norte de Quito, El Ecuador.

Notas culturales V

La lengua, la religión y el alfabeto . . .

(Párrafos tomados de *El continente de siete colores,* publicado en 1965 por el ensayista colombiano Germán Arciniegas.)

Para un indio de Otavalo en el Ecuador, o de la sierra en el Perú, o del sur de México, o de Guatemala, o de los campos de Bolivia, un burro, una gallina° y un puerco representaban más, al cabo de° cuatro siglos y medio, como testimonio de la llegada de los europeos, que la lengua española. Ellos siguen hablando su maya, su quechua, su guaraní o su aymará. Lo que deben a los nuevos amos° son esos animales, que a veces representan la única cosa nueva que se ve en sus chozas.°

Pero hay que convenir en que° también trajo el español un idioma° con raíces° latinas, griegas y árabes. Un idioma, entonces, con toda la fuerza del siglo en que se mostró° más vigoroso y rico, más creador° y poético, más heroico, místico, teatral, jurídico: universal. Es el siglo de Cervantes, de Santa Teresa, de Lope de Vega, de Quevedo . . .

En el Nuevo Mundo, donde el aislamiento° había mantenido las lenguas estancadas,° donde no se podía ir de Centroamérica al sur sirviéndose de° palabras comunes, se introdujo en brevísimo espacio de tiempo una lengua común que permitió comunicarse a todas las colonias° desde México hasta Chile y el Río de la Plata. Cada nueva capital de un virreinato,° de una gobernación,° cada pequeña villa que se fundaba, era una capital o una villa de lengua castellana . . .

Trajeron los españoles una religión nueva con un código° moral diferente del que en cada región de América imperaba.° El bautismo, la misa, la iglesia, las imágenes, las campanas,° las fiestas, las oraciones,° los nuevos principios° sobre el bien y el mal, el cielo y el

gallina *hen*
al cabo de *at the end of*

amos *masters*
chozas *huts, hovels*
convenir en que *(to) agree that*
idioma *language* / **raíces** *roots*

se mostró *it showed itself to be* / **creador** *creative*

aislamiento *isolation*
estancadas *static*
sirviéndose de *making use of*

permitió . . . colonias *permitted all the colonies to communicate with one another*

virreinato *viceroyalty*
gobernación *government; territory*

código *code*
imperaba *prevailed*
campanas *bells* / **oraciones** *prayers*
principios *principles*

181

infierno, la idea del Crucificado,° la Virgen y los santos, la constitución de la familia, cambiaron la base y el tono general de la vida. La conquista se hubiera detenido en el punto a donde llegaban los conquistadores[1] si no hubiera sido por el espíritu misionero de la Iglesia, que continuó penetrando en las regiones más escondidas del continente.

el Crucificado *the Crucified (Christ)*

Se introdujo una nueva división del tiempo: la semana. Y el domingo, como un día no propiamente de reposo,° pero sí de fiesta.° El domingo, día de misa y de mercado,° vino a ser° el de encontrarse los habitantes del pueblo y del campo en una misma plaza,[2] el de juntarse las familias dispersas, el de informarse de muchas cosas—buenas o malas—que le permitieron al indio analfabeto° leer en el aire[3] una gaceta propia.° Con el tiempo,° después de esta lectura, los indios se habituaron a pasar a la venta° para celebrar los encuentros, olvidar y liberarse fugazmente° de su servidumbre, bebiendo. En las fiestas religiosas el indio conoció el único empleo inocente de la pólvora,° y la encontró sublime.

no propiamente de reposo *not exactly of rest* / **sí de fiesta** *indeed of festivity* / **día de misa y de mercado** *a day for Mass and market day* / **vino a ser** *(Sunday) became*

analfabeto *illiterate* / **una gaceta propia** *a gazette (newspaper) of his own* **Con el tiempo** *In time* **venta** *roadside inn*

fugazmente *briefly*

pólvora *gunpowder*

PREGUNTAS

Para contestar en español en oraciones completas:

1. ¿Cuáles son algunos animales que los españoles trajeron a América?   2. ¿Qué representaba más para los indios, la presencia de estos animales o la lengua española? 3. ¿En qué países se habla hoy día la lengua maya?   4. ¿En qué países se habla la lengua quechua?   5. ¿Dónde se habla guaraní?   6. ¿En qué región se habla aymará?

7. ¿Cuáles son las raíces de la lengua española?   8. ¿Qué palabras emplea el Sr. Arciniegas para describir el idioma en la época de la llegada de los españoles? 9. ¿Qué nombres de famosos españoles de aquellos tiempos recuerda Ud.?   10. ¿Qué había mantenido las lenguas estancadas en el Nuevo Mundo?   11. ¿Qué se introdujo en brevísimo espacio de tiempo?

12. ¿Cuáles son algunos elementos de la religión que trajeron los españoles? 13. ¿Qué otros principios e ideas introdujeron?   14. ¿Qué dice el Sr. Arciniegas acerca del espíritu misionero de la Iglesia?

---

[1] **La conquista se hubiera detenido . . . conquistadores,** *The conquest would have stopped at the point* (*place*) *reached by the conquerors.* (The -ra form of the imperfect or pluperfect subjunctive tense is sometimes used instead of the conditional or conditional perfect tense in the main clause of a contrary-to-fact sentence.)
[2] **el de encontrarse . . . plaza,** *that of the inhabitants of the town and country meeting in a* (*the*) *same square.*
[3] **en el aire,** *in the air* (i.e., *in the atmosphere, in the surroundings*).

15. ¿Qué nueva división del tiempo se introdujo?   16. ¿Qué vino a ser el domingo?   17. ¿Qué podía leer en el aire el indio analfabeto?   18. Después de esta lectura, ¿qué se habituaron a hacer los indios?   19. ¿De qué podían liberarse fugazmente en la venta?   20. ¿Qué conoció el indio en las fiestas religiosas?

EJERCICIO ESCRITO

Escriban una carta (de unas ciento veinticinco palabras) a un amigo (una amiga), empleando palabras y expresiones que se encuentran en la sección **Cartas españolas** (Texto, páginas 186–199). Su amigo (amiga) le ha pedido a Ud. informes sobre los cambios que han ocurrido en la vida de los indios de Hispanoamérica después de la llegada de los españoles.

CARTAS ESPAÑOLAS

In the following pages some of the essential principles for business and personal letters in Spanish will be given. Even though many formulas used in Spanish letters are less formal and flowery than formerly, in general they are still less brief and direct than in English letters, and at times they may seem rather stilted. No attempt is made to give a complete treatment of Spanish correspondence, but study of the material included should suffice for ordinary purposes.

The new words and expressions whose English equivalents are given in this section (including the **Vocabulario útil**, page 197) are not listed in the Spanish-English vocabulary unless used elsewhere in the text. However, meanings are listed in the English-Spanish vocabulary for words used in Exercises A, B, and C (page 198).

A. Professional titles

Professional titles are more widely used in Spanish-speaking countries than in the United States. Some titles are:

Arquitecto (Arq.)   Architect
Doctor (Dr.)   Doctor (*m.*)
Doctora (Dra.)   Doctor (*f.*)
Ingeniero (Ing.)   Engineer
Licenciado (Lic.)   Licentiate (lawyer, or person who has a permit to practice a profession)
Profesor (Prof.)   Professor (*m.*)
Profesora (Profa.)   Professor (*f.*)

Normally these professional titles are accompanied by **señor (Sr.)**, **señora (Sra.)**, or **señorita (Srta.)**, and followed by **don** or **Don (D.)**, **doña** or **Doña (D.ª)**:

Dr. D. Felipe Solís
Profesora doña (D.ª) Carmen Valdés

Lic. D. Ramón Estrada
Ing. Don Luis Molina

B. Address on the envelope

The title of the addressee begins with **Señor (Sr.)**, **Señora (Sra.)**, or **Señorita (Srta.)**. **Sr. don (Sr. D.)** may be used for a man, **Sra. doña (Sra. D.ª)** for a married woman, and **Srta.** for an unmarried woman:

Señor don Carlos Morelos
Srta. Isabel Alcalá

Sr. D. Pedro Ortega y Moreno[1]
Sra. D.ª María López de Martín

In the third example note that Spanish surnames often include the name of the father (**Ortega**), followed by that of the mother (**Moreno**). Often the mother's name is dropped (first two examples). A woman's married name is her maiden name followed by **de** and the surname of her husband (fourth example).

The definite article is not used with the titles **don** and **doña**, which have no English equivalents.

---

[1] The conjunction **y** is often not used between the surnames: the person might prefer to be known as **D. Pedro Ortega Moreno.**

Two complete addresses follow:

> **Sr. D. Luis Montoya**   **Srta. Elena Pérez**
> **Calle de San Martín, 25**   **Avenida Bolívar, 245**
> **Santiago, Chile**   **Caracas, Venezuela**

Business letters are addressed to a firm:

> **Señores (Sres.) López Díaz y**   **Suárez Hermanos (Hnos.)**
> **Cía., S.A.**   **Apartado (Postal) 867**
> **Paseo de la Reforma, 12**   **Buenos Aires, Argentina**
> **México, D.F., México**

In an address in Spanish, one writes first **Calle** (**Avenida,** *Avenue;* **Paseo,** *Boulevard;* **Camino,** *Road;* **Plaza,** *Square*) (**de**), then the house number. **Apartado (Postal),** *Post Office Box,* may be abbreviated to **Apdo. (Postal)**; in Spanish America **Casilla postal** is commonly used for *Post Office Box.* The abbreviation **Cía.** = **Compañía; S.A.** = **Sociedad Anónima,** equivalent to English *Inc. (Incorporated)*; and **D.F.** = **Distrito Federal,** *Federal District.*

Airmail letters are marked **Vía aérea, Correo aéreo,** or **Por avión.** Special delivery letters are marked **Urgente** or **Entrega inmediata,** and registered letters, **Certificada.** Other directions on the envelope may be: **Particular,** *Private, Personal;* **Lista de correos,** *General Delivery;* **Para reexpedir,** *(Please) Forward;* **Impresos,** *Printed Matter;* **No doblar,** *Don't Fold.*

C. Heading of the letter

The usual form of the date line is:

> **México, D.F., 27 de enero de 1983**

The month is usually not capitalized unless it is given first in the date. For the first day of the month, 1° (**primero**) is commonly used; the other days are written 2, 3, 4, etc. Other less common forms for the date line are:

> **Lima, a 15 de junio de 1982**
> **Bogotá, 1° agosto 1981**

The address which precedes the salutation of the business and formal social letter is the same as that on the envelope. In familiar letters only the salutation need be used.

D. Salutations

Appropriate salutations for business letters or those addressed to strangers, equivalent to *My dear Sir, Dear Sir, Dear Madam, Gentlemen,* etc., are:

> **Muy señor (Sr.) mío:**   (*from one person to one gentleman*)
> **Muy señores (Sres.) míos:**   (*from one person to a firm*)
> **Muy señor nuestro:**   (*from a firm to one gentleman*)

Muy señores nuestros: (*from one firm to another firm*)
Muy señora (Sra.) mía: (*from one person to a woman*)
Muy señorita (Srta.) nuestra: (*from a firm to a young woman*)

Formulas which may be used in less formal letters are:

Estimado(s) señor(es):   Dear Sir (Gentlemen):
Distinguido(s) señor(es):   Dear Sir (Gentlemen):
Estimado profesor: Dear Professor:
Muy estimado Sr. Salas: Dear Mr. Salas:
Mi (Muy) distinguido amigo (colega):   Dear Friend (Colleague):
(Muy) apreciado señor (amigo):   Dear Sir (Friend):

Forms used in addressing relatives or close friends, equivalent to (*My*) *dear brother, friend,* etc., are:

Querido hermano (Luis):   **(Mi) querida hija:**
Querida amiga mía: **Queridísima[1] mamá:**
Apreciado amigo: **Estimada amiga (Diana):**

Great care must be taken to be consistent in the agreement of salutations and conclusions in Spanish letters, keeping in mind whether the letter is addressed to a man, woman, or firm, and whether it is signed by one person or by an individual for a firm.

Cartero, repartiendo las cartas, Salamanca, España.

---

[1] **Queridísima,** *Dearest.*

E. The body of business letters

The Spanish business letter usually begins with a brief sentence which indicates the purpose of the letter. Some examples, with English translations, follow. Note that the sentences cannot always be translated word for word:

Acabo (Acabamos) de recibir su carta del 10 de septiembre.   I (We) have just received your letter of September 10.

Le acusamos recibo de su atenta[1] del 2 del corriente . . .   We acknowledge receipt of your letter of the 2nd (of this month) . . .

He (Hemos) recibido con mucho agrado su amable carta . . .   I was (We were) very glad to receive your (good) letter . . .

Nos referimos a su favor de . . .   We are referring to your letter of . . .

Tenemos a la vista su carta de fecha 8 del actual . . .   We have (at hand) your letter of the 8th (of this month) . . .

Tengo (Tenemos) el honor de acusar recibo de la mercancía . . .   I am (We are) happy to acknowledge receipt of the merchandise . . .

Tenemos el placer de informar a usted[2] que . . .   We are pleased to inform you that . . .

Me (Nos) es grato comunicarle(s) que . . .   I am (We are) pleased to inform you that . . .

Rogamos a Uds. se sirvan[3] enviarnos a vuelta de correo . . .   We ask that you kindly send us by return mail . . .

Les agradeceremos se sirvan comunicarnos . . .   We shall be grateful if you will please let us know . . .

Mucho agradeceré a Ud. el mandarme . . .   I shall be very glad if you will send me . . .

Obra en mi (nuestro) poder su grata del 30 de marzo p. pdo.[4] . . .   I (We) have at hand your letter of March 30 . . .

Le doy a Ud. las gracias por el pedido que se sirvió hacerme . . .   Thank you for the order which you kindly placed with me . . .

Le envío giro postal por $60.00 . . .   I am sending you a postal money order for $60.00 . . .

Con fecha 8 del actual me permití escribir a usted, informándole . . .   On the 8th of this month I took the liberty of writing to you, informing you . . .

Tengo el agrado de dirigirme a usted para agradecerle el envío de . . .   I have the pleasure of writing to thank you for sending me . . .

---

[1] **Carta** is often replaced with **favor, grata, atenta.**

[2] Since **usted** is technically a noun (coming from **vuestra merced,** *your grace*), the object pronoun **le** may be omitted. This practice is noted particularly in letter writing.

[3] After verbs such as **rogar (ue), pedir (i, i), suplicar, esperar, agradecer,** the conjunction **que** is often omitted. This practice is noted particularly in letter writing.

[4] **p. pdo.** *or* **ppdo.** = **próximo pasado,** *last, past.*

En respuesta a su atenta carta del 15 del corriente, nos es grato remitirles adjunto lista de precios y condiciones de venta.   In reply to your letter of the 15th, we are pleased to send you (enclosed) our price list and conditions of sale.

Sírva(n)se reservarme para el 10 del corriente (del próximo) una habitación con dos camas y con baño. La estancia será de ocho días.   Please reserve for me for the 10th of this month (of next month) a room with two beds and with bath. The length of stay will be for one week.

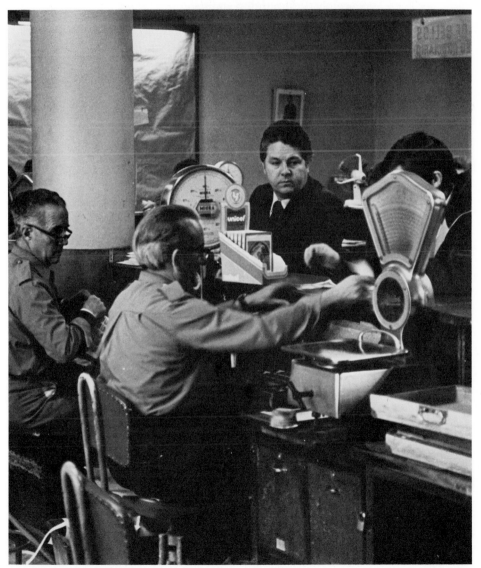

La casa de correos, Salamanca, España.

F. Conclusions

The Spanish conclusion usually requires more than a mere *Very truly yours,* or *Sincerely yours.* However, there is a tendency nowadays to shorten conclusions of business letters, particularly as correspondence continues with an individual or firm. Appropriate conclusions for business letters or those addressed to strangers are:

Queda[1] (Quedo) de Ud(s). atento y seguro servidor,
I remain,

Sincerely (Respectfully) yours,

Aprovecho esta oportunidad para saludarle(s)[2] atentamente,
I am taking advantage of this opportunity to remain,

Sincerely yours,

Aprovechamos esta ocasión para ofrecernos sus attos.[3] y ss. ss.,
We take advantage of this occasion to remain,

Sincerely yours,

Me repito[4] su afmo. s. s. *or* **Nos repetimos sus afmos. ss. ss.,**
I (We) remain,

Sincerely,

Quedamos de ustedes attos. y SS. SS.,
We remain,

Very truly yours,

En espera de sus gratas noticias, les saluda atentamente,
Awaiting the expected good news from you, I remain,

Sincerely,

Anticipándoles las gracias, nos reiteramos de Ud(s). atte.,
Thanking you in advance, we remain,

Sincerely yours,

Les agradecemos su atención, y nos repetimos de Uds. attos. ss. ss.,
We thank you for your attention (to the matter), and we remain,

Sincerely yours,

---

[1] **Queda** is in the third person if the signee is the subject of the verb. Note similar use of other verbs in other examples.

[2] Several formulas used in the **Cartas españolas** section come from letters written in Spain. See page 22, including footnotes 1 and 2, for forms of third person direct object pronouns.

[3] Abbreviations used in the conclusions given are: **atto.** = **atento; attos.** = **atentos; s. s.** or **S. S.** = **seguro servidor** (*sing.*), lit.,*your servant:* **ss. ss.** or **S.S. S.S.** = **seguros servidores** (*pl.*); **afmo. (afma.)** = **afectísimo** (**afectísima**), *sincere(ly), affectionate(ly)*; **afmos. (afmas.)** = **afectísimos (afectísimas); atte.** = **atentamente.**

[4] After the first letter (in which the verb **aprovechar** may have been used), **Me repito** is a good expression.

Lo saludan (muy) atentamente,
   We are (remain),

                        Sincerely yours,

Some conclusions, with many possible variations, for informal social letters equivalent to *Cordially yours, Affectionately yours,* etc., are:

Suyo (Tuyo) afectísimo (afmo.) *or* **Suya (Tuya) afectísima (afma.),**
Suyos afectísimos (afmos.) *or* **Suyas afectísimas (afmas.),**
Queda (Quedo) suyo afmo. (suya afma.),
Le saluda cariñosamente[1] **(muy atentamente),**
Le saluda muy cordialmente (su servidor y amigo),
Se despide afectuosamente[2] **(cordialmente),**
(Con el cariño[3] **de) tu buen amigo (buena amiga),**
Cariñosos saludos[4] **de tu amigo (amiga),**
Sinceramente, Cariñosamente, Afectuosamente,
(Un abrazo[5] **de) tu hijo,** (*one boy signs*)
Tu hijo (hija), que te quiere, (*one boy or girl signs*)
Con todo el cariño (amor)[6] **de tu hermano (hermana),**
Recibe todo mi cariño (amor), (*a young(er) person signs*)

Other phrases which may accompany these formulas are:

Dé (Da) mis mejores recuerdos a toda su (tu) familia,
   Give my best regards to all your family,

Salude afectuosamente de mi parte a sus padres,
   Give my affectionate (cordial) greetings to your parents,

Con mis mejores deseos para Ud. y los suyos, me despido,
   With my best wishes for you and your family, I am (remain),

G. Sample letters

The following letters translated freely from Spanish to English will show how natural, idiomatic phrases in one language convey the same idea in another. Read the following letters aloud for practice, and be able to write any of them from dictation. The teacher may want to test comprehension by asking questions in Spanish on the content of the letters. At the end of this section are listed some words and phrases, not all of which are used in the sample letters, which should be useful in composing original letters.

---

[1] **cariñosamente,** *affectionately.*
[2] **afectuosamente,** *affectionately.*
[3] **cariño,** *affection.*
[4] **saludos,** *greetings.*
[5] **abrazo,** *embrace.*
[6] **amor,** *love.*

1

BIBLOGRAF, S.A.   DEPARTAMENTO EDITORIAL
Calle del Bruch, 151   -   Teléfonos   257 31 58 / 257 18 01   Telegramas: BIBLOGRAF

Barcelona, 3 de enero de 1982
Vía aérea

_____
_____
_____

Muy señores nuestros:

Nos complacemos en acusar recibo de su atenta carta del día 18 de diciembre próximo pasado y de acuerdo con sus deseos les remitimos por correo aéreo aparte un catálogo, folletos y lista de precios de nuestras ediciones.

Sobre los precios de esta lista les ofrecemos el 40% de descuento, con cargo de los gastos de embalaje, envío y seguro y pago por cheque a la recepción de la mercancía.

Les rogamos se sirvan tomar nota de que nuestras obras son de libre adquisición en los Estados Unidos y que no tenemos concedida (ni por el momento entra en nuestros propósitos concederla) la exclusiva de su distribución en ese país.

En espera de sus gratas órdenes, les saludamos muy atentamente,

BIBLOGRAF, S.A.

BIBLOGRAF, S.A.   PUBLISHING (EDITORIAL) DEPARTMENT
151 Bruch Street   Telephones   257 31 58 / 257 18 01   Telegrams: BIBLOGRAF

Barcelona, January 3, 1982
Airmail

_____
_____
_____

Gentlemen:

We are pleased to acknowledge receipt of your (good) letter of (this past) December 18, and in accordance with your wishes we are sending you separately by airmail a catalogue, pamphlets, and a price list of our editions.

We can offer 40 percent discount on prices of this list, less charge for packing, shipment, and insurance. Payment by check (is due) upon receipt of the merchandise.

Please note that our works (publications) can be acquired freely in the United States and that we do not grant (nor for the moment are we thinking of granting) exclusive rights for their distribution in your country.

Awaiting your kind orders, we remain,

Sincerely yours,

BIBLOGRAF, S.A.

2

_____

Madrid, 8 de enero de 1982

_____
_____
_____

Muy Sres. nuestros:

Acusamos recibo de su atenta de fecha 26 de diciembre ppdo., y les notificamos que el precio bruto por un año de suscripción a nuestro diario ABC con destino a Estados Unidos, envío marítimo, es de 23,20$.[1]

La comisión máxima que se les puede abonar es del 10% de la cantidad ya citada.

Las órdenes de suscripción deberán venir acompañadas de su importe líquido, significándoles que el comienzo del servicio ha de ser siempre con el día primero de cada mes.

La remisión de los importes mencionados deberá hacerse por medio de cheque bancario a nombre de Prensa Española, S.A., Serrano, 61, Madrid.

Con este motivo, nos reiteramos suyos affmos. ss. ss.,

POR "PRENSA ESPAÑOLA" S.A.

Madrid, January 8, 1982

Gentlemen:

We acknowledge receipt of your letter of (this past) December 26, and we are notifying you that the gross price for a year's subscription to our newspaper ABC, going to the United States by sea, is $23.20.

The maximum commission which can be granted is 10% of the amount mentioned above.

Subscription orders should be accompanied by the net amount, and we point out to you that the beginning of service (the subscription) must always be as of the first day of each month.

Remittance of the amounts mentioned must be made by (means of) bank check in the name of Spanish Press, S.A., 61 Serrano, Madrid.

(For this purpose), we remain,

Sincerely yours,

For "Spanish Press" S.A.

_____

[1] Read **veintitrés dólares, veinte centavos.** While the comma between the **dólares** and **centavos** has largely been replaced in Spanish by a period, it is still used. (Also, the English comma is often written as a period in Spanish: 1.023,20.) The dollar sign is sometimes placed after the amount in Spanish.

3

AFRODISIO AGUADO, S.A.

Editores—Libreros

LIBRERÍA GENERAL   OFICINAS Y ALMACENES
Marqués de Cubas, 5   Bordadores, 5
Teléfonos   31 88 29 y 21 26 21   Teléfonos   48 63 19 y 48 59 29

MADRID

20 de junio de 1983

Muy Sres. nuestros:

Nos referimos a su atenta del 12 del corriente que agradecemos.

Con esta fecha por correo aéreo, como impresos, les remitimos nuestro catálogo general y folletos de novedades para que se informen de nuestra producción editorial.

Rogamos presten atención a nuestras series "CLÁSICOS Y MAESTROS," donde recientemente hemos incorporado "AL MARGEN DE ESTOS CLÁSICOS," por Julián Marías, en una edición especial dedicada al universitario norteamericano, y "ASPECTOS DEL MUNDO ACTUAL," con tomos de gran interés.

La escala de descuentos que podemos aplicarles para sus encargos es la siguiente:

Pedidos hasta 10,000 Ptas. . . .   35% de descuento
Pedidos hasta 50,000 Ptas. . . .   40% de descuento
Pedidos superiores . . . .   45% de descuento

Nuestros envíos son efectuados por vía marítima en paquetes certificados y asegurados. Les cargamos únicamente los gastos de envío.

Quedamos, pues, en espera de sus noticias y tengan la seguridad de que atenderemos cualquier sugerencia que nos puedan hacer sobre el particular. Atentamente les saludamos,

AFRODISIO AGUADO, S.A.

Publishers—Book Dealers

GENERAL BOOKSTORE
5 Marqués de Cubas
Telephones   31 88 29 and 21 26 21

OFFICES AND WAREHOUSES
5 Bordadores
Telephones   48 63 19 and 48 59 29

MADRID

June 20, 1983

_____
_____
_____

Gentlemen:

Reference is to your letter of June 12 for which we thank you.

By airmail we are sending you today, as printed matter, our general catalogue and pamphlets on recent items in order that you may be informed of our publishing production.

We urge that you note (lit., pay attention to) our series "CLASSICS AND (GREAT) TEACHERS," in which we have recently included "AL MARGEN DE ESTOS CLÁSICOS" (*Marginal Notes on These Classics*), by Julián Marías, in a special edition intended for the American university student, and "ASPECTOS DEL MUNDO ACTUAL" (*Aspects of Today's World*), with volumes of great interest.

The scale of discounts which we can apply for your orders is the following:

Orders up to 10,000 pesetas . . .   35% discount
Orders up to 50,000 pesetas . . .   40% discount
Larger orders . . . .   45% discount

Our shipments are made by sea in registered and insured packages. We charge you only for shipping expenses.

We await, then, word from you, and you may be sure that we shall take care of any suggestion you may wish to make to us concerning the matter.

We are (remain),

Sincerely yours,

4

Madrid, 26 de diciembre de 1982

_____

_____

_____

Muy señores nuestros:

Contestamos a su atenta carta de fecha 18 del corriente mes de diciembre.

Tomamos nota de la próxima visita del Sr. Hurtado de Mendoza, al cual tendremos mucho gusto en saludar personalmente.

Si ustedes desean que vayamos a buscarle al aeropuerto o cualquier otra gestión que podamos hacer desde aquí, saben estamos a su completa disposición.

Sin otro particular y en espera de sus siempre gratas noticias, aprovechamos la ocasión para saludarles muy atentamente y desearles unas Felices Navidades y un venturoso año 1983,

Madrid, December 26, 1982

_____

_____

_____

Gentlemen:

We are replying to your good letter of December 18.

We note the coming visit of Mr. Hurtado de Mendoza, whom we shall be very happy to greet personally.

If you want us to pick him up at the airport, or if there is anything else we can do here, we want you to know that we are completely at your service.

Without anything further and awaiting the good news we always have from you, we take advantage of this opportunity to remain sincerely yours, and to wish you a Merry Christmas and a happy 1983,

Vocabulario útil

abonar to credit
adjunto, -a enclosed, attached; *m. also adv.*
agradecer to be grateful for, thank for
anexo, -a enclosed, attached
aprovechar to take advantage of
el **buzón** mailbox
la **cantidad** quantity, amount
cargar to charge
la **casa de correos** post office
el **catálogo** catalogue
certificar to register
comunicar to inform, tell
dirigir to address, direct
el **ejemplar** copy
el **envío** shipment, remittance
la **estampilla** (postage) stamp (*Am.*)
la **factura** bill, invoice
la **firma** signature
el **franqueo** postage

el **gerente** manager
el **giro** draft
grato, -a pleasing; *f.* letter
el **importe** cost, amount
la **muestra** sample
ofrecer(se) to offer, be, offer one's services
el **pago** payment
el **pasado** last month
el **pedido** order
permitirse to take the liberty (to)
el **recibo** receipt
referir (ie,i) to refer
remitir to remit, send
el **saldo** balance
el **sello** (postage) stamp (*Spain*)
servirse (i, i) to be so kind as to
el **sobre** envelope
la **solicitud** request
suplicar to beg, ask
el **timbre** (postage) stamp (*Am.*)

a la mayor brevedad posible as soon as possible
a las órdenes de Ud(s). at your service
a vuelta de correo by return mail
acusar recibo de to acknowledge receipt of
al cuidado de (a/c) in care of (c/o)
anticipar las gracias to thank in advance
dar(le) las gracias a (uno) to thank (one)
de acuerdo con in compliance with
del corriente (actual) of the present month
echar al correo to mail
en contestación a in reply to
en espera de awaiting
en pago de in payment of
en su cuenta to one's account

estar encargado, -a de to be in charge of
giro postal money order
hacer un pedido to place (give) an order
lista de precios price list
me repito (nos repetimos) I (we) remain
(nos) es grato (we) are pleased
nos place we are pleased
paquete postal parcel post
por separado under separate cover
sírva(n)se + *inf.* please + *verb,* be pleased to + *inf.*
tener el agrado (gusto, placer) de + *inf.* to be pleased (to) + *inf.*
tener la bondad de + *inf.* to have the kindness to + *inf.,* please + *verb*

EJERCICIOS

A. Address envelopes to the following:

1. Mr. Richard Castillo
   10 Santa Ana Square
   Madrid 10, Spain

2. Mrs. Louis Ortiz
   25 Bolívar Avenue
   Lima, Peru

3. Professor George Medina
   Box 546
   Buenos Aires, Argentina

4. López Brothers
   45 Madero Street
   Mexico City, Mexico

B. Give the following date lines and salutations:

1. Buenos Aires, December 10, 1980; Dear Mr. Aguilar: 2. Bogotá, January 1, 1984; Dear Mrs. Rivas: 3. La Paz, October 12, 1982; Dear Miss Ortega: 4. Mexico City, July 14, 1981; Dear Mother: 5. Sevilla, April 20, 1982; Dear Robert: 6. Barcelona, August 15, 1983; Dear daughter:

C. Give in Spanish:

1. Dear Sir: (*from one person*) 2. Dear Sir: (*from a firm*) 3. Dear Madam: (*from one person*) 4. Gentlemen: (*from one person*) 5. Gentlemen: (*from a firm*) 6. My dear Madam: (*to a young woman from one person*)

D. Read in Spanish, then give in correct business English:

1. He recibido su atenta carta del 9 de octubre.
2. Acabo de recibir el libro que se sirvió usted enviarme.
3. Le doy a Ud. las gracias por el pedido que se sirvió hacerme.
4. Tengo el gusto de comunicarle que me fue muy grato recibir su atenta del 16 del corriente.
5. De acuerdo con su solicitud, le remitimos hoy . . .
6. Adjunta le remitimos una muestra.
7. Ruego a ustedes tengan la bondad de darme informes . . .
8. Su carta del 11 del corriente fue referida a nuestro gerente.
9. Tengo el gusto de referirme a su atenta carta del 31 del pasado.
10. Acusamos a usted recibo de su giro postal por la cantidad de . . .

E. Give approximate translations for the following conclusions and indicate whether the signature would be that of an individual or a firm:

1. Aprovecho esta oportunidad para quedar de usted su afectísimo y s. s.,
2. Me pongo a las órdenes de ustedes para todo lo que pueda servirles,
3. En espera de sus noticias, quedo a sus órdenes y le saludo muy cordialmente,
4. Esperando poder servirles en otra ocasión, nos repetimos, atentamente,
5. Agradeciéndoles su atención, saluda a Uds. muy atentamente,

F. Suggestions for original letters in Spanish:

1. Write to a foreign student, describing some of your daily activities. Try to use words which you have had in this text or some previous text.
2. Write to a member of your family, describing some shopping you have done.
3. Assume that you are the Spanish secretary for an American exporting firm. Write a reply to a Spanish-American firm which has asked for a recent catalogue and prices.
4. Write to an individual, thanking him for his check, which has been received in payment of an invoice of a certain date. Give the balance which remains in his account.

APPENDICES

APPENDIX A

Pronunciation

The Spanish Alphabet

Letter	Name	Letter	Name	Letter	Name
a	a	j	jota	r	ere
b	be	k	ka	rr	erre
c	ce	l	ele	s	ese
ch	che	ll	elle	t	te
d	de	m	eme	u	u
e	e	n	ene	v	ve, uve
f	efe	ñ	eñe	w	doble ve
g	ge	o	o	x	equis
h	hache	p	pe	y	ye, i griega
i	i	q	cu	z	zeta

In addition to the letters used in the English alphabet, **ch, ll, ñ,** and **rr** represent single sounds in Spanish and are considered single letters. In dictionaries and vocabularies, words or syllables which begin with **ch, ll,** and **ñ** follow words or syllables that begin with **c, l,** and **n,** while **rr,** which never begins a word, is alphabetized as in English. **K** and **w** are used only in words of foreign origin. The names of the letters are feminine: **la be,** (*the*) *b;* **la jota** (*the*) *j.*

The Spanish alphabet is divided into vowels (**a, e, i, o, u**) and consonants. The letter **y** represents the vowel sound **i** in the conjunction **y,** *and,* and when final in a word, as in **hay,** *there is, there are;* **ley,** *law;* **hoy,** *today;* **muy,** *very.*

The Spanish vowels are divided into two groups, strong vowels (**a, e, o**) and weak vowels (**i, u**).

General Remarks. Definition of Phonetic Terms

Even though Spanish uses practically the same alphabet as English, few sounds are identical in the two languages. In describing the Spanish sounds, it will sometimes be necessary to make comparisons between the familiar English sounds and the unfamiliar Spanish ones in order to show how Spanish is pronounced. The student should avoid, of course, the use of English sounds in Spanish words; he should strive to follow the explanations of the text and imitate the pronunciation of the teacher and of the tapes.

In general, Spanish pronunciation is much clearer and more uniform than the English. The vowel sounds are clipped short and are not followed by the diphthongal glide which is commonly heard in English, as in *no* (*no*[u]), *came* (*ca*[i]*me*), *why* (*why*[e]). Even unstressed vowels are pronounced clearly and distinctly; the slurred sound of English *a* in *fireman,* for example, never occurs in Spanish.

Spanish consonants, likewise, are usually pronounced more precisely and distinctly than English consonants, although a few (especially **b, d,** and **g** between vowels) are pronounced very weakly. Several of them (**t, d, l,** and **n**) are pronounced farther forward in the mouth, with the tongue close to the upper teeth and gums. The consonants **p, t,** and **c** (before letters other than **e** and **i**) are never followed by the *h* sound that is often heard in English: *pen* (*p*[h]*en*), *task* (*t*[h]*ask*), *can* (*c*[h]*an*).

To allow for greater accuracy in the description of Spanish speech sounds, it will be helpful to be familiar with the phonetic terms explained in the following paragraphs:

Voiced and voiceless sounds. A sound is said to be voiceless when, during its articulation, the breath passes through the larynx without the vibration of the vocal cords. When the sound is accompanied by the vibration of the vocal cords, it is called voiced. All vowels are normally voiced sounds; consonants, however, may be voiced or voiceless.[1]

Stop and continuant consonants. A stop consonant is one in the making of which the passage of the air through the mouth is for a brief moment entirely stopped, after which the stoppage is released and the air is allowed to pass; such are the consonants in English, *pat, cub, dog.* Continuants are consonants in the production of which there is a continuous passage of air and, consequently, a continuous sound, capable of being prolonged, such as the consonants in English *thief, save.*

Place of articulation. Sounds are also classified according to the position or place where the chief obstruction to the passage of the breath is made. If this obstruction is formed between the two lips, the sound is called bilabial: *p* in English *pen.* If the obstruction is made between the teeth, the sound is called interdental: English *th* in *thin.* If the tip of the tongue forms the obstruction back of the teeth, the sound is called dental: **t** in Spanish **tú.** If the obstruction is formed at the alveolar ridge (that is, the ridge that covers the base of the upper teeth), the sound is called alveolar: *t* in English *ten.* If the obstruction is between the tongue and the hard palate, the sound is called palatal: *ch* in English *church.* If it is between the tongue and the soft palate or velum, the sound is called velar: *c* in English *cut.*

---

[1]The following Spanish consonants are normally voiced: **b, d, g, l, ll, m, n, ñ, r, rr, v, y.** One can easily learn to perceive the distinction between voiced and voiceless consonants by covering the ears with one's hands during the articulation of the sounds. After covering the ears, pronounce first, for example, the *z* of English *daze* and then the *ss* of English *hiss;* the distinction between voiced *z* and voiceless *ss* can be readily felt.

Division of Words into Syllables

Spanish words are hyphenated at the end of a line and are divided into syllables according to the following principles:

a. A single consonant (including **ch, ll, rr**) is placed with the vowel which follows: **co-sa, mu-cha-cha, si-lla, co-rren.**

b. Two consonants are usually divided: **com-pa-ñe-ro, pre-sen-tan, gus-to, al-mor-zar.** Consonants followed by **l** or **r**, however, are generally pronounced together and go with the following vowel: **o-bra, pa-dre, a-pren-do.** The groups **nl, rl, sl, tl, nr,** and **sr,** however, are divided: **Car-los, En-ri-que.**

c. In combinations of three or more consonants, only the last consonant or the two consonants of the inseparable groups just mentioned (consonant plus **l** or **r**, with the exceptions listed) begin a syllable: **ins-pi-ra-ción, com-pran, in-glés, en-tra.**

d. Two adjacent strong vowels (**a, e, o**) are in separate syllables: **le-o, tra-en, cre-e, em-ple-a-do.**

e. Combinations of a strong and weak vowel (**i, u**), or of two weak vowels, normally form single syllables: **Jai-me, gra-cias, vein-te, bien, sois, es-tu-dio, au-tor, cuar-to, puer-ta, ciu-dad, Luis.** Such combinations of two vowels are called *diphthongs*. (See page 207 for further discussion of diphthongs.)

f. In combinations of a strong and weak vowel, a written accent mark on the weak vowel divides the two vowels into separate syllables: **dí-a, pa-ís, tí-o.** An accent mark on the strong vowel of such combinations does not result in two syllables: **lec-ción, tam-bién.**

Word Stress[1]

a. Most words which end in a vowel, or in **n** or **s** (plural endings of verbs and nouns, respectively), are stressed on the next to the last syllable: *di*-ce, ma-*le*-ta, *to*-mo, *en*-tran, *Car*-men, *ca*-sas.

b. Most words which end in a consonant, except **n** or **s**, are stressed on the last syllable: **pro-fe-*sor*, ha-*blar*, ciu-*dad*, u-ni-ver-si-*dad*, ca-pi-*tal*, I-sa-*bel*, a-*rroz*, fe-*liz*, ge-ne-*ral*.**

c. Words not pronounced according to these two rules have a written accent on the stressed syllable: **ca-*fé*, in-*glés*, lec-*ción*, tam-*bién*, *lá*-piz, *mú*-si-ca.**

d. The written accent is also used to distinguish between two words spelled alike but different in meaning (**si**, *if*, **sí**, *yes*; **el**, *the*, **él**, *he*, etc.), and on the stressed syllable of all interrogative words (¿*dón*-de? *where?*), and a few exclamatory words (¡*Qué* par-*ti*-do! *What a game!*)

---

[1]In this and the following four subsections, the stressed syllable of Spanish examples is italicized.

Vowels

a is pronounced between the *a* of English *ask* and the *a* of *father:* **a***l*-**ta,** **ca**-**sa,** **A**-**na.**

e is pronounced like *e* in *café,* but without the glide sound that follows the *e* in English: **a**-**pa**-*re*-**ce,** *de*-**be,** **us**-*ted.*

i (y) is pronounced like *i* in *machine:* **Fe**-*li*-**pe,** *sí,* **to**-**da**-*ví*-**a,** **y.**

o is pronounced like *o* in *obey,* but without the glide sound that follows the *o* in English: *no, so*-**lo,** *to*-**mo,** **co**-*mi*-**da.**

u is pronounced like *oo* in *cool:* **us**-*ted,* *u*-**no,** *gus*-**to.**

The vowels **e** and **o** also have sounds like *e* in *let* and *o* in *for.* These sounds, as in English, generally occur when the **e** and **o** are followed by a consonant in the same syllable: *él, ser, son,* **es**-**pa**-*ñol.* In pronouncing the **e** in **él** and **ser** and the **o** in **son** and **español,** the mouth is opened wider and the distance between the tongue and the palate is greater than when pronouncing the **e** in **aparece** and **debe,** and the **o** in **no** and **solo.** These more open sounds of **e** and **o** occur also in contact with the strongly trilled **r (rr),** before the **j** sound (written **g** before **e** or **i,** and **j**), and in the diphthongs **ei (ey)** and **oi (oy).** Pay close attention to the teacher's pronunciation of these sounds.

Consonants

b and **v** are pronounced exactly alike. Each has two different sounds, a voiced stop sound and a voiced continuant sound. At the beginning of a breath group (see page 208), or after **m** or **n** (also pronounced **m** in this case), whether within a word or between words, Spanish **b** (or **v**) is a voiced bilabial stop, similar to English *b* in *boy,* but somewhat weaker: *bien,* **bue**-**nas,** *va*-**mos,** *un va*-**so.** In all other positions, it is a voiced bilabial continuant; the lips do not close completely, as in stop **b,** but allow the breath to pass between them through a very narrow passage: *li*-**bro,** *Cu*-**ba,** *no va*-**mos.** When between vowels, the articulation is especially weak. Avoid the English *v* sound.

c before **e** and **i,** and **z** in all positions, are pronounced like the English hissed *s* in *sent* in Spanish America and in southern Spain. In northern and central Spain, this sound is like *th* in *thin.* Examples: *cen*-**tro,** *ci*-**ne,** *gra*-**cias,** *za*-*pa*-**to,** *pi*-*za*-**rra.**

c before all other letters, **k,** and **qu** are like English *c* in *cat,* but without the *h* sound that often follows the *c* in English: *cam*-**po,** *co*-**sa,** *cla*-**se,** ki-*ló*-**me**-**tro,** *que*-**dan,** *par*-**que.** Note both sounds of **c** in *cin*-**co,** **lec**-*ción.*

ch is pronounced like English *ch* in *church:* **mu**-**cho,** *co*-**che,** **cho**-**co**-*la*-**te.**

d has two sounds, a voiced stop sound and a voiced continuant sound. At the beginning of a breath group, or when after **l** or **n,** Spanish **d** is a voiced dental stop, like a weak English *d,* but with the tip of the tongue touching the inner surface of the upper front teeth, rather than the ridge above the teeth, as in English: *dar,* **mun**-**do,** **sal**-*dré.* In all other cases the tongue drops even lower, and the **d** is pronounced as a voiced interdental continuant, like a weak English *th* in *this:* **ca**-**da,** **ma**-**dre,** *to*-**do.** The sound is especially weak in the ending **-ado** and when final in a word before a pause: **es**-*ta*-**do,** **us**-*ted,* **Ma**-*drid.*

f is pronounced like English *f:* *fá*-**cil,** **Fe**-*li*-**pe.**

g before **e** and **i**, and **j** in all positions, have no English equivalent. They are pronounced approximately like a strongly exaggerated *h* in *halt* (rather like the rasping German *ch* in *Buch*): **gen-te, ge-ne-ral, hi-jo, Jor-ge, gim-na-sio.** (The letter **x** in the words **México** and **mexicano,** spelled **Méjico** and **mejicano** in Spain, is pronounced like Spanish **j**).

g in other positions, and **gu** before **e** or **i**, are pronounced alike. Each has two sounds, a voiced stop sound and a voiced continuant sound. At the beginning of a breath group, or when after **n**, Spanish **g** (written **gu** before **e** or **i**) is a voiced velar stop, like a weak English *g* in *go:* **gra-cias, gui-ta-rra, ten-go.** In all other cases, except before **e** or **i** in the groups **ge, gi**, Spanish **g** is a voiced velar continuant, that is, the sound is much weaker, and the breath continues to pass between the back of the tongue and the palate: **a-mi-ga, ha-go, la gui-ta-rra.** (In the combinations **gua** and **guo,** the **u** is pronounced like English *w* in *wet:* **a-gua, len-gua, an-ti-guo;** when the diaeresis is used over **u** in the combinations **güe, güi**, the **u** has the same sound: **ver-güen-za.**)

h is always silent: **ho-ra, ham-bre, hoy.**

l is pronounced like *l* in *leap,* with the tip and front part of the tongue well forward in the mouth: **lu-nes, pa-pel.**

ll is pronounced like *y* in *yes* in most of Spanish America and in some sections of Spain; in other parts of Spain it is somewhat like *lli* in *million:* **e-lla, a-ma-ri-llo, lla-mar.**

m is pronounced like English *m:* **mi-ro, mo-men-to.**

n is pronounced like English *n:* **no, com-pren-den.** Before **b, v, m,** and **p,** however, it is pronounced like *m:* **un ban-co, in-vi-tar.** Before **c, qu, g,** and **j,** it is pronounced like English *n* in *sing:* **blan-co, ven-go, con-Jua-ni-ta.**

ñ is pronounced somewhat like the English *ny* in *canyon:* **se-ñor, ma-ña-na, a-ño, com-pa-ñe-ro.**

p is pronounced like English *p,* but without the *h* sound that often follows the *p* in English: **pa-so, pe-so.**

q (always written with **u**): see page 205, under **c, k,** and **qu.**

r and **rr** represent two different sounds. Single **r**, except when initial in a word and when after **l, n,** or, **s,** is a voiced, alveolar, single trill, that is, it is pronounced with a single tap produced by the tip of the tongue against the gums of the upper teeth. The sound is much like *dd* in *eddy* pronounced rapidly: **ca-ra, o-ro, ha-blar.** When initial in a word, when after **l, n,** or **s,** and when doubled, the sound is a multiple trill, the tip of the tongue striking the gums in a series of very rapid vibrations: **ri-co, ro-jo, pi-za-rra, ca-rre-te-ra, En-ri-que.**

s is a voiceless, alveolar continuant, somewhat like the English hissed *s* in *sent:* **ca-si, es-tos.** Before the voiced **b, d, g, l, ll, m, n, ñ, r, v,** and **y,** however, Spanish **s** becomes voiced and is pronounced like English *s* in *rose:* **las blu-sas, des-gra-cia, mis-mo, los li-bros, es ver-dad.**

t is pronounced with the tip of the tongue touching the back of the upper front teeth (rather than the ridge above the teeth as in English); it is never followed by the *h* sound that is often heard in English: **to-ma, tar-des, tiem-po, tres.**

v: see page 205, under **b.**

x is pronounced as follows: (1) before a consonant it is pronounced like Spanish **s,** that is, it is a voiceless alveolar continuant sound, similar to English hissed *s* in *sent:*

ex-pli-*car*, ex-tran-*je*-ro; (2) between vowels it is usually a double sound, consisting of a Spanish velar continuant g (as in *a*-gua) followed by a voiceless, hissed *s*: e-*xa*-men (eg-*sa*-men), *é*-xi-to (*ég*-si-to); (3) in a few words x may be pronounced s (a voiceless alveolar continuant sound) even between vowels, as in e-*xac*-to, au-xi-*liar* (and in words built on these words).

y is pronounced like a strong English *y* in *you*: *ya*, *yo*, *ma*-yo. The conjunction y, *and*, when combined with the initial vowel of a following word, is similarly pronounced: *Car*-los-*y* A-na.

Diphthongs

As stated on page 204, the weak vowels i (y) and u may combine with the strong vowels a, e, o, or with each other, to form single syllables. Such combinations of two vowels are called diphthongs. In diphthongs the strong vowels retain their full syllabic value, while the weak vowels, or the first vowel in the case of two weak vowels, lose part of their syllabic value.

As the first element of a diphthong, unstressed i is pronounced like a weak English *y* in *yes*, and unstressed u is pronounced like *w* in *wet*. The Spanish diphthongs which begin with unstressed i and u are: ia, ie, io, iu; ua, ue, ui, uo, as in *gra*-cias, *bien*, a-*diós*, ciu-*dad*; *cua*-tro, *bue*-no, *Luis*, an-*ti*-guo.

The dipthongs in which unstressed i and u occur as the second element of the diphthong are nine orthographically, but phonetically only six, since i and y have the same sound here. They are: ai, ay; au; ei, ey; eu; oi, oy; ou. They are pronounced as follows:

> ai, ay like a prolonged English *i* in *mine*: *bai*-le, *hay*
> au like a prolonged English *ou* in *out*: au-to-*bús*, *Lau*-ra
> ei, ey like a prolonged English *a* in *fate*: *seis*, *ley*
> eu has no close equivalent in English. It consists of a clipped *e*, as in English *eh*,
>   followed closely by a glide sound which ends in *oo*, to sound like *ehoo*:
>   Eu-*ro*-pa
> oi, oy like a prolonged English *oy* in *boy*: *sois*, *soy*
> ou like a prolonged English *o* in *note*: lo u-*sa*-mos

Remember that two adjacent strong vowels within a word do not combine in a single syllable, but form two separate syllables: *cre*-o, te-*a*-tro. Likewise, when a weak vowel adjacent to a strong vowel has a written accent, it retains its syllabic value and forms a separate syllable: *dí*-a, pa-*ís*. An accent mark on a strong vowel merely indicates stress: *diá*-lo-go, tam-*bién*.

Triphthongs

A triphthong is a combination in a single syllable of a stressed strong vowel between two weak vowels. Four combinations are of frequent use: iai, iei, uai (uay), uei (uey), as in pro-nun-*ciáis*, es-tu-*diéis*, Pa-ra-*guay*, con-ti-*nuéis*. To indicate the mew of a cat and the bark of a dog the triphthongs iau and uau occur: *miau*, *guau*. In linking vowels between words, four and five vowels may be pronounced in one syllable.

Linking of Words

In reading or speaking Spanish, words are linked together, as in English, so that two or more may sound as one long word. These groups of words are called breath groups. The pronunciation of certain Spanish consonants depends upon their position at the beginning of, or within, a breath group. Similarly, the pronunciation of many individual sounds will be modified depending on the sounds with which they are linked within the breath group. Since the words that make up the breath group are pronounced as if they formed one long word, the principles which govern the structure of the syllable must be observed throughout the entire breath group.

In speech, words normally are uttered in breath groups. Thus it is necessary to practice pronouncing phrases and even entire sentences without a pause between words. Frequently a short sentence will be pronounced as one breath group, while a longer one may be divided into two or more groups. The meaning of what is being pronounced will help you to determine where the pauses ending the breath groups should be made.

The following examples illustrate some of the general principles of linking. The syllabic division in parentheses shows the correct linking; the syllable or syllables italicized bear the main stress.

a. Within a breath group the final consonant of a word is joined with the initial vowel of the following word and forms a syllable with it: **el asiento (e-la-*sien*-to)**.

b. Within a breath group when two identical vowels of different words come to-gether, they are pronounced as one: **el profesor de español (el pro-fe-*sor*-de es-pa-*ñol*)**.

c. When unlike vowels between words come together within a breath group, they are usually pronounced together in a single syllable. Two cases occur: (1) when a strong vowel is followed or preceded by a weak vowel, both are pronounced together in a single syllable and the result is phonetically a diphthong (see page 207): **su amigo (su a-*mi*-go)**, **Juan y Elena (*Jua*-n y E-*le*-na)**, **mi padre y mi madre (mi-*pa*-dre y-mi-*ma*-dre)**; (2) if both vowels are strong, each loses a little of its syllabic value and both are pronounced together in one syllable: **vamos a la escuela (va-mo-sa-la es-*cue*-la)**; **¿Cómo está usted? (¿*Có*-mo es-*tá* us-ted?)**.

Intonation

The term intonation refers to the variations in pitch which occur in speech. Every language has its characteristic patterns of intonation. The intonation of Spanish is quite different from that of English.

The alternate rise and fall of the pitch depends upon the particular meaning of the sentence, the position of stressed syllables, and whether the sentence expresses com-mand, affirmation, interrogation, exclamation, request, or other factors. In general, three meaningful levels of pitch can be distinguished in Spanish: one below the speaker's normal pitch (level 1), the speaker's normal tone (level 2), and a tone higher than the normal one (level 3). With respect to the use of these levels, the following basic principles should be observed:

A. At the beginning of a breath group, the voice begins and continues in a relatively low pitch (level 1) as long as the first accented syllable is not reached.

B. When the first accented syllable of a breath group is reached, the voice rises to the speaker's normal tone (level 2) and continues in the same pitch as long as the last accented syllable is not reached.

C. When the last accented syllable of the breath group is reached, the voice falls or rises, depending on the following circumstances:

1. At the end of a declarative statement, the voice falls to a pitch even lower than that of the initial unaccented syllable or syllables.
2. At the end of an interrogative sentence, or of an incomplete sentence interrupted by a pause, the voice rises to a pitch above the normal tone (level 3).

D. In exclamations, and in questions which begin with an interrogative word, the voice begins in a pitch above the normal tone (level 3) and gradually falls in the following syllables as long as the final accented syllable is not reached; when the last accented syllable is reached, the voice falls to a pitch even lower than that of the initial unaccented syllable or syllables, as in the case of the end of a simple declarative sentence, unless special interest or courtesy is intended, in which case the voice rises to the normal tone or even higher.

EXAMPLES

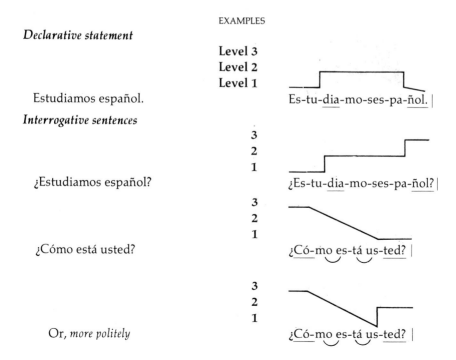

Declarative statement

Level 3
Level 2
Level 1

Estudiamos español.   Es-tu-dia-mo-ses-pa-ñol. |

Interrogative sentences

3
2
1

¿Estudiamos español?   ¿Es-tu-dia-mo-ses-pa-ñol? |

3
2
1

¿Cómo está usted?   ¿Có-mo es-tá us-ted? |

3
2
1

Or, *more politely*   ¿Có-mo es-tá us-ted? |

Exclamatory sentence

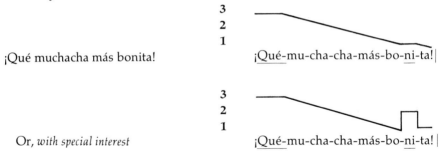

¡Qué muchacha más bonita!

Or, *with special interest*

E. The intonation pattern used to express special interest in an exclamatory sentence may also be used in questions (especially in those beginning with an interrogative word) and in declarative sentences. The voice rises above the normal tone when the last accented syllable is reached (level 3), and falls below the normal tone in the following syllable (or within the accented syllable, if no unstressed syllable follows). In a declarative sentence this pattern may be used to give special emphasis to any word of the breath group. Examples:

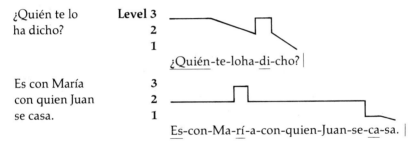

¿Quién te lo ha dicho?

Es con María con quien Juan se casa.

F. The pattern used in exclamations, and in questions which begin with an interrogative word, is typical of commands and requests. The latter differ in that the intervals between accented and unaccented syllables are less than in commands; furthermore, in requests the entire breath group is usually uttered on a higher tone. Examples:

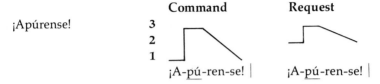

¡Apúrense!

G. If an interrogative sentence consists of two breath-groups, the first group ends below the normal tone. Example:

No saliste anoche, ¿verdad?

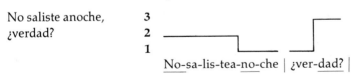

Punctuation

Spanish punctuation is much the same as English. The most important differences are:

1. Inverted question marks and exclamation points precede questions and exclamations. They are placed at the actual beginning of the question or exclamation, not necessarily at the beginning of the sentence:

    ¿Hablan Carlos y Juan?   Are Charles and John talking?
    ¡Qué muchacha más bonita!   What a pretty girl!
    Usted es español, ¿verdad?   You are a Spaniard, aren't you?

2. In Spanish a comma is not used between the last two words of a series, while in English it usually is:

    Tenemos plumas, libros y lápices.   We have pens, books, and pencils.

3. A dash is generally used instead of the quotation marks of English. To denote a change of speaker in dialogue, it appears at the beginning of each speech, but is omitted at the end:

    —¿Es usted español?   "Are you Spanish (a Spaniard)?"
    —Sí, señor. Soy de Toledo.   "Yes, sir. I am from Toledo."

If a direct quotation is followed by its main clause, a second dash is used, to enclose the quotation and separate it from the main clause, just as quotation marks are used in English:

    —¿No viene usted con nosotros?—me preguntó Felipe.   "Aren't you coming with us?" Philip asked me.

If Spanish quotation marks are used, they are placed on the line, as in the example which follows. In current practice English quotation marks are widely used in Spanish:

    Juan dijo: «Pasen ustedes».   John said, "Come in."

Capitalization

Only proper names and the first word of a sentence begin with a capital letter in Spanish. The subject pronoun **yo** (*I* in English), names of months and days of the week, adjectives of nationality and nouns formed from them, and titles (unless abbreviated) are not capitalized. In titles of books or works of art, only the first word is ordinarily capitalized:

    Juan y yo hablamos.   John and I are talking.
    Hoy es lunes.   Today is Monday.
    Buenos días, señor (Sr.) Pidal.   Good morning, Mr. Pidal.
    Son españoles.   They are Spanish.
    La corrida de toros.   The Bullfight

APPENDIX B

Frases para la clase (*Classroom Expressions*)

A number of expressions and grammatical terms which may be used in the classroom are listed below. They are not included in the end vocabulary unless used in the preceding lessons. Other common expressions are used in the text.

Voy a pasar lista.	I am going to call the roll.
Presente.	Present.
¿Qué lección tenemos hoy?	What lesson do we have today?
Tenemos la Lección primera (dos).	We have Lesson One (Two).
¿En qué página empieza?	On what page does it begin?
¿Qué línea (renglón)?	What line?
(La lectura) empieza en la página . . .	(The reading) begins on page . . .
Al principio de la página . . .	At the beginning of (the) page . . .
En el medio (Al pie) de la página . . .	In the middle (At the bottom) of (the) page . . .
Abre (tú) *or* **Abra(n) usted(es) el (los) libro(s).**	Open your book(s).
Cierra (tú) *or* **Cierre(n) usted(es) . . .**	Close . . .
Lee (tú) *or* **Lea(n) usted(es) en español.**	Read in Spanish.
Empieza (tú) *or* **Empiece(n) usted(es) a leer.**	Begin to read.
Sigue (tú) *or* **Siga(n) usted(es) leyendo.**	Continue (Go on) reading.
Traduce (tú) *or* **Traduzca(n) usted(es) al español (inglés).**	Translate into Spanish (English).
Repite (tú) *or* **Repita(n) usted(es) la frase modelo.**	Repeat the model sentence.
Pronuncia (tú) *or* **Pronuncie(n) usted(es) . . .**	Pronounce . . .
Basta.	That is enough. That will do.
Contesta (tú) *or* **Conteste(n) usted(es) (la pregunta) en español.**	Answer (the question) in Spanish.
Ve (tú) *or* **Vaya(n) usted(es) a la pizarra.**	Go to the (chalk)board.
Pasa (tú) *or* **Pase(n) usted(es) a . . .**	Go to . . .
Escucha (tú) *or* **Escuche(n) usted(es) las instrucciones.**	Listen to the directions.
Escribe (tú) *or* **Escriba(n) usted(es) (al dictado).**	Write (at dictation).
Tú has hecho *or* **Usted(es) ha(n) hecho una falta (un error).**	You have made a mistake.

Corrige (tú) *or* Corrija(n) usted(es) . . .	Correct . . .
Borra (tú) *or* Borre(n) usted(es) la frase.	Erase the sentence.
Vuelve (tú) *or* Vuelva(n) usted(es) a su(s) asiento(s).	Return to your seat(s).
Siéntate (tú) *or* Siénte(n)se usted(es).	Sit down.
Haz (tú) *or* Haga(n) usted(es) el favor de (+ *inf.*) . . .	Please (+ *verb*) . . .
Está bien.	All right. That's fine.
¿Qué significa (quiere decir) la palabra . . . ?	What does the word . . . mean?
¿Quién quiere hacer una pregunta?	Who wants to ask a question?
¿Cómo se dice . . . ?	How does one (do you) say . . . ?
Presta (tú) *or* Preste(n) usted(es) atención.	Pay attention.
Prepara (tú) *or* Prepare(n) usted(es) para mañana . . .	Prepare for tomorrow . . .
Ha sonado el timbre.	The bell has rung.
La clase ha terminado.	The class has ended.
Ustedes pueden marcharse.	You (*pl.*) may leave (You are excused).

Términos gramaticales (*Grammatical Terms*)

el **adjetivo**   adjective
   demostrativo   demonstrative
   posesivo   possessive
el **adverbio**   adverb
el **artículo**   article
   definido   definite
   indefinido   indefinite
el **cambio ortográfico**   change in spelling
la **capitalización**   capitalization
la **cláusula**   clause
la **comparación**   comparison
el **comparativo**   comparative
el **complemento**   complement
   directo   direct
   indirecto   indirect
la **composición**   composition
la **concordancia**   agreement
la **conjugación**   conjugation
la **conjunción**   conjunction
la **consonante**   consonant
el **diptongo**   diphthong

el **género**   gender
   femenino   feminine
   masculino   masculine
el **gerundio**   gerund, present participle
el **infinitivo**   infinitive
la **interjección**   interjection
la **interrogación**   interrogation, question
la **letra**   letter (*of the alphabet*)
   mayúscula   capital
   minúscula   small
el **modo indicativo (subjuntivo)**   indicative (subjunctive) mood
el **nombre propio**   proper noun
el **nombre (sustantivo)**   noun (substantive)
el **número**   numeral, number
   cardinal   cardinal
   ordinal   ordinal
el **objeto**   object
   directo   direct
   indirecto   indirect

la **palabra (negativa)**   (negative) word
las **partes de la oración**   parts of speech
el **participio pasado (presente)**   past
    (present) participle
la **persona**   person
    primera   first
    segunda   second
    tercera   third
el **plural**   plural
la **posición**   position
el **predicado**   predicate
la **preposición**   preposition
el **pronombre**   pronoun
    interrogativo   interrogative
    personal   personal
    relativo   relative
la **puntuación**   punctuation
el **radical (la raíz)**   stem
el **significado**   meaning
la **sílaba**   syllable
    penúltima   next to last
    última   last
el **singular**   singular
el **subjuntivo**   subjunctive (mood)
el **sujeto**   subject
el **superlativo (absoluto)**   (absolute)
    superlative
la **terminación**   ending

el **tiempo**   tense
el **tiempo simple (compuesto)**   simple
    (compound) tense
    presente   present
    imperfecto   imperfect
    pretérito   preterit
    futuro   future
    condicional   conditional
    pluscuamperfecto   pluperfect,
    past perfect
    pretérito anterior   preterit perfect
    pretérito perfecto   present perfect
    futuro perfecto   future perfect
    condicional perfecto   conditional
    perfect
el **triptongo**   triphthong
el **verbo**   verb
    auxiliar   auxiliary
    impersonal   impersonal
    (in)transitivo   (in)transitive
    irregular   irregular
    reflexivo   reflexive
    regular   regular
la **vocal**   vowel
la **voz**   voice
    activa   active
    pasiva   passive

Signos de puntuación (*Punctuation Marks*)

,	coma	( )	(los) paréntesis
;	punto y coma	« »	comillas
:	dos puntos	´	acento escrito
.	punto final	¨	(la) diéresis
...	puntos suspensivos	˜	(la) tilde
¿ ?	signo(s) de interrogación	-	(el) guión
¡ !	signo(s) de admiración	—	raya

Abreviaturas y signos (*Abbreviations and Signs*)

adj.	adjective	*aux.*	auxiliary
adv.	adverb	*cond.*	conditional
Am.	America	*conj.*	conjunction

dir.	direct	*obj.*	object
e.g.	for example	*part.*	participle
etc.	and so forth	*perf.*	perfect
f.	feminine	*pl.*	plural
fam.	familiar	*p.p.*	past participle
i.e.	that is	*prep.*	preposition
imp.	imperfect	*pres.*	present
ind.	indicative	*pret.*	preterit
indef.	indefinite	*pron.*	pronoun
indir.	indirect	*reflex.*	reflexive
inf.	infinitive	*sing.*	singular
lit.	literally	*subj.*	subjunctive
m.	masculine	*trans.*	transitive
Mex.	Mexico	*U.S.*	United States

( ) Words in parentheses are explanatory, or they are to be translated in the exercises. In the Glosarios and end vocabularies they are used to indicate that other words or expressions may be substituted (see page 10, footnote 2).

— In the general vocabularies a dash indicates a word repeated, while in the exercises it usually is to be supplied by some grammatical form.

+ = followed by

⌣ ⌢ Linking signs (placed below or above the line) indicate that sounds connected by them are pronounced in one syllable.

APPENDIX C

Cardinal Numerals

0	cero	29	veintinueve (veinte y nueve)
1	un(o), una	30	treinta
2	dos	31	treinta y un(o), -a
3	tres	32	treinta y dos
4	cuatro	40	cuarenta
5	cinco	50	cincuenta
6	seis	60	sesenta
7	siete	70	setenta
8	ocho	80	ochenta
9	nueve	90	noventa
10	diez	100	ciento (cien)
11	once	101	ciento un(o), ciento una
12	doce	110	ciento diez
13	trece	200	doscientos, -as
14	catorce	300	trescientos, -as
15	quince	400	cuatrocientos, -as
16	dieciséis (diez y seis)	500	quinientos, -as
17	diecisiete (diez y siete)	600	seiscientos, -as
18	dieciocho (diez y ocho)	700	setecientos, -as
19	diecinueve (diez y nueve)	800	ochocientos, -as
20	veinte	900	novecientos, -as
21	veintiún, veintiuno, veintiuna [veinte y un(o), -a]	1.000	mil
		1.020	mil veinte
22	veintidós (veinte y dos)	1.500	mil quinientos, -as
23	veintitrés (veinte y tres)	2.000	dos mil
24	veinticuatro (veinte y cuatro)	100.000	cien mil
25	veinticinco (veinte y cinco)	200.000	doscientos, -as mil
26	veintiséis (veinte y seis)	1.000.000	un millón (de)
27	veintisiete (veinte y siete)	2.000.000	dos millones (de)
28	veintiocho (veinte y ocho)	2.500.000	dos millones quinientos, -as mil

Uno and numerals ending in uno drop -o before a masculine noun: un soldado, *one soldier;* veintiún coches, *twenty-one cars;* treinta y un estudiantes, *thirty-one students.* Una is used before a feminine noun: una ciudad, *one city;* veintiuna señoritas, *twenty-one young ladies;* treinta y una páginas, *thirty-one pages.*

When a numeral ending in *one* follows a noun or is used alone, the numeral in Spanish agrees in gender with the noun: —¿Cuántos cuadros hay? —Veintiuno

(Treinta y uno). *"How many pictures are there?" "Twenty-one (Thirty-one)."* —¿Cuántas obras hay? —Veintiuna (Treinta y una). *"How many works are there?" "Twenty-one (Thirty-one)."*

The cardinal numerals precede the nouns they modify unless they are used in a descriptive sense: diez lecciones, *ten lessons,* but Lección dos (veintidós), *Lesson Two (Twenty-two).*

Be sure to note that an accent mark must be written on the forms dieciséis, veintiún, veintidós, veintitrés, veintiséis. Numerals 16 through 19 and 21 through 29 may be written as three words, but they are pronounced as one: diez y seis, diez y siete, veinte y un(o), -a, veinte y dos, etc. Beginning with 31, numerals are written as separate words: treinta y dos.

Ciento becomes cien before nouns and before mil and millones: cien dólares, *one hundred dollars;* cien mil habitantes, *one hundred thousand inhabitants.*

Un is regularly not used with cien(to) and mil: mil estudiantes, *1,000 students;* however, one must say ciento un mil habitantes, *101,000 inhabitants.* Un is used with the noun millón, which requires de when a noun follows: un millón de dólares, *$1,000,000.* For *$2,000,000* one says dos millones de dólares.

The hundreds agree with a feminine noun: doscientas muchachas, *200 girls;* quinientas cincuenta palabras, *550 words.* Beyond nine hundred, mil must be used in counting: mil novecientos setenta, *1970.*

Regardless of the English use of *and* in numbers, y is regularly used in Spanish only between multiples of ten and numbers less than ten: diez y seis, *16;* noventa y nueve, *99;* but seiscientos seis, *606.*

In writing numerals in Spanish, a period is often used where a comma is used in English, and a comma is used for the decimal point: $1.500,75. In current commercial practice, however, the English method is being used more and more.

Ordinal Numerals

1st	primero (primer), -a	4th	cuarto, -a	8th	octavo, -a
2nd	segundo, -a	5th	quinto, -a	9th	noveno, -a
3rd	tercero (tercer), -a	6th	sexto, -a	10th	décimo, -a
		7th	séptimo, -a		

Ordinal numbers agree in gender and number with the nouns they modify. Primero and tercero drop final -o before a masculine singular noun: el primer (tercer) edificio, *the first (third) building,* but los primeros días, *the first days,* la tercera parte, *the third part (one-third).*

The ordinal numerals may precede or follow the noun. Contrast the following:

Lección primera	Lesson One (I)
el capítulo tercero	Chapter Three
la Calle Cuarta	Fourth Street

BUT:	la primera lección	the first lesson
	el tercer capítulo	the third chapter
	la cuarta calle	the fourth street

A cardinal number precedes an ordinal when both are used together: **las tres primeras páginas,** *the first three pages.* (Note that Spanish says *the three first,* not *the first three,* as in English.)

With titles, chapters of books, volumes, etc., ordinal numerals are normally used through *tenth.* For higher numerals, they are regularly replaced by the cardinal numerals; in these cases all numerals follow the noun. With names of rulers and popes the definite article is also omitted in Spanish:

Felipe Segundo	Philip II (the Second)
la página sesenta	page 60
el tomo segundo	Volume Two
el siglo veinte	the twentieth century

Days of the Week/Months/Seasons

domingo	Sunday	**jueves**	Thursday
lunes	Monday	**viernes**	Friday
martes	Tuesday	**sábado**	Saturday
miércoles	Wednesday		

enero	January	**julio**	July
febrero	February	**agosto**	August
marzo	March	**septiembre**	September
abril	April	**octubre**	October
mayo	May	**noviembre**	November
junio	June	**diciembre**	December

la primavera	spring	**el otoño**	fall, autumn
el verano	summer	**el invierno**	winter

Dates

In expressing dates the ordinal numeral **primero** is used for the *first* (day of the month), and the cardinals are used in all other cases. The definite article translates *the, on the,* with the day of the month. (Remember that the definite article also translates *on* with a day of the week: **Yo saldré el lunes,** *I shall leave* [*on*] *Monday.*)

Hoy es el primero de enero.   Today is the first of January (January 1).
Nació el dos de mayo.   He was born (on) the second of May (May 2).

A complete date is expressed:

el diez de abril de mil novecientos ochenta y tres   April 10, 1983

Time of Day

¿**Qué hora es (era)?**   What time is (was) it?

Es (Era) la una.   It is (was) one o'clock.

Son (Eran) las dos.   It is (was) two o'clock.

Es la una y cuarto (media).   It is a quarter after one (half-past one).

Son las nueve menos diez de la mañana.   It is ten minutes before (to) nine A.M. (in the morning).

Son las tres de la tarde en punto.   It is three P.M. (in the afternoon) sharp.

Eran las ocho de la noche.   It was eight at night (in the evening).

Ella saldrá a la una (a las cuatro).   She will leave at one (at four) o'clock.

Acaba de dar la una.   It has just struck one.

Ya han dado las dos.   It has already struck two.

Faltan diez minutos para las once.   It is ten minutes to eleven.

Estarán aquí hasta las cinco.   They will be here until five.

Yo trabajo desde las ocho hasta las doce.   I work from eight until twelve.

APPENDIX D

Regular Verbs

INFINITIVE

tomar, *to take* | **comer,** *to eat* | **vivir,** *to live*

PRESENT PARTICIPLE

tomando, *taking* | **comiendo,** *eating* | **viviendo,** *living*

PAST PARTICIPLE

tomado, *taken* | **comido,** *eaten* | **vivido,** *lived*

The Simple Tenses

Indicative Mood

PRESENT

I take, do take, am taking, etc.	*I eat, do eat, am eating, etc.*	*I live, do live, am living, etc.*
tomo	como	vivo
tomas	comes	vives
toma	come	vive
tomamos	comemos	vivimos
tomáis	coméis	vivís
toman	comen	viven

IMPERFECT

I was taking, used to take, took, etc.	*I was eating, used to eat, ate, etc.*	*I was living, used to live, lived, etc.*
tomaba	comía	vivía
tomabas	comías	vivías
tomaba	comía	vivía

tomábamos	comíamos	vivíamos
tomabais	comíais	vivíais
tomaban	comían	vivían

PRETERIT

I took, did take, etc.	*I ate, did eat, etc.*	*I lived, did live, etc.*
tomé	comí	viví
tomaste	comiste	viviste
tomó	comió	vivió
tomamos	comimos	vivimos
tomasteis	comisteis	vivisteis
tomaron	comieron	vivieron

FUTURE

I shall (will) take, etc.	*I shall (will) eat, etc.*	*I shall (will) live, etc.*
tomaré	comeré	viviré
tomarás	comerás	vivirás
tomará	comerá	vivirá
tomaremos	comeremos	viviremos
tomaréis	comeréis	viviréis
tomarán	comerán	vivirán

CONDITIONAL

I should (would) take, etc.	*I should (would) eat, etc.*	*I should (would) live, etc.*
tomaría	comería	viviría
tomarías	comerías	vivirías
tomaría	comería	viviría
tomaríamos	comeríamos	viviríamos
tomaríais	comeríais	viviríais
tomarían	comerían	vivirían

Subjunctive Mood

PRESENT

(that) I may take, etc.	*(that) I may eat, etc.*	*(that) I may live, etc.*
tome	coma	viva
tomes	comas	vivas
tome	coma	viva
tomemos	comamos	vivamos
toméis	comáis	viváis
tomen	coman	vivan

-ra IMPERFECT

(that) I might take, etc.	*(that) I might eat, etc.*	*(that) I might live, etc.*
tomara	comiera	viviera
tomaras	comieras	vivieras
tomara	comiera	viviera
tomáramos	comiéramos	viviéramos
tomarais	comierais	vivierais
tomaran	comieran	vivieran

-se IMPERFECT[1]

(that) I might take, etc.	*(that) I might eat, etc.*	*(that) I might live, etc.*
tomase	comiese	viviese
tomases	comieses	vivieses
tomase	comiese	viviese
tomásemos	comiésemos	viviésemos
tomaseis	comieseis	vivieseis
tomasen	comiesen	viviesen

Imperative

take	*eat*	*live*
toma (tú)	come (tú)	vive (tú)
tomad (vosotros)	comed (vosotros)	vivid (vosotros)

The Compound Tenses

PERFECT INFINITIVE

haber tomado (comido, vivido), *to have taken (eaten, lived)*

PERFECT PARTICIPLE

habiendo tomado (comido, vivido), *having taken (eaten, lived)*

---

[1] There is also a future subjunctive, used rarely today except in proverbs, legal documents, etc., but which was common in Old Spanish. Forms are:

    tomar: tomare tomares tomare tomáremos tomareis tomaren

    comer: comiere comieres comiere comiéremos comiereis comieren

    vivir: viviere vivieres viviere viviéremos viviereis vivieren

The future perfect subjunctive is: hubiere tomado (comido, vivido), etc.

Indicative Mood

PRESENT PERFECT	PLUPERFECT	PRETERIT PERFECT
I have taken, eaten, lived, etc.	*I had taken, eaten, lived, etc.*	*I had taken, eaten, lived, etc.*

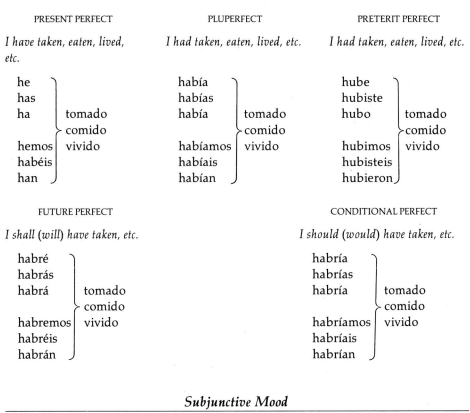

he		había		hube	
has		habías		hubiste	
ha	tomado	había	tomado	hubo	tomado
	comido		comido		comido
hemos	vivido	habíamos	vivido	hubimos	vivido
habéis		habíais		hubisteis	
han		habían		hubieron	

FUTURE PERFECT	CONDITIONAL PERFECT
I shall (will) have taken, etc.	*I should (would) have taken, etc.*

habré		habría	
habrás		habrías	
habrá	tomado	habría	tomado
	comido		comido
habremos	vivido	habríamos	vivido
habréis		habríais	
habrán		habrían	

Subjunctive Mood

PRESENT PERFECT	**-ra** and **-se** PLUPERFECT
(that) I may have taken, etc.	*(that) I might have taken, etc.*

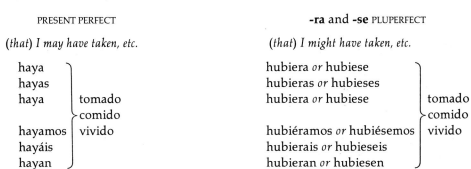

haya		hubiera *or* hubiese	
hayas		hubieras *or* hubieses	
haya	tomado	hubiera *or* hubiese	tomado
	comido		comido
hayamos	vivido	hubiéramos *or* hubiésemos	vivido
hayáis		hubierais *or* hubieseis	
hayan		hubieran *or* hubiesen	

Irregular Past Participles of Regular Verbs

abrir:	**abierto**	escribir:	**escrito**
cubrir:	**cubierto**	romper:	**roto**
describir:	**descrito**		

Comments Concerning Forms of Verbs

INFINITIVE	PRES. PART.	PAST PART.	PRES. IND.	PRETERIT
decir	**diciendo**	**dicho**	**digo**	**dijeron**

IMP. IND.	PROGRESSIVE TENSES	COMPOUND TENSES	PRES. SUBJ.	IMP. SUBJ.
decía	**estoy,** etc. **diciendo**	**he,** etc. **dicho**	**diga**	**dijera** **dijese**

FUTURE			IMPERATIVE	
diré			**di** **decid**	

CONDITIONAL				
diría				

a. From five forms (infinitive, present participle, past participle, first person singular present indicative, and third person plural preterit) all other forms may be derived.

b. The first and second persons plural of the present indicative of all verbs are regular, except in the cases of **haber, ir, ser.**

c. The third person plural is formed by adding **-n** to the third person singular in all tenses, except in the preterit and in the present indicative of **ser.**

d. All familiar forms (second person singular and plural) end in **-s,** except the second person singular preterit and the imperative.

e. The imperfect indicative is regular in all verbs, except **ir (iba), ser (era), ver (veía).**

f. If the first person singular preterit ends in unaccented **-e,** the third person singular ends in unaccented **-o;** the other endings are regular, except that after **j** the ending for the third person plural is **-eron.** Eight verbs of this group, in addition to those which end in **-ducir,** have a u-stem preterit (**andar, caber, estar, haber, poder, poner, saber, tener**); four have an i-stem (**decir, hacer, querer, venir**); **traer** retains the vowel **a** in the preterit. (The third person plural preterit forms of **decir** and **traer** are **dijeron** and **trajeron,** respectively. The third person singular preterit form of **hacer** is **hizo.**) **Ir** and **ser** have the same preterit forms, while **dar** has second-conjugation endings in this tense.

g. The conditional always has the same stem as the future. Only twelve verbs have irregular stems in these tenses. Five drop **e** of the infinitive ending (**caber, haber, poder, querer, saber**), five drop **e** or **i** and insert **d** (**poner, salir, tener, valer, venir**), and two (**decir, hacer**) retain the Old Spanish stems **dir-, har- (far-).**

h. The stem of the present subjunctive of all verbs is the same as that of the first person singular present indicative, except for **dar, estar, haber, ir, saber, ser.**

i. The imperfect subjunctive of all verbs is formed by dropping **-ron** of the third person plural preterit and adding the **-ra** or **-se** endings.

j. The singular imperative is the same in form as the third person singular present indicative, except in the case of ten verbs (**decir, di; haber, he; hacer, haz; ir, ve; poner, pon; salir, sal; ser, sé; tener, ten; valer, val** *or* vale; **venir, ven**). The plural imperative is always formed by dropping final **-r** of the infinitive and adding **-d.** (Remember that the imperative is used only for familiar affirmative commands.)

k. The compound tenses of all verbs are formed by using the various tenses of the auxiliary verb **haber** with the past participle.

Irregular Verbs[1]

1. **andar,** andando, andado, *to go, walk*

PRETERIT	anduve	anduviste	anduvo	anduvimos	anduvisteis	anduvieron
IMP. SUBJ.	anduviera, etc.		anduviese, etc.			

2. **caber,** cabiendo, cabido, *to fit, be contained in*

PRES. IND.	quepo	cabes	cabe	cabemos	cabéis	caben
PRES. SUBJ.	quepa	quepas	quepa	quepamos	quepáis	quepan
FUTURE	cabré	cabrás, etc.				
COND.	cabría	cabrías, etc.				
PRETERIT	cupe	cupiste	cupo	cupimos	cupisteis	cupieron
IMP. SUBJ.	cupiera, etc.		cupiese, etc.			

3. **caer, cayendo, caído,** *to fall*

PRES. IND.	caigo	caes	cae	caemos	caéis	caen
PRES. SUBJ.	caiga	caigas	caiga	caigamos	caigáis	caigan
PRETERIT	caí	caíste	cayó	caímos	caísteis	cayeron
IMP. SUBJ.	cayera, etc.		cayese, etc.			

4. **dar,** dando, dado, *to give*

PRES. IND.	doy	das	da	damos	dais	dan
PRES. SUBJ.	dé	des	dé	demos	deis	den
PRETERIT	di	diste	dio	dimos	disteis	dieron
IMP. SUBJ.	diera, etc.		diese, etc.			

5. **decir, diciendo, dicho,** *to say, tell*

PRES. IND.	digo	dices	dice	decimos	decís	dicen
PRES. SUBJ.	diga	digas	diga	digamos	digáis	digan

---

[1] Participles are given with the infinitive; tenses not listed are regular.

IMPERATIVE		**di**				**decid**	
FUTURE	**diré**	**dirás,** etc.					
COND.	**diría**	**dirías,** etc.					
PRETERIT	**dije**	**dijiste**	**dijo**	**dijimos**		**dijisteis**	**dijeron**
IMP. SUBJ.	**dijera,** etc.		**dijese,** etc.				

6. **estar,** estando, estado, *to be*

PRES. IND.	**estoy**	**estás**	**está**	estamos	estáis	**están**
PRES. SUBJ.	**esté**	**estés**	**esté**	estemos	estéis	**estén**
PRETERIT	**estuve**	**estuviste**	**estuvo**	**estuvimos**	**estuvisteis**	**estuvieron**
IMP. SUBJ.	**estuviera,** etc.		**estuviese,** etc.			

7. **haber,** habiendo, habido, *to have* (auxiliary)

PRES. IND.	**he**	has	ha	**hemos**	habéis	**han**
PRES. SUBJ.	**haya**	**hayas**	**haya**	**hayamos**	**hayáis**	**hayan**
IMPERATIVE		**he**			habed	
FUTURE	**habré**	**habrás,** etc.				
COND.	**habría**	**habrías,** etc.				
PRETERIT	**hube**	**hubiste**	**hubo**	**hubimos**	**hubisteis**	**hubieron**
IMP. SUBJ.	**hubiera,** etc.		**hubiese,** etc.			

8. **hacer,** haciendo, **hecho,** *to do, to make*

PRES. IND.	**hago**	haces	hace	hacemos	hacéis	hacen
PRES. SUBJ.	**haga**	**hagas**	**haga**	**hagamos**	**hagáis**	**hagan**
IMPERATIVE		**haz**			haced	
FUTURE	**haré**	**harás,** etc.				
COND.	**haría**	**harías,** etc.				
PRETERIT	**hice**	**hiciste**	**hizo**	**hicimos**	**hicisteis**	**hicieron**
IMP. SUBJ.	**hiciera,** etc.		**hiciese,** etc.			

9. **ir, yendo, ido,** *to go*

PRES. IND.	**voy**	**vas**	**va**	**vamos**	**vais**	**van**
PRES. SUBJ.	**vaya**	**vayas**	**vaya**	**vayamos**	**vayáis**	**vayan**
IMPERATIVE		**ve**			id	
IMP. IND.	**iba**	**ibas**	**iba**	**íbamos**	**ibais**	**iban**
PRETERIT	**fui**	**fuiste**	**fue**	**fuimos**	**fuisteis**	**fueron**
IMP. SUBJ.	**fuera,** etc.		**fuese,** etc.			

10. **oír, oyendo,** oído, *to hear*

PRES. IND.	**oigo**	**oyes**	**oye**	**oímos**	oís	**oyen**
PRES. SUBJ.	**oiga**	**oigas**	**oiga**	**oigamos**	**oigáis**	**oigan**
IMPERATIVE		**oye**			oíd	
PRETERIT	oí	**oíste**	**oyó**	**oímos**	**oísteis**	**oyeron**
IMP. SUBJ.	**oyera,** etc.		**oyese,** etc.			

11. poder, pudiendo, podido, *to be able*

PRES. IND.	puedo	puedes	puede	podemos	podéis	pueden
PRES. SUBJ.	pueda	puedas	pueda	podamos	podáis	puedan
FUTURE	podré	podrás, etc.				
COND.	podría	podrías, etc.				
PRETERIT	pude	pudiste	pudo	pudimos	pudisteis	pudieron
IMP. SUBJ.	pudiera, etc.		pudiese, etc.			

12. poner, poniendo, puesto, *to put, place*

PRES. IND.	pongo	pones	pone	ponemos	ponéis	ponen
PRES. SUBJ.	ponga	pongas	ponga	pongamos	pongáis	pongan
IMPERATIVE		pon			poned	
FUTURE	pondré	pondrás, etc.				
COND.	pondría	pondrías, etc.				
PRETERIT	puse	pusiste	puso	pusimos	pusisteis	pusieron
IMP. SUBJ.	pusiera, etc.		pusiese, etc.			

13. querer, queriendo, querido, *to wish, want*

PRES. IND.	quiero	quieres	quiere	queremos	queréis	quieren
PRES. SUBJ.	quiera	quieras	quiera	queramos	queráis	quieran
FUTURE	querré	querrás, etc.				
COND.	querría	querrías, etc.				
PRETERIT	quise	quisiste	quiso	quisimos	quisisteis	quisieron
IMP. SUBJ.	quisiera, etc.		quisiese, etc.			

14. saber, sabiendo, sabido, *to know*

PRES. IND.	sé	sabes	sabe	sabemos	sabéis	saben
PRES. SUBJ.	sepa	sepas	sepa	sepamos	sepáis	sepan
FUTURE	sabré	sabrás, etc.				
COND.	sabría	sabrías, etc.				
PRETERIT	supe	supiste	supo	supimos	supisteis	supieron
IMP. SUBJ.	supiera, etc.		supiese, etc.			

15. salir, saliendo, salido, *to go out, leave*

PRES. IND.	salgo	sales	sale	salimos	salís	salen
PRES. SUBJ.	salga	salgas	salga	salgamos	salgáis	salgan
IMPERATIVE		sal			salid	
FUTURE	saldré	saldrás, etc.				
COND.	saldría	saldrías, etc.				

16. ser, siendo, sido, *to be*

PRES. IND.	soy	eres	es	somos	sois	son
PRES. SUBJ.	sea	seas	sea	seamos	seáis	sean
IMPERATIVE		sé			sed	

IMP. IND.	era	eras	era	éramos	erais	eran
PRETERIT	fui	fuiste	fue	fuimos	fuisteis	fueron
IMP. SUBJ.	fuera, etc.		fuese, etc.			

17. tener, teniendo, tenido, *to have*

PRES. IND.	tengo	tienes	tiene	tenemos	tenéis	tienen
PRES. SUBJ.	tenga	tengas	tenga	tengamos	tengáis	tengan
IMPERATIVE		ten			tened	
FUTURE	tendré	tendrás, etc.				
COND.	tendría	tendrías, etc.				
PRETERIT	tuve	tuviste	tuvo	tuvimos	tuvisteis	tuvieron
IMP. SUBJ.	tuviera, etc.		tuviese, etc.			

Like tener: contener, *to contain;* mantener, *to maintain;* obtener, *to obtain;* detenerse, *to stop.*

18. traer, trayendo, traído, *to bring*

PRES. IND.	traigo	traes	trae	traemos	traéis	traen
PRES. SUBJ.	traiga	traigas	traiga	traigamos	traigáis	traigan
PRETERIT	traje	trajiste	trajo	trajimos	trajisteis	trajeron
IMP. SUBJ.	trajera, etc.		trajese, etc.			

Like traer: atraer, *to attract.*

19. valer, valiendo, valido, *to be worth*

PRES. IND.	valgo	vales	vale	valemos	valéis	valen
PRES. SUBJ.	valga	valgas	valga	valgamos	valgáis	valgan
IMPERATIVE		val (vale)			valed	
FUTURE	valdré	valdrás, etc.				
COND.	valdría	valdrías, etc.				

20. venir, viniendo, venido, *to come*

PRES. IND.	vengo	vienes	viene	venimos	venís	vienen
PRES. SUBJ.	venga	vengas	venga	vengamos	vengáis	vengan
IMPERATIVE		ven			venid	
FUTURE	vendré	vendrás, etc.				
COND.	vendría	vendrías, etc.				
PRETERIT	vine	viniste	vino	vinimos	vinisteis	vinieron
IMP. SUBJ.	viniera, etc.		viniese, etc.			

Like venir: convenir, *to be fitting.*

21. ver, viendo, visto, *to see*

PRES. IND.	veo	ves	ve	vemos	veis	ven
PRES. SUBJ.	vea	veas	vea	veamos	veáis	vean
PRETERIT	vi	viste	vio	vimos	visteis	vieron
IMP. IND.	veía	veías	veía	veíamos	veíais	veían

Verbs with Changes in Spelling

	a	o	u	e	i
Sound of *k*	ca	co	cu	que	qui
Sound of *g*	ga	go	gu	gue	gui
Sound of *s* (*th*)	za	zo	zu	ce	ci
Sound of Spanish **j**	ja	jo	ju	ge, je	gi, ji
Sound of *gw*	gua	guo		güe	güi

Changes in spelling are required in certain verbs to preserve the sound of the final consonant of the stem. The changes occur in only seven forms of each verb; in the first four types which follow, the change is in the first person singular preterit, and in the remaining types in the first person singular present indicative, while all types change throughout the present subjunctive.

1. Verbs ending in **-car** change **c** to **qu** before **e: buscar,** *to look for*

PRETERIT	**busqué**	buscaste	buscó, etc.			
PRES. SUBJ.	**busque**	**busques**	**busque**	**busquemos**	**busquéis**	**busquen**

Like **buscar:** acercarse, *to approach;* colocar, *to place;* comunicar, *to communicate;* explicar, *to explain;* indicar, *to indicate;* multiplicar, *to multiply;* practicar, *to practice;* publicar, *to publish;* sacar, *to take out;* tocar, *to play* (music).

2. Verbs ending in **-gar** change **g** to **gu** before **e: llegar,** *to arrive*

PRETERIT	**llegué**	llegaste	llegó, etc.			
PRES. SUBJ.	**llegue**	**llegues**	**llegue**	**lleguemos**	**lleguéis**	**lleguen**

Like **llegar:** agregar, *to add;* colgar (ue),[1] *to hang* (*up*); entregar, *to hand* (*over*); jugar (ue), *to play* (a game); negar (ie), *to deny;* obligar, *to oblige, force;* pagar, *to pay* (*for*).

3. Verbs ending in **-zar** change **z** to **c** before **e: cruzar,** *to cross*

PRETERIT	**crucé**	cruzaste	cruzó, etc.			
PRES. SUBJ.	**cruce**	**cruces**	**cruce**	**crucemos**	**crucéis**	**crucen**

Like **cruzar:** almorzar (ue), *to take* (*eat*) *lunch;* cazar, *to hunt;* comenzar (ie), *to commence, begin;* empezar (ie), *to begin.*

4. Verbs ending in **-guar** change **gu** to **gü** before **e: averiguar,** *to find out*

PRETERIT	**averigüé**	averiguaste	averiguó, etc.			
PRES. SUBJ.	**averigüe**	**averigües**	**averigüe**	**averigüemos**	**averigüéis**	**averigüen**

---

[1] See pages 232–234 for verbs with stem changes.

5. Verbs ending in **-ger** or **-gir** change **g** to **j** before **a** and **o: escoger,** *to choose, select*

PRES. IND.	**escojo**	escoges	escoge, etc.			
PRES. SUBJ.	**escoja**	**escojas**	**escoja**	**escojamos**	**escojáis**	**escojan**

Like **escoger:** diriger, *to direct.*

6. Verbs ending in **-guir** change **gu** to **g** before **a** and **o: distinguir,** *to distinguish*

PRES. IND.	**distingo**	distingues	distingue, etc.			
PRES. SUBJ.	**distinga**	**distingas**	**distinga**	**distingamos**	**distingáis**	**distingan**

Like **distinguir:** conseguir (i, i), *to obtain, attain;* seguir (i, i), *to follow.*

7. Verbs ending in **-cer** or **cir** preceded by a consonant change **c** to **z** before **a** and **o: vencer,** *to overcome, conquer*

PRES. IND.	**venzo**	vences	vence, etc.			
PRES. SUBJ.	**venza**	**venzas**	**venza**	**venzamos**	**venzáis**	**venzan**

8. Verbs ending in **-quir** change **qu** to **c** before **a** and **o: delinquir,** *to be guilty*

PRES. IND.	**delinco**	delinques	delinque, etc.			
PRES. SUBJ.	**delinca**	**delincas**	**delinca**	**delincamos**	**delincáis**	**delincan**

Verbs with Special Endings

1. Verbs ending in **-cer** or **-cir** following a vowel insert **z** before **c** in the first person singular present indicative and throughout the present subjunctive: **conocer,** *to know, be acquainted with*

PRES. IND.	**conozco**	conoces	conoce, etc.			
PRES. SUBJ.	**conozca**	**conozcas**	**conozca**	**conozcamos**	**conozcáis**	**conozcan**

Like **conocer:** amanecer, *to dawn;* aparecer, *to appear;* establecer, *to establish;* ofrecer, *to offer;* parecer, *to seem;* pertenecer, *to belong.*

2. Verbs ending in **-ducir** have the same changes as **conocer,** with additional changes in the preterit and imperfect subjunctive: **conducir,** *to conduct, drive*

PRES. IND.	**conduzco**	conduces	conduce, etc.			
PRES. SUBJ.	**conduzca**	**conduzcas**	**conduzca**	**conduzcamos**	**conduzcáis**	**conduzcan**
PRETERIT	**conduje**	**condujiste**	**condujo**	**condujimos**	**condujisteis**	**condujeron**
IMP. SUBJ.	**condujera,** etc.		**condujese,** etc.			

Like **conducir:** introducir, *to introduce;* producir, *to produce;* reducir, *to reduce;* traducir, *to translate.*

3. Verbs ending in **-uir** (except **-guir** and **-quir**) insert **y** except before **i**, and change unaccented **i** between vowels to **y**: **huir**, *to flee*

PARTICIPLES	**huyendo**			huido			
PRES. IND.	**huyo**	**huyes**	**huye**	huimos	huís	**huyen**
PRES. SUBJ.	**huya**	**huyas**	**huya**	**huyamos**	**huyáis**	**huyan**
IMPERATIVE		**huye**			huid	
PRETERIT	huí	huiste	**huyó**	huimos	huisteis	**huyeron**
IMP. SUBJ.	**huyera**, etc.			**huyese**, etc.		

Like **huir**: construir, *to construct;* incluir, *to include;* substituir, *to substitute.*

4. Certain verbs ending in **-er** preceded by a vowel replace unaccented **i** of the ending by **y**: **creer**, *to believe*

PARTICIPLES	**creyendo**		**creído**			
PRETERIT	creí	**creíste**	**creyó**	**creímos**	**creísteis**	**creyeron**
IMP. SUBJ.	**creyera**, etc.		**creyese**, etc.		

Like **creer**: leer, *to read.*

5. Some verbs ending in **-iar** require a written accent on the **i** in the singular and third person plural in the present indicative and present subjunctive and in the singular imperative: **enviar**, *to send*

PRES. IND.	**envío**	**envías**	**envía**	enviamos	enviáis	**envían**
PRES. SUBJ.	**envíe**	**envíes**	**envíe**	enviemos	enviéis	**envíen**
IMPERATIVE		**envía**			enviad	

Like **enviar**: variar, *to vary.* However, such common verbs as the following do not have the accented **i**: cambiar, *to change;* estudiar, *to study;* pronunciar, *to pronounce.*

6. Verbs ending in **-uar** have a written accent on the **u** in the same forms as verbs in section 5 above:[1] **continuar**, *to continue*

PRES. IND.	**continúo**	**continúas**	**continúa**	continuamos	continuáis	**continúan**
PRES. SUBJ.	**continúe**	**continúes**	**continúe**	continuemos	continuéis	**continúen**
IMPERATIVE		**continúa**			continuad	

Like **continuar**: graduarse, *to graduate;* habituarse a, *to become accustomed to.*

7. Verbs whose stems end in **ll** or **ñ** drop the **i** of the diphthongs **ie (ié)** and **ió.**

bullir, *to boil*

PRES. PART.	**bullendo**					
PRETERIT	bullí	bulliste	**bulló**	bullimos	bullisteis	**bulleron**
IMP. SUBJ.	**bullera**, etc.		**bullese**, etc.		

---

[1] **Reunir(se)**, *to gather, meet,* has a written accent on the **u** in the same forms as **continuar**:

PRES. IND.	**reúno**	**reúnes**	**reúne** . . . **reúnen**
PRES. SUBJ.	**reúna**	**reúnas**	**reúna** . . . **reúnan**
IMPERATIVE		**reúne**	

reñir (i, i), *to scold*

PRES. PART.	**riñendo**						
PRETERIT	reñi	reñiste	**riñó**	reñimos	reñisteis	**riñeron**
IMP. SUBJ.	**riñera,** etc.		**riñese,** etc.				

Stem-Changing Verbs

Class I (-ar, -er)

Many verbs of the first and second conjugations change the stem vowel **e** to **ie** and **o** to **ue** when the vowels **e** and **o** are stressed, i.e., in the singular and third person plural of the present indicative and present subjunctive and in the singular imperative. Class I verbs are designated: **cerrar (ie),**[1] **volver (ue).**[2]

cerrar, *to close*

PRES. IND.	**cierro**	**cierras**	**cierra**	cerramos	cerráis	**cierran**
PRES. SUBJ.	**cierre**	**cierres**	**cierre**	cerremos	cerréis	**cierren**
IMPERATIVE		**cierra**			cerrad	

Like **cerrar:** comenzar, *to commence, begin;* despertar, *to awaken;* empezar, *to begin;* negar, *to deny;* pensar, *to think;* recomendar, *to recommend;* sentarse, *to sit down.*

perder, *to lose, miss*

PRES. IND.	**pierdo**	**pierdes**	**pierde**	perdemos	perdéis	**pierden**
PRES. SUBJ.	**pierda**	**pierdas**	**pierda**	perdamos	perdáis	**pierdan**
IMPERATIVE		**pierde**			perded	

Like **perder:** entender, *to understand.*

contar, *to count; to relate*

PRES. IND.	**cuento**	**cuentas**	**cuenta**	contamos	contáis	**cuentan**
PRES. SUBJ.	**cuente**	**cuentes**	**cuente**	contemos	contéis	**cuenten**
IMPERATIVE		**cuenta**			contad	

---

[1] **Errar,** *to err, miss* (a shot), is designated: **errar (ye).** At the beginning of a verb the initial **i** of the diphthong **ie** is changed to **y,** since no Spanish word may begin with **ie:**

PRES. IND.	**yerro**	**yerras**	**yerra**	erramos	erráis	**yerran**
PRES. SUBJ.	**yerre**	**yerres**	**yerre**	erremos	erréis	**yerren**
IMPERATIVE		**yerra**			errad	

[2] Forms of **oler (ue),** *to smell* (an odor) follow. Spanish words do not begin with **u** followed by **a, e,** or **o;** thus **h** is written before **ue:**

PRES. IND.	**huelo**	**hueles**	**huele**	olemos	oléis	**huelen**
PRES. SUBJ.	**huela**	**huelas**	**huela**	olamos	oláis	**huelan**
IMPERATIVE		**huele**			oled	

Like **contar:** acordarse, *to remember;* acostarse, *to go to bed;* almorzar, *to take (eat) lunch;* colgar, *to hang (up);* costar, *to cost;* encontrar, *to find;* mostrar, *to show;* recordar, *to recall;* sonar, *to sound.*

volver,[1] *to return*

PRES. IND.	**vuelvo**	**vuelves**	**vuelve**	volvemos	volvéis	**vuelven**
PRES. SUBJ.	**vuelva**	**vuelvas**	**vuelva**	volvamos	volváis	**vuelvan**
IMPERATIVE		**vuelve**			volved	

Like **volver:** devolver, *to return, give back;* doler, *to ache, pain;* envolver, *to wrap up;* llover, *to rain;* resolver, *to resolve;* soler, *to be accustomed to.*

jugar, *to play* (a game)

PRES. IND.	**juego**	**juegas**	**juega**	jugamos	jugáis	**juegan**
PRES. SUBJ.	**juegue**	**juegues**	**juegue**	juguemos	juguéis	**jueguen**
IMPERATIVE		**juega**			jugad	

Class II (-ir)

Certain verbs of the third conjugation have the changes in the stem indicated below. Class II verbs are designated: **sentir (ie, e), dormir (ue, u).**

PRES. IND.	1, 2, 3, 6	} e > ie	PRES. PART.		} e > i
PRES. SUBJ.	1, 2, 3, 6	o > ue	PRETERIT	3, 6	o > u
IMPERATIVE	Sing.		PRES. SUBJ.	4, 5	
			IMP. SUBJ.	1, 2, 3, 4, 5, 6	

sentir, *to feel*

PRES. PART.	**sintiendo**					
PRES. IND.	**siento**	**sientes**	**siente**	sentimos	sentís	**sienten**
PRES. SUBJ.	**sienta**	**sientas**	**sienta**	**sintamos**	**sintáis**	sientan
IMPERATIVE		**siente**			sentid	
PRETERIT	sentí	sentiste	**sintió**	sentimos	sentisteis	**sintieron**
IMP. SUBJ.	**sintiera,** etc.		**sintiese,** etc.			

Like **sentir:** adquirir,[2] *to acquire;* consentir, *to consent;* diferir, *to differ;* divertirse, *to amuse oneself;* preferir, *to prefer;* referirse a, *to refer to.*

---

[1] The past participles of **volver, devolver, envolver, resolver** are: **vuelto, devuelto, envuelto, resuelto,** respectively.

[2] Forms of **adquirir (ie)** are:

PRES. IND.	**adquiero**	**adquieres**	**adquiere**	adquirimos	adquirís	**adquieren**
PRES. SUBJ.	**adquiera**	**adquieras**	**adquiera**	adquiramos	adquiráis	**adquieran**
IMPERATIVE		**adquiere**			adquirid	

dormir, *to sleep*

PRES. PART.	**durmiendo**					
PRES. IND.	**duermo**	**duermes**	**duerme**	dormimos	dormís	**duermen**
PRES. SUBJ.	**duerma**	**duermas**	**duerma**	**durmamos**	**durmáis**	**duerman**
IMPERATIVE		**duerme**			dormid	
PRETERIT	dormí	dormiste	**durmió**	dormimos	dormisteis	**durmieron**
IMP. SUBJ.	**durmiera,** etc.		**durmiese,** etc.			

Like **dormir;** morir,[1] *to die.*

Class III (-ir)

Certain verbs in the third conjugation change **e** to **i** in all forms in which changes occur in Class II verbs. These verbs are designated: **pedir (i, i).**

pedir, *to ask*

PRES. PART.	**pidiendo**					
PRES. IND.	**pido**	**pides**	**pide**	pedimos	pedís	**piden**
PRES. SUBJ.	**pida**	**pidas**	**pida**	**pidamos**	**pidáis**	**pidan**
IMPERATIVE		**pide**			pedid	
PRETERIT	pedí	pediste	**pidió**	pedimos	pedisteis	**pidieron**
IMP. SUBJ.	**pidiera,** etc.		**pidiese,** etc.			

Like **pedir:** conseguir, *to obtain, attain;* despedirse, *to take leave;* repetir, *to repeat;* seguir, *to follow;* servir, *to serve;* vestir, *to dress.*

reír, *to laugh*

PARTICIPLES	**riendo**		reído			
PRES. IND.	**río**	**ríes**	**ríe**	reímos	reís	**ríen**
PRES. SUBJ.	**ría**	**rías**	**ría**	**riamos**	**riáis**	**rían**
IMPERATIVE		**ríe**			reíd	
PRETERIT	reí	reíste	**rió**	reímos	reísteis	**rieron**
IMP. SUBJ.	**riera,** etc.		**riese,** etc.			

---

[1] Past participle: **muerto.**

VOCABULARIES

Spanish-English

A

a to, at, in, into, after, *etc.; not translated when used before a personal dir. obj.*
  a clase to class
  a fin de que *conj.* in order that
  a la derecha to (on) the right
  a la iglesia to church
  a (las seis) at (six o'clock)
  a lo lejos in the distance
  a menos que *conj.* unless
  a menudo often, frequently
  a mitad del camino halfway
  a partir de beginning with
  ¿a qué hora? at what time (hour)? when?
  a veces at times
abierto, -a *p.p. of* **abrir** *and adj.* open, opened
el **abogado** lawyer, attorney
el **abrigo** topcoat, overcoat
  abril April
abrir to open; *reflex.* to open (*by itself*), be opened
absolutamente absolutely
el **abuelo** grandfather; *pl.* grandparents
la **abundancia** abundance
  abundar en to abound in
acabar to end, finish
  acabar de + *inf.* to have just + *p.p.*
acaso perhaps
acelerar(se) to accelerate
la **acepción** (*pl.* **acepciones**) acceptation, meaning
aceptar to accept
la **acera** sidewalk
acerca de *prep.* about, concerning
acercar to bring . . . near

acercarse (**a** + *obj. or inf.*) to approach, draw near (to)
acompañado, -a de accompanied by
acompañar to accompany, go with
aconsejar to advise
acordarse (**ue**) (**de** + *obj.*) to remember, recall
  acordarse de + *inf.* to remember to
acostar (**ue**) to put to bed; *reflex.* to go to bed, lie down
actual *adj.* present
adjetivo, -a adjective, adjectival
el **adjetivo** adjective
admitir to admit; to accept
¿adónde? where? (*with verbs of motion*)
adquirir (**ie**) to acquire
adverbial *adj.* adverbial
el **adverbio** adverb
el **aeropuerto** airport
  en el aeropuerto at (in) the airport
aficionado, -a a fond of
  ser aficionado, -a a to be fond of
afirmativamente affirmatively
afirmativo, -a affirmative(ly)
agosto August
agradable agreeable, pleasant
agregar to add
agrupar to group, bring together
el **agua** (*f.*) water
  vaso para agua water glass
ahora now
el **aire** air
  al aire libre open-air
  en el aire in the air (i.e., in the surroundings)
el **aislamiento** isolation
  al = a + el to the
  al + *inf.* on, upon + *pres. part.*
  al año yearly, each year

al poco rato after (in) a short time (while)

la **aldea** village, small town

alegrar to make glad

alegrarse (de + *obj. or inf.*) to be glad (of, to)

alegrarse (de que) to be glad (that)

¡cuánto me alegro (de que) . . . ! how glad I am (that) . . . !

¡cuánto me alegro de verte! how glad I am to see you!

alegre happy, joyful, cheerful

el **alfabeto** alphabet

algo *pron.* something, anything; *adv.* somewhat, rather

alguien *pron.* someone, somebody, anyone, anybody

algún *used for* **alguno** *before m. sing. nouns*

alguno, -a *adj. and pron.* some, any (one), someone; *pl.* some, several, a few

almorzar (ue) to take (eat, have) lunch

el **almuerzo** lunch

para el almuerzo for lunch

los **alrededores** environs, vicinity

alto, -a high, tall

en voz alta aloud

alveolar alveolar

allá there (*often after verbs of motion*)

allí there

por allí around (along) there

amanecer to dawn

amarillo, -a yellow

la **amarilla** the yellow one (*f.*)

el **Amazonas** Amazon (River)

América America

la **América Central** Central America

la **América del Sur** South America

americano, -a American, Spanish American

la **amiga** friend (*f.*), girlfriend

el **amigo** friend, boyfriend

el **amo** master

Ana Ann(e), Anna

analfabeto, -a illiterate

andar to go, walk

los **Andes** Andes (*mountains in South America*)

el **animal** animal

anoche last night

ante *prep.* before (*position*)

anterior: pretérito—, preterit perfect (*tense*)

antes *adv.* before, formerly

antes de *prep.* before (*time*)

antes (de) que *conj.* before

antiguo, -a ancient, old

las **Antillas** Antilles

el **anuncio** ad(vertisement)

el **año** year

al año yearly, each year

¿cuántos años tienes (tiene Ud.)? how old are you?

el **año pasado** last year

tener . . . años to be . . . years old

tener dos años más que to be two years older than

aparecer to appear

apenas scarcely, hardly

la **aplicación** (*pl.* **aplicaciones**) application

aprender (a + *inf.*) to learn (to + *inf.*)

apurarse to hurry (up)

aquel, aquella (-os, -as) *adj.* that, those (*distant*)

aquél, aquélla (-os, -as) *pron.* that (one), those; the former

aquello *neuter pron.* that

aquí here

por aquí around (by) here, this way

el **árabe** Arabic (*language*)

el **árbol** tree

el **arcaísmo** archaism

arcaizante *adj.* obsolescent

la **Argentina** Argentina

argentino, -a (*also noun*) Argentine

arreglo: con—a according to

el **arte** art

el **artículo** article

el (la) **artista** artist

el **asiento** seat

asistir a to attend

Asociado: Estado Libre—, Commonwealth (Associated Free State)

el **aspecto** aspect, appearance

aspirado, -a aspirate

aspirarse to be aspirated

el **ataúd** coffin

atraer to attract

atraído *p.p. of* **atraer**

atreverse (a) to dare (to)

aumentar to increase

el **aumento**   increase

aun, aún   even, still

aunque *conj.*   although, even though, even if

el **auricular**   receiver (*telephone*)

el **autobús** (*pl.* **autobuses**)   bus

 autobús de las ocho   eight-o'clock bus

 en autobús   by (in a) bus

el **autor**   author

auxiliar *adj.*   auxiliary

averiguar   to find out

el **avión** (*pl.* **aviones**)   (air)plane

 avión de las tres   three-o'clock plane

 en avión   by (in a) plane

ayer   yesterday

 ayer por la mañana (tarde)   yesterday morning (afternoon)

el **aymará**   Aymara (*language of Aymara Indians in Bolivia and Peru*)

ayudar (**a** + *inf.*)   to help (to + *inf.*)

el **azúcar**   sugar

azul   blue

B

bailar   to dance

el **baile**   dance

 en el baile   at the dance

bajo *prep.*   under

bajo, -a   low, lower

 piso bajo   lower (first) floor

la **base**   base, basis

el **básquetbol**   basketball

bastante *adj. and adv.*   quite, rather, enough, sufficient

bastar   to be enough (sufficient)

el **bautismo**   baptism

beber   to drink

la **beca**   scholarship

la **biblioteca**   library

la **bicicleta**   bicycle

bien *adv.*   well

 más bien   rather

el **bien**   good

el **billete**   ticket

blanco, -a   white

 las blancas   the white ones (*f.*)

la **blusa**   blouse

el **boleto**   ticket (*Am.*)

bonito, -a   beautiful, pretty

el **Brasil**   Brazil

el **brazo**   arm

brevísimo, -a   very short

buen *used for* **bueno** *before m. sing. nouns*

bueno, -a   good; well (*with* **estar**)

 lo bueno   what is good, the good thing (part)

bullir   to boil

burlarse (**de**)   to make fun (of)

 se burlan uno de otro   they make fun of each other (one another)

el **burro**   burro, donkey

buscar   to look (for), search (for), seek

C

caber   to fit, be contained in

la **cabeza**   head

 tener dolor de cabeza   to have a headache

el **cabo**   end

 al cabo de *prep.*   at the end of

cada   each

caer   to fall

el **café**   coffee; café

 taza para café   coffee cup

la **cafetería**   cafeteria

caído *p.p. of* **caer**   fallen

calcular   to calculate, estimate

el **calendario**   calendar

 Calendario Turístico   Tourist Calendar

la **calidad**   quality, grade

caliente   warm, hot

el **calor**   heat, warmth

 hacer más calor   to be warmer (warmest) (*weather*)

 hacer (mucho) calor   to be (very) warm (*weather*)

 tener (mucho) calor   to be (very) warm (*living beings*)

el **Callao**   Callao (*port near Lima, Peru*)

la **calle**   street

 salir a la calle   to go out into the street

la **cámara**   camera

cambiar   to change

el **cambio**   change
　　en cambio   on the other hand
el **camino**   road, way
la **camisa**   shirt
la **campana**   bell
el **campo**   country, field, countryside
　　caso de campo   country house
el **Canadá**   Canada
　Canarias: Islas—   Canary Islands
la **canción** (*pl.* **canciones**)   song
la **cancha**   (tennis) court
　cansado, -a   tired
　　estar cansado, -a (**de** + *inf.*)   to be
　　　tired (of + *pres. part.*)
　cantar   to sing; to sing of; to chant
la **capital**   capital (*city*)
la **cara**   face
el **carácter** (*pl.* **caracteres**)   character
　cardinal   cardinal
el **Caribe**   Caribbean (*region*)
　Carlos   Charles
　Carlota   Charlotte
　Carmen   Carmen
　caro, -a   expensive
　Carolina   Caroline
la **carretera**   highway, road
la **carta**   letter
el **cartel**   poster
la **cartera**   purse
el **cartero**   postman
la **casa**   house, home
　　a casa de Ramón   to Raymond's
　　　(house)
　　casa de campo   country house
　　casa de piedra   stone house
　　en casa   at home
　　salir de casa   to leave home
　　(traer) a casa   (to bring) home
　casar   to marry
　casi   almost
el **caso**   case
　cazar   to hunt
　celebrar   to celebrate, hold; *reflex.* to be
　　celebrated (held), take place
　cenar   to eat (take, have) supper
　central   central
el **centro**   center, downtown
　　del centro   from downtown
　　(estar) en el centro   (to be) downtown
　　(ir) al centro   (to go) downtown
　Centroamérica   Central America

　cerca de *prep.*   near, close to
　cerrado, -a *p.p. of* **cerrar** *and adj.*   closed
　cerrar (ie)   to close; *reflex.* to close (*by
　　itself*), be closed
　Cervantes, (Miguel de) (1547-1616)
　　famous Spanish novelist, author of
　　Don Quijote, *short stories, comic
　　interludes*
el **ciclo**   cycle
el **cielo**   sky; heaven
　ciento (cien)   a (one) hundred
　cientos   hundreds
　cierto, -a   (a) certain, sure
　　por cierto   certainly
　cinco   five
　　a las cinco   at five o'clock
　　eran las cinco   it was five o'clock
　cincuenta   fifty
el **cine**   movie(s)
la **cinta**   tape
el **cinturón** (*pl.* **cinturones**)   belt
la **cita**   date, appointment
　citado, -a   cited, above-mentioned
la **ciudad**   city
　　ciudad de México   Mexico City
　Clara   Clara
　claramente   clearly
　claro, -a   clear
la **clase**   class; kind
　　a clase   to class
　　en clase   in class
　　la clase media   middle class
　　¿qué clase de . . . ?   what kind of . . . ?
　　sala de clase   classroom
　clásico, -a   classic
la **cláusula**   clause
la **clínica**   clinic, hospital
　cobrar   to cash
la **cocina**   kitchen
el **coche**   car
el **código**   code
la **coexistencia**   coexistence
　coincidir   to coincide, concur
　colgar (ue)   to hang (up)
la **colocación**   position, place
　colocar   to place, put
　colombiano, -a (*also noun*)   Colombian
la **colonia**   colony
el **color**   color
la **combinación**   combination
　combinar   to combine

comenzar (ie) (a + *inf.*)   to commence
(to), begin (to), start (to)

comer   to eat

la comida   meal, food

el comienzo   beginning

como   as, like; since

como si   as if

tan . . . como   as (so) . . . as

tanto como   as (so) much as

tanto, -a (-os, -as) . . . como   as (so)
much (many) . . . as

¿cómo?   how? what? in what way?

cómodo, -a   comfortable

el compañero   companion (*m.*)

compañero de cuarto   roommate (*m.*)

la comparación   comparison

comparativo, -a   comparative

el compendio   summary

completar   to complete

completo, -a   complete

por completo   completely

la composición (*pl.* composiciones)
composition

la compra   purchase

ir de compras   to go shopping

comprar   to buy

comprender   to comprehend, understand

compuesto, -a   composed; compound
(*tense*)

común *adj.*   common, ordinary

comunicar   to communicate; *reflex.* to
communicate with one another

con   with

concentrar   to concentrate, bring
together; *reflex.* to concentrate,
be concentrated

el concierto   concert

la concordancia   agreement

el concurso   competition, contest

la condición (*pl.* condiciones)   condition

condicional *adj.*   conditional

el condicional   conditional (*tense*)

conducir   to conduct, drive

la conferencia   lecture

confundirse   to be (become) confused
or mixed

la confusión   confusion

la conjunción (*pl.* conjunciones)   conjunction

conmigo   with me

conocer   to know, be acquainted with,
meet; to recognize

mucho gusto en conocerlo (-la)   (I'm)
very glad *or* pleased to meet (know)
you (*formal sing.*)

conocido, -a   known, well-known

la conquista   conquest

el conquistador   conqueror

conseguir (i, i)   to get, obtain, attain

consentir (ie, i) en   to consent to,
agree to

la conservación   conservation,
preservation

conservar   to conserve, preserve

considerablemente   considerably

consigo   with himself, herself, itself, etc.

la consonante   consonant

la constitución   constitution, makeup

la construcción   construction

construido, -a *p.p. of* abrir *and adj.*
constructed, built

construir   to construct, build

contar (ue)   to count; to tell, relate

contener   to contain

contento, -a   content(ed), happy,
pleased; *adv.* contentedly

estar contento, -a de (+ *inf.*)   to be
happy (pleased) (to)

estar contento, -a (de que)   to be
happy (that)

lo contentos que están   how happy
they are

la contestación   answer, reply

contestar   to answer, reply

contigo   with you (*fam. sing.*)

el continente   continent

la continuación   continuation

continuar   to continue, go on

contra *prep.*   against

contrario: por el—,   on the contrary, on
the other hand

convenir   to agree; to be fitting
(advisable)

convenir en que   to agree that

la cooperación   cooperation

la corbata   necktie

correctamente   correctly

correcto, -a   correct

correr   to run

corresponder a   to correspond to,
belong to

correspondiente (a)   corresponding (to)

la corrida de toros   bullfight

corriente *adj.* current, ordinary, popular, common

la **corriente** current, stream

cortar to cut

cortés (*pl.* **corteses**) courteous

cortésmente courteously

corto, -a short

la **cosa** thing

alguna cosa something, anything

cualquier cosa anything

costar (ue) to cost

la **costumbre** custom

creador, -ora creative

creer to believe, think

creído *p.p. of* **creer** believed, thought

el **Crucificado** the Crucified (Christ)

cruzar to cross

el **cuaderno** notebook

el **cuadro** picture

cual: el—, la—(los, las cuales) that, which, who, whom

lo cual which (fact)

¿cuál(es)? which one (ones)? what?

cualquier(a) (*pl.* **cualesquier[a]**) any *or* anyone (at all), just any

cualquier(a) cosa anything

cuando when

¿cuándo? when?

cuanto: en— *conj.* as soon as

en cuanto a *prep.* as for

¿cuánto, -a (-os, -as)? how much (many)?

¿cuánto tiempo? how long?

¡cuánto + verb! how ... !

el **cuarto** room; quarter

compañero de cuarto roommate (*m.*)

(son las diez) y cuarto (it is) a quarter after (ten), (it is) 10:15

cuatro four

a las cuatro at four o'clock

cubano, -a (*also noun*) Cuban

cubierto, -a (de) *p.p. of* **cubrir** *and adj.* covered (with)

cubrir to cover

cubrirse de to be covered with

la **cuenta** account; bill

tener en cuenta to bear in mind, take into account

el **cuento** (short) story, tale

el **cuidado** care

con cuidado carefully

tener (mucho) cuidado to be (very) careful

la **culpa** fault, blame

tener la culpa to be at fault, be to blame

el **cultivo** crop

culto, -a cultured, learned, correct

la **cultura** culture

cultural cultural

curioso, -a curious; quaint, unusual, strange

cursiva: en—, in italics

el **curso** course

curso de inglés English course

cuyo, -a whose, of whom, of which

el **Cuzco** Cuzco (*Andean city in Peru, former capital of the Inca empire*)

Ch

charlar to chat

el **cheque** check

Chiapas Chiapas (*a state in southern Mexico*)

la **chica** girl, child (*f.*), youngster (*f.*)

el **chico** boy, child, youngster; *pl.* boys, boy(s) and girl(s), children, youngsters

el **chocolate** chocolate

la **choza** hut, hovel

D

dame = da (tú) + me give me

la **danza** dance

dar to give

dar un paseo to take a walk (stroll)

dar una vuelta to take a walk (stroll)

darse prisa to hurry (up)

de of, from, by, about, to, concerning, with, in (*after a superlative*); than (*before a numeral*)

de dos maneras in two ways

de manera (modo) que *conj.* so that

no ... más de not ... more than (*before a numeral*)

deber to owe; must, ought to, should
  deber de + *inf.* must, probably + *verb*
  debería I (he, she, you *formal sing.*) should
  debiera I (he, she, you *formal sing.*) should *or* ought to
  debieras you (*fam. sing.*) should *or* ought to
decidir to decide
decir to say, tell
  decir que sí to say yes
  se lo dije I told him (her, you *formal*, them)
  se lo diré (a Uds.) I'll tell you
  sin decírmelo without telling me
el **dedo** finger
definido, -a definite
dejar to leave (*behind*); to let, allow, permit
  dejar de + *inf.* to fail *or* cease to + *inf.*
del = **de** + **el** of (from) the
delinquir to be guilty
demasiado *adv.* too, too much
demostrativo, -a demonstrative
el **deporte** sport
derecho, -a right (*direction*)
  a la derecha to (on) the right
desarrollar to develop (*something*); *reflex.* to develop, evolve
desayunarse to take (have, eat) breakfast
el **desayuno** breakfast
  para el desayuno for breakfast
  tomar el desayuno to take (have, eat) breakfast
descansar to rest
describir to describe
desde *prep.* from, since, for (*time*)
  desde hace una hora for an hour
  desde hacía un mes (for) a month
  desde ... hasta from ... (up) to
desear to desire, wish, want
desechar to cast aside, reject
el **deseo** desire
  tener muchos deseos de to be very eager (wish very much) to
desfavorable unfavorable
desgracia: por—, unfortunately
designar to designate, denote

despacio slowly
  lo más despacio posible the slowest possible, as slowly as possible
despedirse (i, i) (de) to take leave (of), say goodbye (to)
despejado, -a clear (*weather*)
despertar (ie) to awaken, wake up, arouse; *reflex.* to wake up (*oneself*)
después de *prep.* after
  después (de) que *conj.* after
detenerse to stop
devolver (ue) to return, give back
devuelto *p.p. of* **devolver** returned, given back
el **día** day
  buenos días good morning (day)
  con nuestros días with today (the present)
  día de fiesta holiday, festival day
  hoy día nowadays, today
  quince días two weeks, fifteen days
  todo el día all day, the whole (entire) day
  todos los días every day
el **diálogo** dialogue
la **diana** reveille (call, summons)
  Diana Diana, Diane
el **diccionario** dictionary
diciembre December
el **dictado** dictation
  dicho *p.p. of* **decir** said
  lo dicho what is (was) said
  dieciocho eighteen
  dieciséis sixteen
el **diente** tooth
  diez ten
  a (hasta) las diez at (until) ten o'clock
  eran las diez it was ten o'clock
  son las diez y cuarto it is a quarter after ten (10:15)
la **diferencia** difference
  a diferencia de unlike
diferente different
diferir (ie, i) to differ
difícil difficult, hard
  lo difícil what is difficult, the difficult thing (part)
  lo difíciles que son how difficult (hard) they are
la **dificultad** difficulty

el **diminutivo**   diminutive
el **dinero**   money
  Dios   God
    ¡por Dios!   heavens!
  directo, -a   direct
  dirigir   to direct, manage
el **disco**   record (*phonograph*)
  disperso, -a   scattered, separated
  distinguido, -a   distinguished, famous
  distinguir   to distinguish
  distinto, -a   different
la **diversión** (*pl.* **diversiones**)   diversion, amusement
  diverso, -a   diverse, different
  divertir (ie, i)   to amuse; *reflex.* to have a good time, amuse oneself
    divertirse mucho   to have a very good time
    ¡que te diviertas mucho!   may you (I want you to, I hope you) have a very good time!
la **división**   division
  doce   twelve
    antes de las doce   before twelve o'clock
el **dólar**   dollar (*U.S.*)
  doler (ue)   to ache, hurt
    a ella le duele la garganta   her throat hurts
    me (le) duele la cabeza   my (his) head aches
el **dolor**   ache, pain
    dolor de cabeza   headache
    tener dolor de cabeza   to have a headache
  Domingo   Dominic
  Santo Domingo   St. Dominic
el **domingo**   (on) Sunday
    todos los domingos   every Sunday
  don   Don (*title used before first names of men*)
  donde   where, in which
  ¿dónde?   where?
    ¿por dónde se va . . . ?   how (i.e., *by what route*) does one go . . . ?
  doña   Doña (*title used before first names of women*)
  dormir (ue, u)   to sleep; *reflex.* to fall asleep, go to sleep
    dormir la siesta   to take a nap

  dos   two
    son las dos y media   it is 2:30 (half past two)
la **duda**   doubt
    sin duda alguna   without any doubt
  dudar   to doubt
  dudoso, -a   doubtful
    lo dudoso   what is doubtful
  durante *prep.*   during, in, for

E

  e   and (*used for* **y** *before* **i-, hi-,** *but not* **hie-**)
el **Ecuador**   Ecuador
el **edificio**   building
  efectivo, -a   effective
el **ejemplo**   example
    por ejemplo   for example
el **ejercicio**   exercise
  el (*pl.* **los**)   the (*m.*)
    del (de los) que   than
    el (los) de   that (those) of, the one(s) of (with, in)
    el (los) que   that, who, which, he (those) who (whom), the one(s) who (that, which)
  él   he; him, it (*m.*) (*after prep.*)
el **elemento**   element
  Elena   Ellen, Helen
  eliminar   to eliminate
  ella   she; her, it (*f.*) (*after prep.*)
  ello *neuter pron.*   it
    a todo ello   to all of it
  ellos, -as   they; them (*after prep.*)
  empezar (ie) (**a** + *inf.*)   to begin (to), start (to)
el **empleado**   employee, clerk
  emplear   to employ, use
el **empleo**   use
  en   in, on, at
    en autobús (avión, coche)   by *or* in a bus (plane, car)
    en cuanto   as soon as
    en (el aeropuerto)   at *or* in (the airport)
    en la escuela   at (in) school
    en lugar de   instead of, in place of
    en seguida   at once, immediately
    en voz alta   aloud

el **encierro taurino**   driving of bulls into
  pen before fight
encontrar (ue)   to encounter, find, meet;
  reflex. to find oneself, be found, be
el **encuentro**   encounter, meeting
enero   January
enfermo, -a   ill, sick; sickly (*with* **ser**)
Enrique   Henry
la **ensalada**   salad
el (la) **ensayista**   essayist
enseñar   to show, teach, point out
  enseñar a + *inf.*   to show (teach)
    how to
entender (ie)   to understand
entonces   then, at that time
entrar (en + *obj.***)**   to enter, come (go) in
entre *prep.*   between, among, in
entregar   to hand (over, in), turn in,
  deliver
enviar   to send
envolver (ue)   to wrap (up)
envuelto *p.p. of* **envolver**   wrapped (up)
la **época**   epoch; season
el **equipo**   team
el **equivalente**   equivalent
errar (ye)   to err
escoger   to choose, select
escondido, -a   hidden, out-of-the-way
escribir   to write
escrito, -a *p.p. of* **escribir** *and adj.*   written
  lo escrito   what is (has been, was)
    written
la **escritora**   writer (*f.*)
escuchar   to listen (to)
  ¿escuchamos un disco?   shall we
    listen to a record?
la **escuela**   school
  a (en) la escuela   to (at, in) school
ese, esa (-os, -as) *adj.*   that, those (*nearby*)
ése, ésa (-os, -as) *pron.*   that (one), those
  (*nearby*)
eso *neuter pron.*   that
  por eso   therefore, because of that,
    for that reason, that's why
el **espacio**   space; period
España   Spain
español, -ola (*also noun*)   Spanish;
  Spaniard
  la española   the Spanish one (*f.*)
el **español**   Spanish (*language*)

(profesor) de español   Spanish
  (teacher)
especial   special
especialmente   especially
la **especie**   kind
esperar   to wait (for); to hope, expect
  (no) esperar más   (not) to wait (any)
    longer
el **espíritu**   spirit
la **esquina**   corner (*street*)
establecer   to establish, settle; *reflex.*
  to establish oneself, settle
la **estación** (*pl.* **estaciones**)   season
el **estadio**   stadium
el **estado**   state
  Estado Libre Asociado   Common-
    wealth (Associated Free State)
  los Estados Unidos   United States
estancado, -a   static, stagnant
estar   to be; to look, taste, feel
  está de fiesta   (it) has a holiday
    celebration
  está por escribir   it is to be written
  estar para   to be about to, be on the
    point of
este, esta (-os, -as) *adj.*   this (these)
éste, ésta (-os, -as) *pron.*   this, this one
  (these); the latter
el **estilo**   style
estimar   to esteem
esto *neuter pron.*   this
estrecho, -a   narrow
el (la) **estudiante**   student
  residencia de estudiantes   student
    residence hall (dormitory)
estudiar   to study
etc.   etc., and so forth
Europa   Europe
europeo, -a (*also noun*)   European
evidente   evident
evidentemente   evidently
evitar   to avoid
exacto, -a   exact
el **examen** (*pl.* **exámenes**)   exam(ination),
  test
excelente   excellent, fine
la **exclamación** (*pl.* **exclamaciones**)
  exclamation
la **excursión** (*pl.* **excursiones**)   excursion,
  trip

hacer una (la) excursión　to make *or* take an (the) excursion *or* a (the) trip

el **exiliado**　exile

existir　to exist, be

el **éxito**　success

　con éxito　successfully

　tener (mucho) éxito　to be (very) successful

explicar　to explain

la **exposición** (*pl.* **exposiciones**)　exposition, exhibition

expresar　to express

la **expresión** (*pl.* **expresiones**)　expression

extenso, -a　extensive, vast

exterior *adj.*　exterior, outer

el **extranjerismo**　foreignism

extranjero, -a　foreign, strange

extraño, -a　strange, unusual

extraordinario, -a　extraordinary

F

fácil　easy

falta: por—de *prep.*　for lack of

faltar　to be lacking (missing), need

la **familia**　family

familiar *adj.*　familiar, everyday

famoso, -a　famous

el **favor**　favor

　por favor　please (*at end of request*)

favorito, -a　favorite

febrero　February

fecundo, -a　fruitful

la **fecha**　date

felicitar　to congratulate

Felipe　Philip

feliz (*pl.* **felices**)　happy; *adv.* happily

felizmente　happily

el **fenómeno**　phenomenon

la **feria**　fair, holiday

festejar　to celebrate

el **festejo**　celebration

la **festividad**　festivity, celebration

la **fiesta**　fiesta, festival, party; holiday

　de fiesta　of festivity

　día de fiesta　holiday, festival day

　está de fiesta　(it) has a holiday celebration

la **fila**　row

Filipinas: las—,　the Philippines (*islands*)

el **fin**　end

　a fin de que *conj.*　in order that

　fin de semana　weekend

　por fin　finally, at last

final *adj.*　final

el **flan**　flan (*a custard*)

la **flor**　flower

la **Florida**　Florida

la **forma**　form

la **formación**　formation

formar　to form, make up

la **foto**　photo

la **fotografía**　photograph

francés, -esa　French

el **francés**　French (*language*)

　profesora de francés　French teacher (*f.*)

Francisco　Francis

la **frase**　phrase, sentence

el **fresco**　coolness

　hacer (mucho) fresco　to be (very) cool (*weather*)

　frío, -a　cold

el **frío**　cold

　hacer (mucho) frío　to be (very) cold (*weather*)

　tener (mucho) frío　to be (very) cold (*living beings*)

　frito, -a　fried

la **frontera**　frontier, border

fuera de *prep.*　outside (of)

fuerte: plato—,　main course

la **fuerza**　force, strength, power

fugazmente　briefly, for a short time

fundar　to found

el **fútbol**　football

　(partido) de fútbol　football (game)

futuro, -a　future

el **futuro**　future; future tense

G

la **gaceta**　gazette, newspaper

la **gallina**　hen

la **gana**　desire

　tener (muchas) ganas de　to desire *or* wish (very much) to, be (very) eager to, feel (very much) like

el **ganado vacuno**　cattle

ganar　to gain, earn, win

la **garganta** throat
gastronómico, -a gastronomic, pertaining to good eating
general general
  en general in general, generally
  por lo general generally
generalmente generally
el **género** gender
la **gente** people
geográfico, -a geographic
el **gimnasio** gym(nasium)
el **glosario** glossary
la **gobernación** government; territory
el **golf** golf
el **golpe** blow
gracias thanks
  dar las gracias a to thank, give thanks to
graduarse to graduate
gramaticalmente grammatically
gran *used for* **grande** *before sing. nouns* great, grand
grande large, big, great
grave grave, serious
griego, -a Greek
gritar to shout
el **grupo** group
el **guante** glove
guapo, -a handsome
el **guaraní** Guarani (*language of Guarani Indians in Paraguay*)
la **guerra** war
la **guitarra** guitar
gustar to be pleasing (to), like
  ¿cómo te gusta . . . ? how do you like . . . ?
  gustarle a uno más to like better (best), prefer
  me gustaría I should (would) like
el **gusto** pleasure
  mucho gusto en conocerlo(-la) (I'm) very glad *or* pleased to know (meet) you (*formal sing.*)

H

La **Habana** Havana
haber to have (*aux.*); to be (*impersonal*)
  ha habido there has (have) been

haber de + *inf.* to be (be supposed) to
había there was (were)
había que + *inf.* it was necessary to
habrá there will be
habría there would be
hay there is (are)
hay (mucho) sol it is (very) sunny, the sun is shining (brightly)
hay que + *inf.* it is necessary to, one must
hubo *pret.* there was (were)
el **habitante** inhabitant
habituarse a to become accustomed to
el **habla** (*f.*) speech
  de habla española Spanish-speaking
hablador, -ora talkative
hablar to speak, talk
hacer to do, make; to have, cause
  ¿cuánto tiempo hace? how long (much time) has it been?
  desde hace una hora for an hour
  hace media hora que llegaron they arrived a half hour ago (it is a half hour since they arrived)
  hace (mucho) sol it is (very) sunny, the sun is shining (brightly)
  hace (mucho) tiempo it is a long time, for a long time
  hace (unos minutos) (a few minutes) ago
  hacer buen tiempo to be good (nice) weather
  hacer el favor de + *inf.* please + *verb*
  hacer el (un) viaje to make *or* take the (a) trip
  hacer la (una) excursión to make *or* take the (an) excursion *or* the (a) trip
  hacer mal tiempo to be bad weather
  hacer más calor to be warmer (warmest) (*weather*)
  hacer (mucho) calor (fresco, frío, viento) to be (very) warm (cool, cold, windy)
hacerse + *noun* to become
hacía tiempo for a long time
hacía un mes que yo vivía allí I had been living there (for) a month
haga(n) Ud(s). (*formal pl.*) **el favor de** + *inf.* please + *verb*

hazme (tú) (*fam. sing.*) **el favor de** +
inf.   please + *verb*
hizo poner los paquetes   (he) had the
packages put
¿qué tiempo hace?   what kind of
weather is it? (what is the weather
like?)
hacia *prep.*   toward, to
hallar   to find; *reflex.* to find oneself, be
found, be
el **hambre** (*f.*)   hunger
tener (mucha) hambre   to be (very)
hungry
hasta *prep.*   until, to, up to, as far as
desde . . . hasta   from . . . (up) to
hasta (las ocho)   until (eight o'clock)
hasta que *conj.*   until
hay   there is (are)
hecho *p.p. of* **hacer**   done, made
lo hecho   what is (was) done
la **hermana**   sister
la **hermanita**   little sister
el **hermanito**   little brother
el **hermano**   brother; *pl.* brothers, brother(s)
and sister(s)
hermosísimo, -a   very pretty (beautiful)
hermoso, -a   pretty, beautiful
heroico, -a   heroic
el **hielo**   ice
la **hija**   daughter
el **hijo**   son; *pl.* children
hispánico, -a   Hispanic
el **hispano**   person of Hispanic origin
Hispanoamérica   Spanish America
hispanoamericano, -a (*also noun*)
Spanish American
hispanoparlante *adj.*   Spanish-speaking
el (la) **hispanoparlante**   speaker of
Spanish
histórico, -a   historical
el **hombre**   man
el **honor**   honor
hacer honores a   to do (show) honor to
la **hora**   hour, time (*of day*)
¿a qué hora?   at what time (hour)?
when?
¿qué hora es (era)?   what time is
(was) it?
hoy   today
hoy día   nowadays, today
periódico de hoy   today's newspaper

el **huevo**   egg
huir   to flee

_____ I

la **idea**   idea
idéntico, -a   identical
el **idioma**   language, idiom
ido *p.p. of* **ir**   gone
la **iglesia**   church
a la iglesia   to church
la **igualdad**   equality
la **imagen** (*pl.* **imágenes**)   image
imperar   to prevail
el **imperfecto**   imperfect (*tense*)
el **imperio**   empire
la **importancia**   importance
importante   important
lo importante   what is important, the
important thing (part)
importar   to be important, matter
imposible   impossible
lo imposible   what is impossible,
the impossible thing (part)
incluir   to include
incompleto, -a   incomplete
indefinido, -a   indefinite
indicado, -a   indicated
indicar   to indicate
el **indicativo**   indicative (*mood*)
(presente) de indicativo   (present)
indicative
indígena (*m. and f.*)   native, Indian,
indigenous
el **indio**   Indian
indirecto, -a   indirect
Inés   Inez, Agnes
el **infierno**   hell
el **infinitivo**   infinitive
el **influjo**   influence
informarse   to inform oneself, get
information
el **informe**   report; *pl.* information
el **ingeniero**   engineer
el **inglés**   English (*language*)
curso de inglés   English course
profesora de inglés   English teacher
(*f.*)
inglés, -esa   English

la **inglesa**   the English one (*f.*)
inicial   initial
la **inmigración**   immigration
el **inmigrante**   immigrant
inocente   innocent
insistir (en + *obj.***)**   to insist (on)
   insistir en que   to insist that
la **inspiración**   inspiration
intenso, -a   intense, intensive
el **interés** (*pl.* **intereses**) **(por)**   interest (in)
interesante   interesting
   lo interesante que es   how interesting
   it is
interior *adj.*   interior
el **interior**   interior, inside
interrogativo, -a   interrogative
introducido, -a por   introduced by
introducir   to introduce
introdujo *pret. of* **introducir**
el **invierno**   winter
la **invitación** (*pl.* **invitaciones**)   invitation
invitar (a + *inf. or obj.***)**   to invite (to)
ir (a + *obj. or inf.***)**   to go (to); *reflex.* to go
   away, leave
   ir + *pres. part.*   to be (*progressive form*),
   go on, keep on, be gradually
   (+ *pres. part.*)
   ir a la iglesia   to go to church
   ir al centro   to go downtown
   ir de compras   to go shopping
   ir en autobús (avión, coche)   to go by
   or in a bus (plane, car)
   va terminando   (it) is gradually ending
   vámonos   let's go (be going)
   vamos a + *inf.*   we are going to *or*
   let's (let's go to)
irregular   irregular
Isabel   Isabel, Betty, Elizabeth
la **isla**   island
   las Islas Canarias   the Canary Islands

J

Jaime   James
jamás   ever, never, (not) . . . ever
el **jardín** (*pl.* **jardines**)   garden
Jorge   George
la **jornada**   day, work day
José   Joseph

joven (*pl.* **jóvenes**)   young
   el (ese) joven   the (that) young man
   la (una) joven   the (a) young lady
   (woman)
   las jóvenes   young ladies (women)
   los jóvenes   young people, young
   men
Juan   John
Juanita   Jane
Juanito   Johnny
el **judío**   Jew
   judíos sefarditas   Sephardic Jews
   (= the Jews who are descendants of
   the former Jews of Spain and
   Portugal)
el **jueves**   (on) Thursday
el **jugador**   player
   jugar (ue) (a + *obj.***)**   to play (*a game*)
   jugar al (tenis)   to play (tennis)
juntar   to bring together; *reflex.* to gather
   (together)
junto con   along with
jurídico, -a   juridical, legal

K

el **kilómetro**   kilometer (*5/8 mile*)

L

la (*pl.* **las**)   the (*f.*)
   de la(s) que   than
   la(s) de   that (those) of, the one(s) of
   (with, in)
   la(s) que   who, that, which, she who,
   the one(s) *or* those who (that, whom,
   which)
la *dir. obj. pron.*   her, it (*f.*), you
   (*formal f.*)
la **lamprea**   eel
el **langostino**   prawn
el **lápiz** (*pl.* **lápices**)   pencil
largo, -a   long
   lo largas que son   how long (*f.*) they
   are
las *dir. obj. pron.*   them (*f.*), you (*f. pl.*)
   (*also see* **la**)

la **lástima**   pity, shame
  ¡qué lástima!   what a pity (shame)!
  ser lástima   to be a pity (too bad)
  latino, -a   Latin
  Laura   Laura
  lavar   to wash; *reflex.* to wash (*oneself*)
  le *dir. obj. pron.*   him, you (*formal m. sing.*);
    indir. obj. pron. (to) him, her, it, you
    (*formal sing.*)
la **lección** (*pl.* **lecciones**)   lesson
    toda la lección   all the lesson, the
      whole (entire) lesson
la **lectura**   reading
la **leche**   milk
  leer   to read
  leído *p.p. of* **leer**   read
  lejos: a lo —,   in the distance
la **lengua**   tongue, language
el **lenguaje**   language
  les *indir. obj. pron.*   (to) them, you (*pl.*)
  levantar   to raise, lift; *reflex.* to rise,
    get up
la **ley**   law
  liberarse   to free oneself
  libre   free
    al aire libre   open-air
la **librería**   bookstore
el **libro**   book
    libro (de español)   (Spanish) book
la **licencia**   license
    sacar la licencia   to get (obtain)
      the license
  lindísimo, -a   very pretty
  lindo, -a   pretty, beautiful
la **linea**   line
  listo, -a   ready; clever (*with* **ser**)
  lo *neuter article*   the; what is (was, *etc.*)
    a lo lejos   in the distance
    de lo que   than
    lo + *adj. or adv.* + **que**   how . . .
    lo (bueno)   what is good, the (good)
      thing *or* part
    lo de   that (matter, affair) of
    lo (largas) que son   how (long) (*f.*)
      they are
    lo más pronto posible   the soonest
      possible, as soon as possible
    lo peor   what is worse (worst), the
      worse (worst) thing *or* part
    lo que   what, that which

  por lo general   in general, generally
  por lo tanto   therefore
  todo lo que   all that, all that which
  lo *dir. obj. pron.*   him, it (*m. and neuter*),
      you (*formal m. sing.*)
    (ella) no lo parece   (she) doesn't seem
      so
    lo soy   I am
la **localidad**   locality, place; town
  localizado, -a   localized; located
el **lodo**   mud
    hay (mucho) lodo   it is (very) muddy
  lograr + *inf.*   to succeed in + *pres. part.*
  Lola   Lola
  Lope de Vega   *see* **Vega (Carpio)**
  los   the (*m. pl.*)
    de los que   than
    los de   those of, the ones of (with, in)
    los que   who, that, which, the ones *or*
      those who (that, whom, which)
  los *dir. obj. pron.*   them (*m.*), you (*m. pl.*)
  Los Ángeles   Los Angeles
  Lucía   Lucy
  luego   then, next, later
el **lugar**   place, hamlet, settlement
    en lugar de *prep.*   in place of,
      instead of
    tener lugar   to take place, occur
  Luis   Louis
  Luisa   Louise
la **luna**   moon
    hay luna   the moon is shining, there
      is moonlight
el **lunes**   (on) Monday
  Lupe   Lupe

Ll

  llamar   to call; to knock; *reflex.* to call
    oneself, be named
    (ella) la mandó llamar   (she) had her
      called, (she) sent for her
    llamar por teléfono   to telephone, call
      by (on the) telephone
la **llave**   key
  llegar (a)   to arrive (at), reach, come *or*
    go (to)
    llegar a tiempo   to arrive on time

llegar tarde   to arrive (be) late
llevar   to take, carry; to wear; *reflex.*
    to take (with oneself), take away
llover (ue)   to rain

M

la **madre**   mother
magnífico, -a   magnificent, fine,
    wonderful, great
mal   *used for* **malo** *before m. sing. nouns*
mal *adv.*   bad, badly
el **mal**   evil
la **maleta**   suitcase
malo, -a   bad; ill (*with* **estar**)
    lo malo   what is bad, the bad thing
    (part)
la **mamá**   mama, mother, mom
mandar   to send; to order, command;
    to have (*someone do something or*
    something done)
    (ella) la mandó llamar   (she) had her
    called, (she) sent for her
    le mandé esperar   I ordered him to
    wait (had him wait)
el **mandato**   command
la **manera**   manner, way
    de distintas maneras   in different
    ways
    de dos maneras   in two ways
    de manera que *conj.*   so that
manifestarse (ie)   to be (become)
    manifest, be seen
la **mano**   hand
mantener   to maintain, keep
la **manzana**   apple
mañana *adv.*   tomorrow
    mañana por la mañana (tarde,
    noche)   tomorrow morning
    (afternoon, evening
    or night)
    pasado mañana   day after tomorrow
la **mañana**   morning
    ayer (mañana) por la mañana   yester-
    day (tomorrow) morning
    de la mañana   in the morning, A.M.
    por la mañana   in the morning
el **mapa**   map

el **mar**   sea
la **marca**   brand, make, kind
Margarita   Margaret, Marguerite
María   Mary
marítimo, -a   maritime; sea (*adj.*)
Marta   Martha
el **martes**   (on) Tuesday
más   more, most
    lo más (pronto) posible   the
    (soonest) possible, as (soon) as
    possible
    más bien   rather
    más o menos   more or less,
    approximately
    (no) esperar más   (not) to wait (any)
    longer
    no . . . más de   not . . . more than
    (*before a numeral*)
    no . . . más que   only
    ¡qué libro más interesante!   what an
    interesting book!
materno, -a   maternal, mother (*tongue*)
el **maya**   Maya(n) (*Indian language*
    spoken largely in Yucatan and northern
    Guatemala)
mayor   greater, greatest; older, oldest
    la mayor parte de   most (of), the
    greater part of
la **mayoría**   majority, most
    en su mayoría   for the most part
me *obj. pron.*   me, to (from) me, (to)
    myself
el **médico**   doctor, physician
medio, -a   half, a half; middle
    a (las siete) y media   at half past
    (seven), at (7):30
    es la una y media   it is half past one
    (1:30)
    hace media hora   a half hour ago
    la clase media   the middle class
    un mes y medio   a month and a half
    una hora y media   an hour and a half
el **medio**   means
    por medio de *prep.*   by means of
mejor   better, best
    lo mejor   what is better (best), the
    better (best) part *or* thing
menor   smaller, smallest; younger,
    youngest; lesser, least
menos   less, least, fewer; except

a menos que *conj.*   unless

más o menos   more or less, approximately

no menos de   no less (fewer) than (*before a numeral*)

por lo menos   at least

menudo: a —,   often, frequently

el **mercado**   market

día de mercado   market day

el **mes**   month

el mes pasado   last month

la **mesa**   table, desk

la **metrópoli**   metropolis

mexicano, -a (*also noun*)   Mexican

México   Mexico

mi   my

mí *pron.*   me, myself (*after prep.*)

el **miedo**   fear

tener miedo (de que)   to be afraid (that)

tener (mucho) miedo (de)   to be (very much) afraid *or* frightened (of, to)

mientras (que) *conj.*   while, as long as

el **miércoles**   (on) Wednesday

Miguel   Michael

mil   a (one) thousand

el **millón** (*pl.* **millones**)   million

mínimo -a   minimum

el **minuto**   minute

mío, -a *adj.*   my, (of) mine

¡Dios mío!   heavens!

(el) mío, (la) mía, (los) míos, (las) mías *pron.*   mine

mirar   to look (at), watch

la **misa**   Mass

la **misión** (*pl.* **misiones**)   mission

misionero, -a   missionary

mismo, -a   same; -self

él mismo   he himself

lo mismo que   the same as

místico, -a   mystical

la **mitad**   half

a mitad del camino   halfway

más de la mitad   more than half

la **modalidad**   type, variety

el **modelo**   model

moderno, -a   modern

el **modo**   mode, manner, way; mood (*grammar*)

de modo que *conj.*   so that

el **momento**   moment

en este (ese) momento   at this (that) moment

la **montaña**   mountain

moral   moral

morir (ue, u)   to die

moscatel   muscatel

mostrar (ue)   to show; *reflex.* to show oneself to be

la **muchacha**   girl

el **muchacho**   boy; *pl.* boys, boy(s) and girl(s)

muchísimo *adv.*   very much

muchísimo, -a (-os, -as)   very much (many), a lot of

mucho *adv.*   much, very much, a great deal, a lot of

mucho, -a (-os, -as)   much, a lot of, many; very

la **muerte**   death

la **mujer**   woman

multiplicar   to multiply

mundial   world (*adj.*)

el **mundo**   world

todo el mundo   everybody, the whole (entire) world

la **música**   music

muy   very

N

nacer   to be born

la **nación** (*pl.* **naciones**)   nation

nacional   national

nada *pron.*   nothing, (not) . . . anything; *adv.* (not) at all

nadie   no one, nobody, (not) . . . anyone (anybody)

natural   natural

la **neblina**   mist

había neblina   it was misty

necesario, -a   necessary

lo necesario   what is necessary

necesitar   to need

negar (ie)   to deny

negativamente   negatively

negativo, -a   negative

negro, -a   black

el **neologismo**   neologism

neutro, -a   neuter
ni *conj.*   neither, nor, (not) . . . or
  ni . . . ni   neither . . . nor, (not) . . .
    either . . . or
la **niebla**   fog
  había niebla   it was foggy
la **nieve**   snow
ningún *used for* **ninguno** *before m. sing.*
  nouns
ninguno, -a *adj. and pron.*   no, no one,
  none, (not) . . . any (anybody, anyone)
la **niña**   little girl, child
el **niño**   little boy, child; *pl.* children
no   no, not
  todavía no   not yet
  yo no   not I
la **noche**   night, evening
  de la noche   in the evening, P.M.
  (el sábado) por la noche   (Saturday)
    night
  esta noche   tonight, this evening
  mañana por la noche   tomorrow
    night (evening)
el **nombre**   name
la **norma**   norm, standard
normal   normal
el **norte**   north
  Norteamérica   North America
  norteamericano, -a   North American
nos *obj. pron.*   us, (to) us, (to) ourselves;
  reciprocal pron. (to) each other,
  one another
nosotros, -as   we, us (*after prep.*);
  ourselves
la **nota**   note
notablemente   notably
la **noticia**   news (item), information, notice;
  pl. news, news items
la **novela**   novel
noventa   ninety
  noventa y dos   ninety-two
la **novia**   sweetheart, fiancée, girlfriend
el **novio**   sweetheart, boyfriend, fiancé
la **nube**   cloud
nublado, -a   cloudy
nuestro, -a *adj.*   our, of ours
  (el) nuestro, (la) nuestra, (los)
    nuestros, (las) nuestras *pron.*   ours
  lo nuestro   what is ours
nueve   nine

son las nueve   it is nine o'clock
nuevo, -a   new, brand-new
  Nueva York   New York
  Nuevo México   New Mexico
el **número**   number, numeral
nunca   never, (not) . . . ever

O

o   or
  o . . . o   either . . . or
el **objeto**   object
obligar (a + *inf.***)**   to oblige *or* force (to)
la **obra**   work (*art, literature, etc.*)
obscuro, -a   dark
la **observación** (*pl.* **observaciones**)
  observation
el **obstáculo**   obstacle
obtener   to obtain, get
ocupado, -a   busy, occupied
ocurrir   to occur, take place
ocho   eight
  a (hasta) las ocho   at (until) eight
    o'clock
  antes de las ocho   before eight o'clock
  autobús de las ocho   eight-o'clock bus
el **oeste**   west
la **oficina**   office
ofrecer   to offer
oído *p.p. of* **oír**   heard
oír   to hear
¡ojalá!   God grant it! I hope so!
  ¡ojalá (que)!   would that! I wish that!
oler (hue)   to smell (*an odor*)
el **olivo**   olive tree
olvidar   to forget (to)
  olvidarse (de + *obj.***)**   to forget (to)
la **omisión**   omission
once   eleven
  a las once y media   at half past
    eleven (o'clock)
  son las once   it is eleven o'clock
la **oportunidad**   opportunity
la **oración** (*pl.* **oraciones**)   sentence;
  prayer
ordinal   ordinal
el **origen** (*pl.* **orígenes**)   origin
original   original

el **oro**   gold
> **de oro**   (of) gold

la **orquesta**   orchestra

os *obj. pron.*   you (*fam. pl.*), to you, (to)
> yourselves; *reciprocal pron.* (to) each
> other, one another

el **otoño**   fall, autumn
> **otro, -a**   other, another
>> **el otro**   the other one (*m.*)
>> **la otra**   the other one (*f.*)
>> **otra vez**   again, another time
>> **otras muchas**   many others (*f.*)

P

Pablo   Paul

el **padre**   father; *pl.* parents

la **paella**   *a rice dish containing meat,*
> *vegetables, and shellfish*

pagar   to pay (for)

la **página**   page

el **país**   country, nation

el **pájaro**   bird

la **palabra**   word

el **papá**   papa, father, dad

el **papel**   paper

el **paquete**   package

para *prep.*   for, to, in order to, by (*time*)
> **para que** *conj.*   in order that
> **¿para qué?**   why? for what purpose?
> **taza para café**   coffee cup
> **taza para té**   teacup
> **vaso para agua**   water glass

el (los) **paraguas**   umbrella(s)

el **Paraguay**   Paraguay

parecer   to appear, seem, appear *or*
> seem to be
> **(ella) no lo parece**   (she) doesn't
> seem so
> **¿qué (te) parece . . . ?**   what do (you)
> think of . . . ? how do (you) like . . . ?

la **pared**   wall

el (los) **paréntesis**   parenthesis
> (*pl.* parentheses)

el **parque**   park

el **párrafo**   paragraph

la **parte**   part
> **la mayor parte de**   most (of), the
> greater part of

participar en   to participate in,
> take part in

el **participio**   participle

el **partido**   game, match
> **partido (de fútbol)**   (football) game

partir (de + *obj.***)**   to depart, leave
> **a partir de**   beginning with
> **partir para**   to leave for

pasado, -a   past, last
> **la semana pasada**   last week
> **pasado mañana**   day after
> tomorrow

pasar   to pass, pass on, go; to spend
> (*time*)
> **pasa (tú), pase(n) Ud(s).**   come in
> **pasar a ser**   to become
> **pasar por**   to pass (go, come) by *or*
> along

el **paseo**   walk, stroll, ride, drive
> **dar un paseo**   to take a walk (stroll)
> **dar paseos**   to take walks

pasivo, -a   passive

el **patio**   patio, courtyard

la **patrona**   patroness

la **paz**   peace

pedir (i, i)   to ask, ask for, request

la **película**   film

el **peligro**   danger

el **pelo**   hair

penetrar (en)   to penetrate, enter

la **Península**   Peninsula (= Spain and
> Portugal)
> **peninsular**   peninsular (*of Spain*)

pensar (ie)   to think, believe; + *inf.*
> to intend to, plan to
> **pensar en** + *obj. or inf.*   to think of
> (about)

peor   worse, worst
> **lo peor**   what is worse (worst), the
> worse (worst) thing *or* part

Pepe   Joe

pequeño, -a   small, little (*size*)
> **el más pequeño**   the smaller
> (smallest) one (*m.*)

perder (ie)   to lose, miss

perfecto, -a (also *m. noun*)   perfect
> **pretérito perfecto**   present perfect

el **periódico**   newspaper
> **el periódico de hoy**   today's newspaper

permitir   to permit, allow, let

pero   but

la **persona**   person; *pl.* persons, people
personal   personal
personalmente   personally
pertenecer   to belong
el **Perú**   Peru
peruano, -a   Peruvian
el **peso**   peso (*monetary unit of several countries*)
el **pie**   foot
la **piedra**   stone
de piedra   (of) stone
la **pierna**   leg
la **pintura**   painting
el **piso**   floor, story
piso bajo   lower (first) floor
la **pizarra**   (chalk)board
el **placer**   pleasure
el **plan**   plan
Plata: el Río de la —,   La Plata River, River Plate
el **plato**   dish, plate, course (*at meals*)
plato fuerte   main course
la **playa**   beach
la **plaza**   square
la **pluma**   pen
el **plural**   plural
el **pluscuamperfecto**   pluperfect (*tense*)
la **población**   population; city, town
pobre   poor
poco, -a *adj., pron., and adv.*   little (*quantity*); *pl.* (a) few
al poco rato   after (in) a short time (while)
un poco   a little, a little while
un poco de   a little (of)
poder   to be able, can; may, might, could
puede ser que   it may be that
¿se puede entrar?   may I (one, we) come in?
poético, -a   poetic
político, -a   political
el **polvo**   dust
haber (mucho) polvo   to be (very) dusty
la **pólvora**   powder, gunpowder
poner   to put, place, put on (*records*); turn on (*television*); *reflex.* to put on (*clothes*); + *adj.* to become
popular   popular
por *prep.*   for, during, in, through, along, by, for the sake of, because of, on

behalf of, in exchange for, about, as (a), around; + *inf.* to be + *p.p.*
pasar por   to pass (go, come) by *or* along
por allí   around, (along) there
por aquí   around, (by) here, this way
por cierto   certainly
por completo   completely
por desgracia   unfortunately
¡por Dios!   heavens!
por ejemplo   for example
por eso   therefore, because of that, for that reason, that's why
por falta de *prep.*   for lack of
por favor   please (*at end of request*)
por fin   finally, at last
por la mañana (tarde, noche)   in the morning (afternoon, evening)
por lo general   in general, generally
por lo menos   at least
por lo tanto   therefore
por medio de *prep.*   by means of
por primera vez   for the first time
¿por qué?   why? for what reason?
por supuesto   of course, certainly
por teléfono   by (on the) telephone
por último   finally, ultimately
porque   because, for
el **portugués**   Portuguese (*language*)
posesivo, -a   possessive
posible   possible
la **posición**   position, place
el **postre**   dessert
postrer(o), -a   last
practicar   to practice
precedido, -a de   preceded by
preciso, -a   necessary
lo preciso   what is necessary
predominantemente   predominantly
preferir (ie, i)   to prefer
la **pregunta**   question
preguntar   to ask (*a question*)
preguntar por   to ask for (about), inquire about
pregúntaselo a ellos   ask them
se lo preguntaré   I shall ask them (him, her, you *formal*)
la **preparación** (*pl.* **preparaciones**) preparation

preparado -a   prepared, ready
preparar   to prepare
   preparar el terreno   to pave the way
la **preposición**   preposition
   preposicional   prepositional
la **presencia**   presence
   presentar   to present, give
   presente *adj.*   present
el **presente**   present, present tense
el **pretérito**   preterit (*tense*)
   pretérito anterior   preterit perfect
   pretérito perfecto   present perfect
la **prima**   cousin (*f.*)
la **primavera**   spring
   primer *used for* **primero** *before m. sing. nouns*
   primero *adv.*   first
   primero, -a   first
      la primera   the first one (*f.*)
      Lección primera   Lesson One
      Repaso primero   Review One
el **primo**   cousin
   principalmente   principally
el **principio**   principle, beginning
la **prisa**   haste
   darse prisa   to hurry
   tener (mucha) prisa   to be in a (big)
      hurry
la **probabilidad**   probability
   probable   probable
el **problema**   problem
   procedente *adj.*   originating, coming
la **procesión** (*pl.* **procesiones**)   procesión
   producir   to produce
el **producto**   product
   profesional   professional
el **profesor**   professor, teacher, instructor
   profesor de español   Spanish teacher
la **profesora**   teacher, instructor (*f.*)
   profesora (de francés)   (French)
      teacher (*f.*)
el **programa**   program
   programa de televisión   television
      program
   prometer   to promise
el **pronombre**   pronoun
   pronto   soon, quickly
      lo más pronto posible   the soonest
         possible, as soon as possible
la **pronunciación**   pronunciation
   pronunciar   to pronounce
   propiamente   properly; exactly

propio, -a   (one's) own
la **protesta**   protest
   próximo, -a   next
   publicar   to publish
el **pueblecito**   small town, village
el **pueblo**   town, village
el **puerco**   pig, hog
la **puerta**   door
   puertorriqueño, -a   Puerto Rican
   puesto *p.p. of* **poner**   put, placed
el **puesto**   position, job, employment;
      place
el **pulpo**   octopus
la **pulsera**   bracelet
   reloj de pulsera   wristwatch
el **punto**   point; place
   **en el punto a donde llegaban los
      conquistadores**   at the point (place)
      that the conquerors reached
   en punto   sharp (*time*)

Q

que   that, which, who, whom; as; than;
   since; *indir. command* have, let, may, *etc.*
   antes (de) que *conj.*   before
   de lo que   than (what)
   del (de la, de los, de las) que   than
   el (la, los, las) que   that, which, who,
      whom, he (she, those) who (*etc.*), the
      one(s) who (*etc.*)
   lo + *adj. or adv.* + **que**   how...
   lo interesante que es   how interesting
      it is
   lo que   what, that which, whatever
   no ... más que   only
   tener que + *inf.*   to have to, must
   todo lo que   all that, all that which
¿**qué?**   what? which?
   ¿**para qué?**   why? for what purpose?
   ¿**por qué?**   why? for what reason?
   ¿**qué tal?**   how are you? how goes it?
   ¡**qué** + *adj. or adv.!*   how...! what...!;
      + *noun!* what (a, an)...!
   ¡**qué libro más (tan) interesante!**
      what an interesting book!
el **quechua**   Quechua (*language of the
      Quechua Indians in Ecuador and Peru*)
   quedar(se)   to remain, stay; to be, be left

quejarse (de) to complain (of, about)
  quejarse uno de otro to complain of
    one another (each other)
querer to wish, want; to be willing;
    in pret. to try to
  (él) quiso llamarla (he) tried to call
    her
  no quieren (quedarse) (they) won't
    or are unwilling to (stay)
  (él) no quiso quedarse (he) wouldn't
    or refused to stay
  querer (a) to love, like, feel affection
    for
  ¿quieres (quiere Ud.) + *inf.?* will you
    (are you willing to) + *verb?*
  quisiera (I) should *or* would like
querido, -a dear
  querida mía my dear (*f.*)
Quevedo, (Francisco Gómez de)
  (1580-1645) *noted Spanish satirical*
    writer of prose and poetry
quien (*pl.* **quienes)** who, whom, he
    (those) who, the one(s) who
¿quién(es)? who? whom?
  ¿de quién es (la bicicleta)? whose
    (bicycle) is it?
quince fifteen
  quince días two weeks, fifteen days
quisiera (I) should *or* would like
quitar to take away (off), remove; *reflex.*
    to take off (*oneself*)
quizá(s) perhaps

R

radical stem *adj.*
el **radio** radio, radio set
la **radio** radio (*as a means of communication*)
la **raíz (** *pl.* **raíces)** root
Ramón Raymond
rápidamente rapidly, fast
  lo más rápidamente posible the
    fastest possible, as fast (rapidly) as
    possible
rápido, -a rapid, fast
el **rasgo** characteristic, trait
el **rato** while, short time (while)
  al poco rato after (in) a short time
    (while)

la **razón (** *pl.* **razones)** reason
  no tener razón to be wrong
  tener (mucha) razón to be (quite)
    right
la **realidad** reality
  en realidad in reality, in fact
recibir to receive, get
reciente recent
recomendar (ie) to recommend
recordar (ue) to recall, remember
reducirse a to be reduced to
redundante redundant
referirse (ie, i) to refer
  por lo que se refiere al verano
    referring to the summer
reflejar to reflect
reflexivo, -a reflexive
el **refresco** refreshment, cold (soft) drink
el **regalo** gift
la **región (** *pl.* **regiones)** region
regresar to return, come back
regular regular
reír (i, i) to laugh
relativo, -a relative
la **religión** religion
religioso, -a religious
el **reloj** watch, clock
  reloj de pulsera wristwatch
reñir (i, i) to scold
el **reparo** objection
repartir to deliver, distribute
el **repaso** review
  Repaso primero Review One
repetir (i, i) to repeat
el **reposo** rest
representar to represent
la **residencia** residence, residence hall
  residencia de estudiantes student
    residence hall (dormitory)
residir to reside, live
resolver (ue) to resolve, solve; *reflex.*
    to be resolved (solved)
respectivo, -a respective
restante *adj.* remaining
el **restaurante** restaurant
el **resumen (** *pl.* **resúmenes)** summary
la **reunión (** *pl.* **reuniones)** meeting
reunirse to gather, meet
la **revista** magazine, journal
ricamente richly
Ricardo Richard

rico, -a   rich, wealthy
el **río**   river
   Río de la Plata   La Plata River, River
      Plate
   Rita   Rita
   Roberto   Robert
   rogar (ue)   to ask, beg
   rojo, -a   red
   la roja   the red one (*f.*)
la **romería**   pilgrimage; excursion, picnic
   en romería   on a pilgrimage (picnic)
   romper   to break
la **rosa**   rose
   roto, -a *p.p. of* **romper** *and adj.*   broken
   él tiene el dedo roto   his finger is
      broken, he has a broken finger
   rubio, -a   blond(e)
   Ruiz   Ruiz (*family name*)
   los Ruiz   the Ruiz family
   los señores Ruiz   Mr. and Mrs. Ruiz

S

el **sábado**   (on) Saturday
   el sábado por la noche   Saturday
      night (evening)
   saber   to know (*a fact*), know how, can
      (*mental ability*); *in pret.* to learn,
      find out
   no lo sé   I don't know
   sacar   to take, take out
   sacar (fotos)   to take (photos)
   sacar la licencia   to get (obtain) the
      license
la **sala**   living room, classroom
   sala (de clase)   classroom
   salir (de + *obj.*)   to leave, go out (of)
   salir a   to come *or* go out on (to, into)
   salir de casa   to leave home
el **salón** (*pl.* **salones**)   salon, (large) hall,
      meeting room
   saludar   to greet, say hello to
El **Salvador**   El Salvador, The Savior
   san *used for* **santo** *before m. saint's name not
      beginning with* **Do-** *or* **To-**
   San Francisco   St. Francis
   San Pablo   St. Paul
   Santa Teresa   *see* **Teresa (de Jesús)**

   santo, -a   holy, saint, St(e).
el **santo**   saint
la **sardina**   sardine
   se *obj. pron. used for* **le** *or* **les** (to) him,
      her, it, them, you (*formal sing.*); *reflex.*
      pron. (to) himself, herself, *etc.; reciprocal*
      pron. (to) each other, one another;
      indef. subject one, people, they, you,
      etc. used with verb as substitute for the
      passive voice
la **secretaria**   secretary (*f.*)
la **sed**   thirst
   tener (mucha) sed   to be (very) thirsty
   sefarditas   *see* **el judío**
   seguida: en—,   at once, immediately
   seguido, -a de   followed by
   seguir (i, i)   to follow, continue;
      + *pres. part.* to continue, go (keep)
      on + *pres. part.*
   según *prep.*   according to
   segundo, -a   second
   el segundo   the second one (*m.*)
   seguro, -a   sure, certain
   estar seguro, -a de   to be sure of
   estar seguro, -a de que   to be sure that
   seis   six
   a las seis   at six o'clock
   para las seis   by six o'clock
la **semana**   week
   fin de semana   weekend
   la semana pasada   last week
   la semana que viene   next week
el **semestre**   semester
   sentado, -a   seated
   sentar (ie)   to seat; *reflex.* to sit down
   sentir (ie, i)   to feel, regret, be sorry
   ¡cuánto siento . . . !   how sorry I
      am . . . !
   sentir mucho   to be very sorry
   sentirse bien   to feel well
   señor   Mr.
   los señores (Ruiz)   Mr. and Mrs. (Ruiz)
el **señor**   gentleman
   señora   Mrs.
la **señora**   lady, woman
   señorita   Miss
la **señorita**   Miss, young lady (woman)
   septentrional *adj.*   northern
   ser   to be

cuando sea necesario   when it is (may be) necessary
es ella   it is she
pasar (venir) a ser   to become
puede ser que   it may be that
soy yo   it is I
ya sea   whether it is (may be)
la **servidumbre**   servitude
servir (i, i)   to serve
al servirse   upon being served
servirse de   to use, make use of
sesenta   sixty
si   if, whether
sí   yes; indeed
sí *reflex pron.*   himself, herself, *etc.* (*after prep.*)
entre sí   among themselves
siempre   always
siempre que *conj.*   provided that
la **sierra**   sierra, mountain range
la **siesta**   nap, siesta
dormir (ue, u) la siesta   to take a nap
siete   seven
a las siete y media   at 7:30, at half past seven
el **siglo**   century
el **significado**   meaning
siguiente *adj.*   following
los siguientes   the following ones (*m.*)
la **sílaba**   syllable
silencioso, -a   silent
la **silla**   chair
simbólico, -a   symbolic
simpático, -a   likeable, charming, nice
sin *prep.*   without
sin que-conj.*   without
el **singular**   singular
sino *conj.*   but
no sólo . . . sino (que)   not only . . . but
sino que *conj.*   but
la **situación**   situation
sobre   on, upon, on top of, over, about, concerning
sobre todo   above all, especially
social   social
la **sociedad**   society
el **sol**   sun
hace *or* **hay (mucho) sol**   it is (very) sunny, the sun is shining (brightly)
solamente   only
soler (ue)   to be accustomed to
solicitar   to solicit, apply for
la **solicitud**   application
solo, -a   sole, single, lone
ni uno solo   not (a single) one
sólo *adv.*   only
no sólo . . . sino (que)   not only . . . but
el **sombrero**   hat
sonar (ue)   to sound, ring
el **sonido**   sound
sorprendente   surprising
sorprender   to surprise
me (nos) sorprende   (it) surprises me (us), I'm (we're) surprised
sorprendido, -a   surprised
la **sorpresa**   surprise
su   his, her, your (*formal*), its, their
subjuntivo, -a   subjunctive
el **subjuntivo**   subjunctive (*mood*)
sublime   sublime, beautiful
substituir   to substitute
substitúyan(lo)   substitute (it)
substituyendo   substituting
el **sueño**   sleep
tener (mucho) sueño   to be (very) sleepy
la **suerte**   luck
¡qué suerte tienes!   how lucky (fortunate) you are!
tener (mucha) suerte   to be (very) lucky *or* fortunate
el **sujeto**   subject
superior *adj.*   superior
el **supermercado**   supermarket
suplir   to supply
supuesto: por—,   of course, certainly
el **sur**   south
la América del Sur   South America
el **suroeste**   southwest
sustantivo, -a (*also m. noun*)   substantive, noun
suyo, -a *adj.*   his, her, its, your (*formal sing., pl.*), their, of his (hers, its, yours (*formal sing., pl.*), theirs)
(el) suyo, (la) suya, (los) suyos, (las) suyas *pron.*   his, hers, its, yours (*formal sing. pl.*), theirs

T

tal   such (a)
   con tal (de) que *conj.*   provided that
   ¿qué tal?   how are you? how goes it?
   tal vez   perhaps
también   also, too
tampoco   neither, (not *or* nor) . . . either
tan   as, so; such (a *or* an)
   ¡es una obra tan excelente!   it is such
   an excellent work!
   ¡qué noche tan bonita!   what a
   beautiful night!
   tan + *adj. or adv.* + **como**   as (so) . . .
   as
tanto, -a (-os, -as) *adj. and pron.*   as (so)
   much (many); *adv.* as (so) much
   por lo tanto   therefore
   tanto . . . como   as (so) much . . . as, as
   (so) well as
   tanto como   as (so) much as
tardar   to delay
   tardar menos (tiempo)   to take less
   time
   tardar (mucho) en   to take (very) long
   to, be (very) long in, delay (long) in
tarde *adv.*   late
   lo más tarde posible   the latest
   possible, as late as possible
   llegar tarde   to arrive (be) late
la tarde   afternoon
   ayer (mañana) por la tarde   yesterday
   (tomorrow) afternoon
   buenas tardes   good afternoon
   por la tarde   in the afternoon
   todas las tardes   every afternoon
la tarjeta   card (*postal*)
   taurino: el encierro—,   driving of bulls
   into pen before fight
la taza   cup
   taza para café   coffee cup
   taza para té   teacup
te *obj. pron.*   you (*fam. sing.*), to you, (to)
   yourself
el té   tea
   taza para té   teacup
   teatral   theatrical
el teatro   theater
el teléfono   telephone

   llamar por teléfono   to telephone,
   call by (on the) telephone
la televisión   television
   programa de televisión   television
   program
el tema   theme, topic, subject
   temer   to fear
la temperatura   temperature
   temprano   early
tener   to have (*possess*), hold; *in pret.* to
   get, receive
   aquí tienes (tiene Ud.) el libro   here
   is the book
   ¿cuántos años tienes (tiene Ud.)?   how
   old are you?
   él tiene un dedo roto   his finger is
   broken, he has a broken finger
   no tener nada que hacer   not to have
   anything to do
   no tener razón   to be wrong
   ¡qué suerte tienes!   how lucky
   (fortunate) you are!
   ¿qué tiene (Luis)?   what's the matter
   with (Louis)?
   tener . . . años   to be . . . years old
   tener dolor de cabeza   to have a
   headache
   tener en cuenta   to bear in mind, take
   into account
   tener la culpa   to be at fault, be to
   blame
   tener lugar   to take place
   tener (mucha) hambre   to be (very)
   hungry
   tener (mucha) prisa   to be in a (big)
   hurry
   tener (mucha) razón   to be (quite)
   right
   tener (mucha) sed   to be (very) thirsty
   tener (mucha) suerte   to be (very)
   lucky *or* fortunate
   tener (mucha) vergüenza   to be (very
   much) ashamed
   tener (muchas) ganas de   to desire *or*
   wish (very much) to, be (very) eager
   to, feel (very much) like
   tener (mucho) calor   to be (very)
   warm
   tener (mucho) cuidado   to be (very)
   careful

tener (mucho) frío   to be (very) cold
tener (mucho) miedo (de)   to be (very much) afraid *or* frightened (of, to)
tener (mucho) sueño   to be (very) sleepy
tener muchos deseos de   to be very eager (wish very much) to
tener que + *inf.*   to have to, must + *inf.*
tener tiempo para   to have time to
el **tenis**   tennis
(cancha) de tenis   tennis (court)
la **teoría**   theory
tercer *used for* **tercero** *before m. sing. nouns*
tercero, -a   third
Teresa (de Jesús), Santa (1515-1582)
outstanding Spanish writer of the Mystic school
terminar   to end, finish
va terminando   (it) is gradually ending
el **terreno**   terrain, area
preparar el terreno   to pave the way
el **territorio**   territory
el **testimonio**   testimony
el **texto**   text
libro de texto   textbook
ti *pron.*   you (*fam. sing.*), yourself (*after prep.*)
la **tía**   aunt
el **tiempo**   time (*in general sense*); tense; weather
con el tiempo   in time
¿cuánto tiempo (hace)?   how long (much time) has it been?
hace buen (mal) tiempo   it is good *or* nice (bad) weather
llegar a tiempo   to arrive on time
¿qué tiempo hace?   what kind of weather is it? (what is the weather like)?
tardar menos (tiempo)   to take less time
tener tiempo para   to have time to
la **tienda**   store, shop
la **tierra**   land
el **timbre**   (door)bell
el **tío**   uncle; *pl.* uncles, uncle(s) and aunt(s)
típico, -a   typical
el **tipo**   type
el (los) **tocadiscos**   record player(s)
tocar   to touch, play (*music*)

todavía   still, yet
todavía no   not yet
todo, -a   all, every; *pl.* all, all of them, everybody, everyone; *neuter pron.* all, everything
sobre todo   above all, especially
toda la (lección)   all the (lesson), the whole *or* entire (lesson)
todas ellas   all of them (*f.*)
todas las tardes   every afternoon
todo el día   all day, the whole (entire) day
todo el mundo   everybody, the whole (entire) world
todo lo que   all that, all that which
todos los días   every day
tomar   to take, drink, eat
tomar el desayuno   to take (have, eat) breakfast
Tomás   Thomas
el **tono**   tone
el **toro**   bull
corrida de toros   bullfight
el **total**   total
trabajar   to work
trabajar mucho   to work hard
el **trabajo**   work
la **tradición** (*pl.* **tradiciones**)   tradition
la **traducción**   translation
traducir   to translate
traer   to bring
el **tráfico**   traffic
traído, -a *p.p. of* **traer** *and adj.*   brought
el **traje**   suit
transportar   to transport, carry
tratar   to treat
tratar de + *inf.*   to try to; + *obj.* to deal with, treat of (about)
tratarse de   to be a question of
el **tratado**   treaty
el **trato**   relations
treinta   thirty
tres   three
eran las tres   it was three o'clock
trescientos, -as   three hundred
triste   sad
lo tristes que están   how sad they are
tristemente   sadly
tu   your (*fam.*)
tú   you (*fam. sing.*)

turístico, -a   tourist *adj.*
tuyo, -a *adj.*   your (*fam. sing.*), of yours
(el) tuyo, (la) tuya, (los) tuyos, (las)
    tuyas, *pron.*   of yours (*fam. sing.*)
    lo tuyo   what is yours (*fam. sing.*)

U

u   or (*used for* **o** *before* **o-, ho-**)
Ud(s). = usted(es)   you (*formal*)
últimamente   ultimately; recently,
    lately
último, -a   last (*in a series*)
    el último   the last one (*m.*)
    este último   this last one (*m.*)
    la última   the last one (*f.*)
    por último   finally, ultimately
un, uno, -a   a, an, one
    es la una (y media)   it is (half past)
        one
    hasta (a) la una   until (at) one o'clock
    se gritaron el uno al otro   they
        shouted to each other (one another)
único, -a   only
unido, -a   united
    los Estados Unidos   United States
uniforme   uniform
unir   to join, unite; to add
universal   universal
la **universidad**   university
unos, -as   some, a few, any, several;
        about (*quantity*)
    unos guantes   some (a pair of) gloves
urgente   urgent
urgentemente   urgently
el **Uruguay**   Uruguay
usar   to use
el **uso**   use
usted   you (*formal sing.*); *pl. used also for
    fam. pl.*
la **uva**   grape

V

las **vacaciones**   vacation
    valer   to be worth
        más vale (vale más)   it is better
        valer más   to be better

vamos   we are going, let's go
    vamos a + *inf.*   we are going to, let's
        (let's go to)
variar   to vary
la **variedad**   variety
varios, -as   various, several
el **vaso**   glass
    vaso para agua   water glass
Vd(s). = usted(es)   you (*formal*)
Vega (Carpio), Lope (Félix) de (1563-1635)
    *renowned national Spanish dramatist
    and poet*
veinte   twenty
vencer   to overcome, conquer
vender   to sell
venir (a + *inf. or obj.*)   to come (to)
    (la semana) que viene   next (week)
    venir a ser   to become
la **venta**   roadside inn
la **ventana**   window
la **ventanilla**   ticket window
    ver   to see; *reflex.* to see oneself, be
        seen, be
    a ver   let's see
    nos vemos   we see (we'll see, we'll be
        seeing) each other *or* one another
veraniego, -a   summer (*adj.*)
el **verano**   summer
    el verano que viene   next summer
el **verbo**   verb
la **verdad**   truth
    es verdad   it is true
    ¿no es verdad? *or* **¿verdad?**   isn't it
        true? weren't they? *etc.*
la **vergüenza**   shame
    tener (mucha) vergüenza   to be (very
        much) ashamed
verificar   to verify
el **vestido**   dress
    vestir (i, i)   to dress (*someone*); *reflex.* to
        dress (*oneself*), get dressed
la **vez** (*pl.* **veces**)   time (*in a series*)
    a veces   at times
    alguna vez   ever, sometime, (at)
        anytime
    dos veces   two times, twice
    otra vez   again, another time
    por primera vez   for the first time
    tal vez   perhaps
viajar   to travel

el **viaje**   trip
   hacer el (un) viaje   to make *or* take
     the (a) trip
la **vida**   life
   de vida   (of) living
  viejo, -a   old
el **viento**   wind
   hacer (mucho) viento   to be (very)
     windy
el **viernes**   (on) Friday
  vigoroso, -a   vigorous
la **villa**   town (= a town enjoying certain
     privileges by charter)
el **vino**   wine
la **virgen** (*pl.* **vírgenes**)   virgin
    la Virgen del Carmen   Our Lady of
     Mount Carmel
  Virgen   Virgin Mary
el **virreinato**   viceroyalty
  visitar   to visit, call on
  visto *p.p. of* **ver**   seen
  vivir   to live
el **vocabulario**   vocabulary
la **vocal**   vowel
  volver (ue)   to return, come back
   volver a (llamar)   (to call) again
   vuelvo en seguida   I'll return at once
    (be right back)
  vosotros, -as   you (*fam. pl. subject pron.*);
    you, yourselves (*fam. pl.*) (*after prep.*)
la **voz** (*pl.* **voces**)   voice
   en voz alta   aloud
la **vuelta**   return
   dar una vuelta   to take a walk (stroll)
   estar de vuelta   to be back
  vuelto *p.p. of* **volver**   returned
  vuestro, -a *adj.*   your (*fam. pl.*), of yours
   (el) vuestro, (la) vuestra, (los) vuestros,
   (las) vuestras *pron.*   yours (*fam. pl.*)
  vulgar *adj.*   popular; vernacular

Y

y   and
ya   already, now; *sometimes not translated,*
  merely emphasizing the verb
yo   I
  yo no   not I

Z

el **zapato**   shoe
la **zona**   zone

English-Spanish

A

a, an un, una; *often not translated*
able: be—, poder
abound abundar
about *prep.* de, acerca de, sobre; *(quantity)* unos, -as
  be about to estar para
  for about two years desde hace unos dos años
accelerate acelerar
accept aceptar
accompanied by acompañado, -a de
accompany acompañar
according to *prep.* según
ache doler (ue)
  his head aches le duele a él la cabeza, él tiene dolor de cabeza
  my head aches me duele la cabeza, tengo dolor de cabeza
acquainted: be well—with conocer bien
advise aconsejar
afraid: be—(that) tener miedo (de que)
after *prep.* después de; *conj.* después (de) que
  day after tomorrow pasado mañana
afternoon la tarde
  good afternoon buenas tardes
  yesterday (tomorrow) afternoon ayer (mañana) por la tarde
again otra vez
Agnes Inés
  St. Agnes Santa Inés
ago: (a few minutes)—, hace (unos minutos)
airport el aeropuerto
  at the airport en el aeropuerto

all todo, -a; *pl.* todos, -as
  all day todo el día
allow dejar, permitir
almond la almendra
almost casi
along por
already ya
also también
although aunque
always siempre
A.M. de la mañana
America: Spanish—, Hispanoamérica
and y, *(before* i-, hi-, *but not* hie-) e
Ann Ana
another otro, -a
  (look at) one another (mirar)se
answer contestar
any *adj. and pron.* alguno, -a, *(before m. sing. nouns)* algún, *(after negative or comparative)* ninguno, -a (ningún); *often not translated*
  any woman (at all) cualquier mujer
anyone alguien, *(after negative or comparative)* nadie
  anyone (at all) cualquier(a)
  anyone of them cualquiera de ellos, -as
  anyone of us (at all) cualquiera de nosotros, -as
anything algo, alguna cosa, *(after negative)* nada
  not to have anything to do no tener nada que hacer
application la solicitud
appointment la cita
apply for solicitar
approach acercarse (**a** + *obj.*)
April abril
Argentina la Argentina
Argentine argentino, -a

264

arm el brazo
arrive llegar
  arrive at llegar a
  arrive home llegar a casa
  arrive on time llegar a tiempo
  how sorry I am to arrive late! ¡cuánto
    siento llegar tarde!
art el arte
article el artículo
artist el (la) artista
as tan, como
  as . . . as tan . . . como
  as if como si
  as (so) much as tanto como
ask (a question) preguntar; (request) pedir
    (i, i)
  ask for preguntar por, (request) pedir (i, i)
  ask (formal sing.) her (it) pregúnteselo
    Ud. (a ella)
  ask (fam. sing.) him (it) pregúntaselo
    (a él)
  we asked him se lo preguntamos (a él)
asleep: fall—, dormirse (ue, u)
at a; en
  at once en seguida
  at (the airport) en (el aeropuerto)
  at this moment en este momento
attend asistir a
attract atraer
August agosto
aunt la tía
author el autor
avenue la avenida
awaken (someone) despertar (ie)
away: go—, irse

___ B ___

back: be—, estar de vuelta
bad malo, -a, (before m. sing. nouns) mal
  it is too bad es lástima
  the bad thing lo malo
basketball el básquetbol
  basketball game partido de básquetbol
be estar, ser; encontrarse (ue), hallarse;
    (visible phenomena) haber; (weather) hacer
  be able poder
  be about to estar para

be afraid (that) tener miedo (de que)
be back estar de vuelta
be dusty haber polvo
be foggy haber niebla
be fond of ser aficionado, -a a
be found hallarse, encontrarse (ue)
be glad that alegrarse de que
be good (bad) weather hacer buen (mal)
  tiempo
be right tener razón
be sleepy tener sueño
be successful tener éxito
be thirsty tener sed
be to, be supposed to haber de + inf.
be (very) careful tener (mucho) cuidado
be (very) cold (living beings) tener
  (mucho) frío
be (very) cool (weather) hacer (mucho)
  fresco
be (very) hungry tener (mucha) hambre
be (very) lucky tener (mucha) suerte
be (very) windy hacer (mucho) viento
be warm (weather) hacer calor
be . . . years old tener . . . años
he is (él) lo es
her finger is broken (ella) tiene el dedo
  roto
here is (the letter) aquí tienes or tiene
  Ud. (la carta)
how fortunate our team is! ¡qué suerte
  tiene nuestro equipo!
how glad I am to see you (pl.)! ¡cuánto
  me alegro de verlos!
how old is (he)? ¿cuántos años tiene (él)?
it has been bad weather ha hecho mal
  tiempo
it is too bad es lástima
it is (very) sunny hace or hay (mucho) sol
it may be that puede (ser) que
it was two o'clock eran las dos
she is (ella) lo es
the moon was shining había luna
there have been ha habido
there is (are) hay
there was (were) había, hubo
what's the matter with (Louis)? ¿qué
  tiene (Luis)?
what time can it be? ¿qué hora será?
weren't they? ¿(no es) verdad?
beach la playa

at (on) the beach   en la playa
beautiful   bonito, -a, hermoso, -a, lindo, -a
  what a beautiful day!   ¡qué día más (tan)
    bonito (hermoso, lindo)!
  what beautiful hair she has!   ¡qué pelo
    tan (más) hermoso *or* bonito tiene (ella)!
because   porque
bed: go to —,   acostarse (ue)
beef   la carne de vaca
  ground beef   carne de vaca picada
before *adv.*   antes; *conj.* antes (de) que;
    prep. antes de
  at twenty minutes before nine   a las
    nueve menos veinte
beg   rogar (ue)
begin (to)   comenzar (ie) (a + *inf.*),
    empezar (ie) (a + *inf.*)
beginning with   a partir de
believe   creer
belong to   pertenecer a
belt   el cinturón (*pl.* cinturones)
best   mejor
  the best thing   lo mejor
better   mejor
  like better   gustarle más a uno
Betty   Isabel
between   entre
bicycle   la bicicleta
bill   la cuenta
black   negro, -a
  black pepper   la pimienta
blouse   la blusa
blue   azul
book   el libro
  (French) books   libros (de francés)
bookstore   la librería
  at the bookstore   en la librería
box (*postal*)   el apartado (postal)
boy   el chico, el muchacho
boyfriend   el novio
bracelet   la pulsera
brand   la marca
break   romper
  break one's arm   romperse el brazo
breakfast   el desayuno
  eat (have, take) breakfast   desayunarse,
    tomar el desayuno
bring   traer
broken   roto, -a
brother   el hermano
  little brother   el hermanito

building   el edificio
bus   el autobús (*pl.* autobuses)
  by bus   en autobús
busy   ocupado, -a
but   pero, sino
buy   comprar
by   por, de, para, en
  by (bus)   en (autobús)
  by working   trabajando

C

café   el café
call   llamar
  call by telephone   llamar por teléfono
camera   la cámara
can   poder, (*mental ability*) saber; *for
    conjecture use future tense*
Canada   el Canadá
car   el coche
card   la tarjeta
careful: be (very) —,   tener (mucho) cuidado
carefully   con cuidado
Caroline   Carolina
case   el caso
cash   cobrar
cattle   el ganado vacuno
center   el centro
century   el siglo
certain   cierto, -a, seguro, -a
  a certain   cierto, -a
chair   la silla
chalkboard   la pizarra
change   el cambio
Charles   Carlos
Charlotte   Carlota
charming   simpático, -a
chat   charlar
check   el cheque
cheese   el queso
chicken   el pollo
children   los niños, los hijos
chili   el chile
  chili sauce   salsa de chile
chocolate   el chocolate
choose   escoger
church   la iglesia
  to church   a la iglesia
city   la ciudad

class la clase
  after class después de (la) clase
  to class a clase
  Spanish class clase de español
classroom la sala de clase
clear (*weather*) despejado, -a
clearly claramente
  clearly and correctly clara y
    correctamente
clever listo, -a
clinic la clínica
close cerrar (ie)
closed cerrado, -a
cloud la nube
cloudy nublado, -a
coexistence la coexistencia
coffee el café
  coffee cup taza para café
cold *adj.* frío, -a; (*noun*) el frío
  be (very) cold (*weather*) hacer (mucho)
    frío; (*living beings*) tener (mucho) frío
  cold drink el refresco
Colombian (*also noun*) colombiano, -a
color el color
come venir
  come for venir por
  come in entrar (en + *obj.*); (*formal sing.
    command*) pase Ud.; (*pl. command*) pasen
    (entren) Uds.
comfortable cómodo, -a
complete completar
composition la composición (*pl.*
  composiciones)
concert el concierto
  at the concert en el concierto
contain contener
content(ed) contento, -a
continue continuar, seguir (i, i)
cool fresco, -a; *noun* el fresco
  be (very) cool (*weather*) hacer (mucho)
    fresco
corn el maíz
  corn cake tortilla de harina de maíz
correct correcto, -a
correctly correctamente
  clearly and correctly clara y
    correctamente
cost costar (ue)
could *imp., pret., or cond. tense of* poder
count contar (ue)
country el campo, (*nation*) el país

course el curso
court: tennis—, la cancha (de tenis)
courteous cortés
courtyard el patio
cousin el primo, la prima
crab el cangrejo
Cuban (*also noun*) cubano, -a
culture la cultura
cup la taza
  coffee cup taza para café
cut cortar, (*oneself*) cortarse
  you (*fam. sing.*) **have cut your foot!** ¡(tú)
    te has cortado el pie!

D

dance el baile
dare to atreverse a
date la fecha
daughter la hija
day el día
  all day todo el día
  day after tomorrow pasado mañana
  every day todos los días
  what a beautiful day! ¡qué día más *or*
    tan hermoso (bonito)!
deal: a great—, *adv.* mucho
dear querido, -a
  my dear Madam muy señora (señorita)
    mía
December diciembre
decide decidir
deliver entregar
describe describir
Diane Diana
different diferente, distinto, -a
difficult difícil
dish (*food*) el plato
do hacer; *not translated as an auxiliary*
  doesn't he? ¿(no es) verdad?
doctor el médico
dollar el dólar
door la puerta
dormitory la residencia de estudiantes
doubt la duda; dudar
  without any doubt (whatever) sin duda
    alguna
down: sit—, sentarse (ie)
downtown el centro

(be) downtown   (estar) en el centro
drive (go) downtown   conducir (ir)
  al centro
dress   el vestido; (*someone*) vestir (i, i);
  (*oneself*) vestirse (i, i)
dressed: get—,   vestirse (i, i)
drink: cold—,   el refresco
drive   conducir
drop by   pasar por
during   durante

E

each   cada
  (see) each other   (ver)se
  (they) used to make fun of each other
    se burlaban uno de otro
early   temprano
easily   fácilmente
easy   fácil
eat   comer
  eat breakfast   desayunarse, tomar
    el desayuno
  eat lunch   almorzar (ue)
  eat supper   cenar
eight   ocho
  (before) eight o'clock   (antes de) las ocho
  eight hundred   ochocientos, -as
  it is eight o'clock   son las ocho
eighteen   diez y ocho (dieciocho)
eighth   octavo, -a
eighty   ochenta
  eighty(-nine)   ochenta (y nueve)
either (*after negative*)   tampoco
  (not) . . . either . . . or   (no) . . . ni . . . ni
eleven   once
  it was eleven P.M.   eran las once de
    la noche
eliminate   eliminar
Elizabeth   Isabel
employee   el empleado
enchilada   la enchilada
engineer   el ingeniero
English   el inglés
  English course   curso de inglés
enough   bastante
enter   entrar (en + *obj.*)
environs   los alrededores
even though   aunque

evening   la noche
  this evening   esta noche
every   todo, -a
  every day (Sunday)   todos los días
    (domingos)
everybody   todo el mundo
examination   el examen (*pl.* exámenes)
excellent   excelente
excursion   la excursión (*pl.* excursiones)
  make *or* **take an (the) excursion**   hacer
    una (la) excursión
exercise   el ejercicio
exhibition   la exposición (*pl.* exposiciones)
exile   el exiliado
expect   esperar
explain   explicar
expression   la expresión (*pl.* expresiones)
extraordinary   extraordinario, -a

F

face   la cara
fail: (not) to—to   (no) dejar de + *inf.*
fall asleep   dormirse (ue, u)
famous   famoso, -a, distinguido, -a
fastest: the—possible   lo más rápidamente
  posible
father   el padre, el papá
favorite   favorito, -a
February   febrero
feel   sentir (ie, i)
  feel well   sentirse (ie, i) bien
few: (a)—,   unos, -as
fifteen   quince
fifth   quinto, -a
  Charles the Fifth   Carlos Quinto
fifty   cincuenta
fill with   rellenar de
film   la película
finally   por fin, por último
find   encontrar (ue), hallar
  be found   hallarse, encontrarse (ue)
  find out (*in pret.*)   saber
finger   el dedo
  her finger is broken   ella tiene el dedo
    roto
finish   terminar
first   primero, -a (*before m. sing. nouns*)
  primer; *adv.* primero

for the first time   por primera vez
  the first year   el primer año
fish   el pescado
  pickled fish   el escabeche
five   cinco
  at (until) five o'clock   a (hasta) las cinco
five hundred   quinientos, -as
floor   el piso
Florida   la Florida
flower   la flor
  what pretty flowers!   ¡qué flores más *or*
    tan hermosas (bonitas, lindas)!
foggy: be—,   haber niebla
follow   seguir (i, i)
fond: be—of   ser aficionado, -a a
food   la comida
foot   el pie
  you (*fam. sing.* **) have cut your foot!**   ¡(tú)
    te has cortado el pie!
football   el fútbol
  football (game)   (partido) de fútbol
for *prep.*   para, por
  for (six months)   desde hace (seis meses)
  for yourself (*formal* **)**   para sí
  we haven't seen her for a long time
    hace mucho tiempo que no la vemos
    (hemos visto)
foreign   extranjero, -a
forget   olvidar, olvidarse de (+ *obj.*)
  forget that   olvidarse de que,
    olvidar que
form   la forma
forty   cuarenta
  forty-seven   cuarenta y siete
found: be—   hallarse, encontrarse (ue)
four   cuatro
  four hundred   cuatrocientos, -as
  it is four P.M.   son las cuatro de la tarde
fourteen   catorce
French *adj.*   francés, -esa; (*language*)
    el francés
  French books   libros de francés
Friday: on—,   el viernes
fried   frito, -a
friend   el amigo, la amiga
from   de, desde
fruitful   fecundo, -a
fun: make—of   burlarse de
  (they) used to make fun of each other   se
    burlaban uno de otro
future   el futuro

G

game   el partido
  (football) game   partido (de fútbol)
garnished with   aderezado, -a de
general: in—,   en general, por lo general
gentleman   el señor
  gentlemen   muy señores (Sres.) míos
    (nuestros)
George   Jorge
get   obtener, conseguir (i, i)
  get dressed   vestirse (i, i)
  get the license   sacar la licencia
  get up   levantarse
  let's get up   vamos a levantarnos,
    levantémonos
  let's not get up   no nos levantemos
gift   el regalo
girl   la chica, la muchacha
girlfriend   la amiga, la novia
give   dar
glad: be (very)—to   alegrarse (mucho)
    de + *inf.*
  be glad that   alegrarse de que
  how glad I am to see you (*pl.* **)!**   ¡cuánto
    me alegro de verlos!
glass   el vaso
  water glass   vaso para agua
glove   el guante
go   ir (a + *inf.*)
  go away   irse
  go downtown   ir al centro
  go for   ir por
  go out into the street   salir a la calle
  go shopping   ir de compras
  go to bed   acostarse (ue)
  go to church   ir a la iglesia
  go to sleep   dormirse, (ue, u)
  let's not go (to the bookstore)   no
    vayamos (a la librería)
gold   el oro
  gold (watch)   (reloj) de oro
good   bueno, -a, (*before m. sing. nouns*) buen
  be good weather   hacer buen tiempo
  have a (very) good time   divertirse (ie, i)
    (mucho)
  the good thing   lo bueno
gradually   *use* ir + *pres. part.*
  (they) are gradually learning   van
    aprendiendo

graduate   graduarse
grandparents   los abuelos
great   gran (*before sing. nouns*); *pl.* grandes
  a great deal *adv.*   mucho
ground   picado, -a
  ground beef   carne de vaca picada
  ground pork   carne de cerdo picada
group   el grupo
guitar   la guitarra

H

hair   el pelo
  what beautiful hair she has!   ¡qué pelo
    tan (más) hermoso *or* bonito *or* lindo
    tiene (ella)!
half   medio, -a
  an hour and a half   una hora y media
  at half past (seven)   a las (siete) y media
  for a half hour   desde hace media hora
    or hace media hora que + *verb*
  it was half past (twelve)   eran las (doce)
    y media
hall   el salón (*pl.* salones)
  residence hall   la residencia de
    estudiantes
hand   la mano
  hand (over, in)   entregar
handsome   guapo, -a
hang   colgar (ue)
happen   pasar
happy   feliz (*pl.* felices), contento, -a
  how happy she is   lo contenta que está
    ella
  to be happy that   estar contento, -a de
    que
hard: work—,   trabajar mucho
hat   el sombrero
Havana   La Habana
have   tener; (*aux.*) haber
  have (*someone do something* *or* *have something*
    *done***)**   hacer *or* mandar + *inf.*
  have (*indir. command***)**   que + *pres. subj.*
  have a headache   tener dolor de cabeza
  have a (very) good time   divertirse (ie, i)
    (mucho)
  have just   acabar de + *inf.*
  have lunch   almorzar (ue)

have time to   tener tiempo para
have to   tener que + *inf.*
  not to have anything to do   no tener
    nada que hacer
he   él
head   la cabeza
  does your (*formal sing.***) head ache?**   ¿le
    duele a Ud. la cabeza? ¿tiene Ud. dolor
    de cabeza?
  my (his) head aches   me (le) duele la
    cabeza, tengo (él tiene) dolor de cabeza
headache: have a—,   tener dolor de cabeza
hear   oír
heavens!   ¡por Dios!
Helen   Elena
help   ayudar (a + *inf.*)
Henry   Enrique
her *adj.*   su(s); su(s) *or* el (la, los, las) . . .
    de ella
her *dir. obj.*   la; *indir. obj.* le, se; *after*
    prep. ella
  with her(self)   consigo
here   aquí
  here is (the letter)   aquí tienes *or* tiene
    Ud. (la carta)
  by here   por aquí
hers *pron.*   (el) suyo, (la) suya, (los) suyos,
    (las) suyas *or* (el, la, los, las) de ella
him *dir. obj.*   le, lo; *indir. obj.* le, se; *after*
    prep. él
his *adj.*   su(s); su(s) *or* el (la, los, las) . . . de
    él; *pron.* (el) suyo, (la) suya, (los) suyos,
    (las) suyas *or* (el, la, los, las) de él
  of his   suyo(s), -a(s), de él
Hispanic   hispano, -a
home   la casa
  (go) home   (ir) a casa
  leave home   salir de casa
hope   esperar
  I hope so!   ¡ojalá!
hot *adj.*   caliente
hour   la hora
  a half hour   media hora
  an hour and a half   una hora y media
house   la casa
  stone house   casa de piedra
  to Martha's house   a casa de Marta
how?   ¿cómo?
  how much (many)?   ¿cuánto, -a (-os, -as)?

how + *adj. or adv.!* ¡qué . . . ! ¡lo . . . que!
 how + *verb!* ¡cuánto . . . !
 how sick she is! ¡lo enferma que está (ella)!
hundred: a (one)—, cien(to)
 five hundred quinientos, -as
 four (eight, nine, seven, two) hundred cuatro- (ocho-, nove-, sete-, dos-) cientos, -as
 one hundred (sixteen) ciento (diez y seis, dieciséis)
hungry: be (very)—, tener (mucha) hambre
hurry (up) darse prisa
hurt doler (ue)
 does your (*fam. sing.*) leg hurt? ¿te duele la pierna?
 her throat hurts le duele a ella la garganta
husk: corn—, hoja de la mazorca del maíz

I

I yo
if si
ill enfermo, -a
immediately en seguida
immigrant el inmigrante
immigration la inmigración
important importante
 the important thing lo importante
impossible imposible
in en, de, a, por; (*after a superlative*) de
 in order to *prep.* para
increase el aumento; aumentar
Inez Inés
ingredient el ingrediente
inhabitant el habitante
insist that insistir en que
intend to pensar (ie) + *inf.*
interest el interés
interesting interesante
invitation la invitación (*pl.* invitaciones)
invite invitar (a + *inf.*)
Isabel Isabel
it *dir. obj.* lo (*m. and neuter*), la (*f.*); *indir. obj.* le; (*usually omitted as subject*) él (*m.*), ella (*f.*); *after prep.* él (*m.*), ella (*f.*)

J

James Jaime
Jane Juanita
January enero
job el puesto; el trabajo
Joe Pepe
John Juan
Johnny Juanito
Joseph José
June junio
just: have—, acabar de + *inf.*

K

kind la especie, la clase
know (*facts*) saber, (*be acquainted with*) conocer
 I don't know no lo sé
 know how to saber + *inf.*

L

lady: young—, la joven, la señorita
land la tierra
large grande
 a large one (*f.*) una grande
 the largest one (*f.*) la más grande
last pasado, -a, (*in a series*) último, -a
 last night anoche
 last (year) (el año) pasado
late tarde
latter: the—, éste, ésta (-os, -as)
Laura Laura
lawyer el abogado
learn aprender (a + *inf.*)
 (they) are gradually learning van aprendiendo
leave salir (de + *obj.*), partir (de + *obj.*); *trans.* dejar
 leave for salir (partir) para
 leave home salir de casa
lecture la conferencia
leg la pierna
 does your (*fam. sing.*) leg hurt? ¿te duele la pierna?

less   menos

lesson   la lección (*pl.* lecciones)

let   dejar, permitir; *indir. command* que +
pres. subj.

  let (*formal sing.***) me** + *verb*   déjeme Ud.
  or permítame Ud. + *inf.*

  let's (let us) + *verb*   vamos a + *inf.* or
  first pl. pres. subj.

  let's not + *verb*   no + *first pl. pres. subj.*

letter   la carta

library   la biblioteca

  at the library   en la biblioteca

license   la licencia

  get the license   sacar la licencia

like   gustarle a uno, (*person*) querer (a)

  I should (would) like   (yo) quisiera, me
  gustaría

  like better   gustarle a uno más

  Louise would like to go   le gustaría a
  Luisa ir, a Luisa le gustaría ir

  she would like   le gustaría a ella

  we should (would) like   quisiéramos,
  nos gustaría

listen to   escuchar

little (*quantity***)**   poco, -a

  little brother   el hermanito

  little sister   la hermanita

live   vivir, residir

Lola   Lola

long   largo, -a

  for a long time   hace tiempo

  how long have you (*pl.***) been in . . . ?**
  ¿cuánto tiempo hace que Uds. están
  en . . . ?

  how long have you (*fam. sing.***) been
  playing?**   ¿cuánto tiempo hace que
  juegas?

longer: wait—,   esperar más

look at   mirar

  look at one another   mirarse

look for   buscar

Los Angeles   Los Ángeles

lose   perder (ie)

lot: a—, *adv.*   mucho

  a lot of *adj.*   mucho, -a, -os, -as

Louis   Luis

Louise   Luisa

love   querer

  love each other   quererse

lucky: be (very)—,   tener (mucha) suerte

lunch   el almuerzo

  for lunch   para el almuerzo

  have (eat, take) lunch   almorzar (ue)

M

Madam   señora, señorita

  (my) dear Madam   muy señora (señorita)
  mía

made *p.p. and adj.*   hecho, -a

magazine   la revista

magnificent   magnífico, -a

make   la marca; hacer

  (he) was making (*progressive***)**   (él) estaba
  haciendo

  make a trip   hacer un viaje (una
  excursión)

  make the excursion   hacer la excursión

man   el hombre

  that young man   ese (aquel) joven

  the young men   los jóvenes

many   muchos, -as

  how many?   ¿cuántos, -as?

  so many *adj.*   tantos, -as

map   el mapa

March   marzo

Margaret   Margarita

maritime   marítimo, -a

Martha   Marta

Mary   María

  St. Mary   Santa María

maternal   materno, -a

matter: that—of   lo de

  what's the matter with (him)?   ¿qué tiene
  (él)?

may *indir. command (wish)*   que + *pres. subj.*;
sign of pres. subj.; poder

  (he) may have to (wait)   es posible que
  (él) tenga que esperar

  it may be that   puede (ser) que

  may you (*pl.***) have a good time!**   ¡que se
  diviertan Uds.!

  you (*pl.***) may sit down**   Uds. pueden
  sentarse

May   mayo

me *dir. and indir. obj.*   me; *after prep.* mí

  with me   conmigo

meal   la comida
meat   la carne
meet   encontrar (ue), (*gather*) reunirse,
   (*be introduced to*) conocer
  (I'm) pleased to meet you (*formal m. sing.*)
   mucho gusto en conocerlo
meeting   la reunión (*pl.* reuniones)
  at the meeting   en la reunión
metropolis   la metrópoli
Mexican (*also noun*)   mexicano, -a
Mexico   México
  Mexico City   México, D.F.
Michael   Miguel
might   *sign of the imp. subj. tense*
million   el millón (*pl.* millones)
  a (one) million   un millón (de)
  five million   cinco millones (de)
mine *pron.*   (el) mío, (la) mía, (los) míos,
  (las) mías
minute   el minuto
  it is ten minutes to (two)   son las (dos)
   menos diez, faltan diez minutos para las
   (dos)
miss   perder (ie)
Miss   (la) señorita, (la) Srta.
modern   moderno, -a
moment   el momento
  at this moment   en este momento
Monday   el lunes
  on Monday   el lunes
money   el dinero
month   el mes
moon   la luna
  the moon was shining   había luna
more   más
morning   la mañana
  it is two o'clock in the morning   son las
   dos de la mañana
  until one o'clock in the morning   hasta
   la una de la mañana
  yesterday (tomorrow) morning   ayer
   (mañana) por la mañana
most   más
  most (of)   la mayor parte de, la mayoría de
mother   la madre, la mamá
mountains   las montañas
movie   el cine
Mr.   (el) señor, (el) Sr.
  Mr. and Mrs. (Ruiz)   los señores (Ruiz)
Mrs.   (la) señora, (la) Sra.

much *adj.*   mucho, -a; *adv.* mucho
  as (so) much   tanto, -a
  as (so) much as   tanto como
  too much *adv.*   demasiado
  very much *adv.*   mucho, muchísimo
music   la música
must   deber, haber de + *inf.*, tener que +
  inf.; for probability use future, cond., future
  perf. or cond. perf. tense or deber de + *inf.*
  one must (remember)   hay que
  (recordar), es necesario *or* preciso
  (recordar)
my   mi(s)

N

name: be named   llamarse
  what is (his) name?   ¿cómo se llama (él)?
nap   la siesta
  take a nap   dormir (ue, u) la siesta
near *prep.*   cerca de
necessary   necesario, -a, preciso, -a
  be necessary to   haber que (ser necesario
  or preciso) + *inf.*
need   necesitar
never   nunca, jamás
new   nuevo, -a
  New York   Nueva York
news   las noticias
  news item(s)   la(s) noticia(s)
newspaper   el periódico
next   próximo, -a
  next (week)   la (semana) que viene
night   la noche
  last night   anoche
nine   nueve
  it is nine A.M.   son las nueve de la mañana
  it must be nine o'clock   serán las nueve
  nine hundred   novecientos, -as
ninety   noventa
  ninety-two   noventa y dos
no, not *adv.*   no; *adj.* ninguno, -a, (*before m.*
  sing. nouns) ningún; *often not translated*
none   ninguno, -a
notably   notablemente
notebook   el cuaderno
nothing   nada

to have nothing to do   no tener nada que
  hacer
November   noviembre
now   ahora
number   el número

O

obstacle   el obstáculo
obtain   obtener, conseguir (i, i)
occur   ocurrir
o'clock: at (five)—,   a las (cinco)
  before eight o'clock   antes de las ocho
  by seven o'clock   para las siete
  it was two o'clock   eran las dos
  two-o'clock plane   el avión de las dos
October   octubre
of   de
off: take—(*clothes*)   quitarse
office   la oficina
often   a menudo
old   viejo, -a
  be ... years old   tener ... años
  how old is (he)?   ¿cuántos años tiene (él)?
older   mayor
olive oil   el aceite
on   en, sobre
  put on (*clothes***)**   ponerse
once: at—,   en seguida
one   un, uno, una; *indef. subject* se, uno
  a large one (*f.*)   una grande
  (look at) one another   (mirar)se
  the one in (of, with)   el (la) de
  the ones who   los (las) que
  the white one (*m.***)**   el blanco
  until one o'clock in the morning   hasta
    la una de la mañana
  which one(s)?   ¿cuál(es)?
onion   la cebolla
only   solamente, no ... más que
open   abrir
or   o, (*before* o-, ho-) u
  (not) ... either ... or   (no) ... ni ... ni
order: in—that *conj.*   para que, a fin de que
  in order to *prep.*   para
origin   el origen (*pl.* orígenes)
other   otro, -a
  (see) each other   (ver)se
  (they) used to make fun of each other
    se burlaban uno de otro

ought: you (*fam. sing.*)—**to**   (tú) debieras *or*
  debes + *inf.*
our   nuestro, -a
ours *pron.*   (el) nuestro, (la) nuestra,
    (los) nuestros, (las) nuestras
out: go—into the street   salir a la calle

P

package   el paquete
paella   la paella
page   la página
painting   la pintura, el cuadro
paper   el papel
parents   los padres
park   el parque
part: our—,   lo nuestro
participate   participar
party   la fiesta
  at the party   en la fiesta
pass by   pasar por
past: half—(twelve)   (las doce) y media
patio   el patio
Paul   Pablo
  St. Paul   San Pablo
pay (for)   pagar
pen   la pluma
pencil   el lápiz (*pl.* lápices)
people   la gente; *indef. subject* se, uno
  young people   los jóvenes
pepper   el chile
  black pepper   la pimienta
perhaps   tal vez, quizá(s), acaso
permit   permitir, dejar
person   la persona
Peru   el Perú
Peruvian   peruano, -a
Philip   Felipe
photo   la foto
photograph   la fotografía
pickled fish   el escabeche
picture   el cuadro
pie: small (meat)—,   la empanada
pity   la lástima
  what a pity!   ¡qué lástima!
place   el lugar; poner
plan   el plan; pensar (ie) + *inf.*
plane   el avión (*pl.* aviones)
  by plane   en avión
  two-o'clock plane   el avión de las dos

play (*game*)   jugar (ue) (a + *obj.*); (*music*)
 tocar
  play (tennis)   jugar al tenis
player   el jugador
pleasant   agradable
please (*after request*)   por favor
  please + *verb* (*formal command*)   hága(n)me
 Ud(s). el favor de + *inf.*; (*fam. sing.*
 command) hazme (tú) el favor de
 + *inf.*
pleased: (I'm)—to meet you (*formal m.*
 sing.)   mucho gusto en conocerlo
pleasure   el placer
P.M.   de la tarde (noche)
  at (three) P.M.   a las (tres) de la tarde
  before six P.M.   antes de las seis de la tarde
  it was three P.M.   eran las tres de la tarde
  it was (ten) P.M.   eran las (diez) de la noche
popular   popular
pork   la carne de cerdo (puerco)
  ground pork   la carne de cerdo (puerco)
 picada
Portuguese (*language*)   el portugués
position   el puesto
possible   posible
  as rapidly as possible   lo más rápidamente
 posible, tan rápidamente como posible
  as soon as (the soonest) possible   lo más
 pronto posible, tan pronto como posible
  (the fastest) possible   (lo más rápidamente)
 posible
poster   el cartel
practice   practicar
prefer   preferir (ie, i)
prepare   preparar
prepared   preparado, -a
present   presentar
present *adj.*   actual
pretty   bonito, -a, hermoso, -a, lindo, -a
probably   *use future, cond., future perf. or cond.*
 perf. tense
problem   el problema
produce   producir
professor   el profesor, la profesora
program   el programa
  television program   el programa de
 televisión
promise   prometer
provided that *conj.*   con tal (de) que
Puerto Rican (*also noun*)   puertorriqueño, -a
purchase   la compra

purse   la cartera
put   poner
  put on (*clothes*)   ponerse

Q

quarter   el cuarto
  at a quarter to nine   a las nueve menos
 cuarto
  it is (at) a quarter after (one)   es (a) la
 (una) y cuarto
question   la pregunta
quickly   pronto

R

radio (*set*)   el radio, (*communication*) la radio
  radio program   el programa de radio
rain   llover (ue)
raise   levantar
raisin   la pasa
rapidly   rápidamente
  as rapidly as possible   lo más rápidamente
 posible, tan rápidamente como posible
Raymond   Ramón
read   leer
ready   listo, -a
receive   recibir
recent   reciente
recommend   recomendar (ie)
record (*phonograph*)   el disco
red   rojo, -a
  the red one (*f.*)   la roja
refreshment   el refresco
refused: (he)—to (go)   (él) no quiso (ir)
region   la región (*pl.* regiones)
remember   recordar (ue)
repeat   repetir (i, i)
reply   contestar
reside   residir, vivir
residence hall   la residencia de estudiantes
rest   descansar
restaurant   el restaurante
return (*come back*)   volver (ue), regresar,
 (*give back*) devolver (ue)
  return home   volver (regresar) a casa
rice   el arroz
rich   rico, -a
Richard   Ricardo

right   derecho, -a
  be right   tener razón
  to the right   a la derecha
Rita   Rita
road   la carretera, el camino
roast(ed)   asado, -a
Robert   Roberto
rolled corn cake   tortilla de harina de maíz
    enrollada
room   el cuarto
roommate   el compañero de cuarto (*m.*)
rose   la rosa
run   correr
  run along   correr por

S

salad   la ensalada
salon   el salón (*pl.* salones)
same   mismo, -a
Saturday   el sábado
  on Saturday   el sábado
sauce   la salsa
say   decir
  say yes   decir que sí
scholarship   la beca
school   la escuela
  to school   a la escuela
seasoning   el condimento
seated   sentado, -a
second   segundo, -a
  Philip the Second   Felipe Segundo
see   ver
  we shall see each other   nos veremos
seek   buscar
seem   parecer
  (they) don't seem so   no lo parecen
sell   vender
semester   el semestre
send   enviar, mandar
  send for   enviar (mandar) por
sentence   la frase, la oración (*pl.* oraciones)
September   septiembre
serious   grave
serve   servir (i, i)
settle   establecerse
seven   siete
  at (half past) seven o'clock   a las siete
    (y media)

by seven o'clock   para las siete
seven hundred   setecientos, -as
seventeen   diez y siete, diecisiete
seventy   setenta
  seventy-(nine)   setenta (y nueve)
several   varios, -as, unos, -as
shall   *sign of the future tense; occasionally*
    translated by the present tense
  shall I buy . . . ?   ¿compro . . . ?
  shall we watch . . . ?   ¿miramos . . . ?
sharp   en punto
she   ella
  she is   (ella) lo es
shellfish   los mariscos
shining: the moon was—,   había luna
shirt   la camisa
shoe   el zapato
shopping: go—,   ir de compras
short   corto, -a
should   *sign of cond. ind. and imp. subj. tenses;*
    deber
  I should like   (yo) quisiera, me gustaría
  we should like   nos gustaría, quisiéramos
  you (*fam. sing.* **) should**   tú debieras
sick   enfermo, -a
  how sick she is!   ¡lo enferma que está
    (ella)!
since   como, (*time*) desde
  it is two days since my father returned
    hace dos días que mi padre volvió
    (regresó) *or* mi padre . . . hace dos días
sing   cantar
sir   señor
  Dear Sir   muy señor (Sr.) mío (nuestro);
    also see Cartas españolas, *pages 187–188*
sister   la hermana
  little sister   la hermanita
sit down   sentarse (ie)
  let's not sit down   no nos sentemos
  let's sit down   vamos a sentarnos,
    sentémonos
  shall we sit down?   ¿nos sentamos?
  sit down (*formal sing. command* **)**   siéntese
    Ud.
six   seis
  at (until) six o'clock   a (hasta) las seis
  at six A.M.   a las seis de la mañana
sixteen   diez y seis, dieciséis
sixty   sesenta
  sixty-five   sesenta y cinco
sky   el cielo

sleep   dormir (ue, u)
  go to sleep   dormirse (ue, u)
sleepy: be—,   tener sueño
slowly   despacio
small   pequeño, -a
  small (meat) pie   la empanada
  small town   el pueblecito
snow   la nieve
so   tan
  so (as) much as   tanto como
  so many   tantos, -as
  so much   tanto, -a
  so that *conj.*   de manera (modo) que
  (they) don't seem so   no lo parecen
social   social
some *adj. and pron.*   alguno, -a, (*before m. sing.*
  nouns) algún; *pl.* algunos, -as unos, -as;
  often not translated
someone   alguien
something   algo, alguna cosa
song   la canción (*pl.* canciones)
soon   pronto
  as soon as possible (the soonest possible)
  lo más pronto posible, tan pronto como
  posible
sorry: be—,   sentir (ie, i)
  how sorry I am (to arrive late)!   ¡cuánto
  siento (llegar tarde)!
southwest   el suroeste
Spain   España
Spanish *adj.*   español, -ola; (*language*)
  el español
  Spanish America   Hispanoamérica
  Spanish (class)   (clase) de español
  Spanish teacher   profesor (profesora) de
  español
Spanish-American   hispanoamericano, -a
speak   hablar
special   especial
spend (*time*)   pasar
sport   el deporte
square   la plaza
St.   san, santo, -a
  St. Agnes   Santa Inés
  St. Mary   Santa María
  St. Paul   San Pablo
  St. Thomas   Santo Tomás
stadium   el estadio
start (to)   comenzar (ie) (a + *inf.*), empezar
  (ie) (a + *inf.*)
state   el estado

United States   los Estados Unidos
stay   quedarse
  let's not stay   no nos quedemos
  let's stay   vamos a quedarnos,
  quedémonos
steep   macerar
still   todavía
stone   la piedra
  stone house   casa de piedra
stop + *pres. part.*   dejar de + *inf.*
store   la tienda
story   el cuento
strange   extraño, -a
street   la calle
  go out into the street   salir a la calle
strike (*clock*)   dar
  strike eight (o'clock)   dar las ocho
student   el (la) estudiante, el alumno,
  la alumna
stuffed   relleno, -a
successful: be—,   tener éxito
such (a, an)   tal
  such an interesting work   una obra tan
  interesante
  such as (*pl.*)   tales como
suit   el traje
suitcase   la maleta
summer   el verano
  next summer   el verano que viene
Sunday   el domingo
  every Sunday   todos los domingos
  on Sunday(s)   el (los) domingo(s)
sunny: it is (very)—,   hace *or* hay (mucho)
  sol
supper: eat—,   cenar
suppose   *for conjecture use future, cond., future*
  perf., or cond. perf. tense
supposed: be—to   haber de + *inf.*
sure   seguro, -a
  be sure that   estar seguro, -a de que
surprise   la sorpresa
  I am (we are) surprised that   me (nos)
  sorprende que
  what a surprise!   ¡qué sorpresa!

T

table   la mesa
taco   el taco

take   tomar, (*carry*) llevar, (*photos*) sacar
  did you (*formal sing.***) take her
    temperature?**   ¿le tomó Ud. a ella la
    temperatura?
  he is going to (will) take your (*fam. sing.***)
    temperature**   (él) va a tomarte la tem-
    peratura
  take a nap   dormir (ue, u) la siesta
  take a walk   dar un paseo (una vuelta)
  take breakfast   desayunarse, tomar el
    desayuno
  take lunch   almorzar (ue)
  take off (from) (*oneself***)**   quitarse
  take the (a) trip   hacer el (un) viaje *or* la
    (una) excursión
talk   hablar
  talk on the telephone   hablar por teléfono
tall   alto, -a
  very tall   muy alto, -a, altísimo, -a
tamale   el tamal
tape   la cinta
tea   el té
teacher   el profesor, la profesora
  Spanish teacher   profesor (profesora) de
    español
team   el equipo
  (tennis) team   equipo (de tenis)
telephone   el teléfono
  call by (on the) telephone   llamar por
    teléfono
  talk on the telephone   hablar por teléfono
television   la televisión
  shall we watch television?   ¿miramos la
    televisión?
  television program   el programa de
    televisión
  turn on the television   poner la televisión
tell   decir
  I didn't tell her   no se lo dije a ella
  I shall tell them (it)   se lo diré (a ellos)
temperature   la temperatura
  did you (*formal sing.***) take her temperature?**
    ¿le tomó Ud. a ella la temperatura?
  he is going to (will) take your (*fam. sing.***)
    temperature**   (él) va a tomarte la
    temperatura
ten   diez
  it is ten A.M.   son las diez de la mañana
  it was ten P.M.   eran las diez de la noche
tennis   el tenis
  play tennis   jugar (ue) al tenis
  tennis court   cancha (de tenis)

tenth   décimo, -a
than   que, (*before a numeral*) de, (*before a
    clause*) del (de la, de los, de las) que, de
    lo que
thank   dar las gracias a
that *adj.* (*near person addressed*) ese, esa (-os,
    as); (*distant*) aquel, aquella (-os, -as);
    pron.
  that (one)   ése, ésa (-os, -as), aquél,
    aquélla (-os, -as); (*neuter*) eso, aquello;
    relative pron. que
the   el, la, los, las; (*neuter article*) lo
  the (good thing)   lo (bueno)
theater   el teatro
theirs *pron.*   (el) suyo, (la) suya, (los) suyos,
    (las) suyas *or* (el, la, los, las) de ellos, -as
  of theirs *adj.*   suyo(s), -a(s), de ellos, -as
them *dir. obj.*   los, las; *indir. obj.* les, se; *after
    prep.* ellos, -as
then   luego
there   allí, allá (*often after verbs of motion*)
therefore   por eso, por lo tanto
these *adj.*   estos, -as; *pron.* éstos, -as
they   ellos, -as
thing   la cosa
  the (good) thing   lo (bueno)
think   pensar (ie), creer
  what do you (*fam. sing.***) think of (the plan)?**
    ¿qué te parece (el plan)?
third   tercero, -a, (*before m. sing. nouns*) tercer
thirsty: be —,   tener sed
thirty   treinta
  thirty-five   treinta y cinco
this *adj.*   este, esta; *pron.* **this (one)** éste, ésta
Thomas   Tomás
  St. Thomas   Santo Tomás
those *adj.* (*near person addressed*) esos, -as,
    (*distant*) aquellos, -as; *pron.* ésos, -as,
    aquéllos, -as
  those which   los (las) que
thousand: a (one) —,   mil
three   tres
  at three P.M.   a las tres de la tarde
  it was three P.M.   eran las tres de
    la tarde
  three hundred   trescientos, -s
throat   la garganta
through   por
ticket   el boleto (*Am.*), el billete
time   (*in a general sense*) el tiempo; (*of day*)
    la hora; (*series*) la vez (*pl.* veces)
  arrive on time   llegar a tiempo

at times a veces
at what time? ¿a qué hora?
for a long time hace tiempo
for the first time por primera vez
have a (very) good time divertirse (ie, i) (mucho)
have time to tener tiempo para
may you (*pl.***) have a good time!** ¡que se diviertan Uds.!
what time can it be? ¿qué hora será?
what time was it? ¿qué hora era?
tired cansado, -a
  be tired of (watching) estar cansado, -a de (mirar)
to a, de, para, que
  at twenty minutes to nine a las nueve menos veinte
  it is ten minutes to two son las dos menos diez, faltan diez minutos para las dos
today hoy, hoy día
tomorrow mañana
  day after tomorrow pasado mañana
  tomorrow morning (afternoon) mañana por la mañana (tarde)
tongue la lengua
tonight esta noche
too también
  it is too bad es lástima
  too much *adv.* demasiado
topcoat el abrigo
tostada la tostada
toward *prep.* hacia
town el pueblo
  small town el pueblecito
traffic el tráfico
travel viajar
  travel in (through) viajar por
trip el viaje, la excursión (*pl.* excursiones)
  make *or* **take the (a) trip** hacer el (un) viaje *or* la (una) excursión
true: be—, ser verdad
truth la verdad
try to tratar de + *inf.*; (*in pret.*) querer + *inf.*
Tuesday el martes
turn in entregar
turn on (*television*) poner
twelve doce
  it was half past twelve eran las doce y media
twenty veinte
  twenty-nine veinte y nueve, veintinueve

twenty-one veinte y un(o), -a (veintiún, veintiuno, veintiuna)
twenty-two veinte y dos, veintidós
two dos
  at (two) P.M. a las (dos) de la tarde
  it is a quarter after two son las dos y cuarto
  it is ten minutes to two son las dos menos diez, faltan diez minutos para las dos
  two hundred doscientos, -as
  two-o'clock plane el avión de las dos
type el tipo
typical típico, -a

U

umbrella el paraguas
uncle el tío
understand comprender, entender (ie)
united unido, -a
  United States los Estados Unidos
university la universidad
  at the university en la universidad
  university bus autobús de la universidad
unless a menos que
until *prep.* hasta; *conj.* hasta que
up: get—, levantarse
  hurry up darse prisa
  wake up (*oneself*) despertarse (ie)
upon + *pres. part.* al + *inf.*
Uruguay el Uruguay
us *dir. and indir. obj.* nos; *after prep.* nosotros, -as
use emplear, usar
used to *sign of imp. ind. tense*

V

vacation las vacaciones
verb el verbo
very *adv.* muy; *adj.* mucho, -a
  very much *adv.* mucho, muchísimo
vinegar el vinagre
visit visitar

W

wait   esperar
  wait longer   esperar más
wake up (*oneself*)   despertarse (ie)
walk   el paseo, la vuelta; andar
  (he) was walking (*progressive*)   (él) iba andando
  take a walk   dar un paseo (una vuelta)
wall   la pared
want   querer, desear
war   la guerra
warm (*noun with* hacer *and* tener)   el calor
  be warm (*weather*)   hacer calor
  be very warm (*persons*)   tener mucho calor
wash   lavar, (*oneself*) lavarse
  (she) will wash his face   (ella) le lavará a él la cara
  will you (*formal sing.*) **wash my hand?**   ¿quiere Ud. lavarme la mano?
watch   el reloj; mirar
  gold watch   reloj de oro
  shall we watch television?   ¿miramos la televisión?
water   el agua (*f.*)
  water glass   vaso para agua
we   nosotros, -as; *indef. subject* se, uno
wealthy   rico, -a
weather   el tiempo
  be good (bad) weather   hacer buen (mal) tiempo
  it has been bad weather   ha hecho mal tiempo
week   la semana
  last week   la semana pasada
  next week   la semana que viene
  two weeks   quince días, dos semanas
weekend   el fin de semana
well *adv.*   bien
what   lo que
what?   ¿qué? ¿cómo?
  at what time?   ¿a qué hora?
  what is his name?   ¿cómo se llama (él)?
  what's the matter with (Louis)?   ¿qué tiene (Luis)?
what + *noun!*   ¡qué . . . !
  what a beautiful day!   ¡qué día más *or* tan hermoso (bonito, lindo)!

what a pity (surprise)!   ¡qué lástima (sorpresa)!
whatever   lo que
when   cuando
where?   ¿dónde? (*with verbs of motion*) ¿adónde?
whether   si
which *relative pron.*   que, el (la) cual, los (las) cuales, el (la, los, las) que
  which (fact)   lo que, lo cual
which?   ¿qué? ¿cuál?
  which one(s)?   ¿cuál(es)?
while   el rato; *conj.* mientras (que)
white   blanco, -a
  the white one (*m.*)   el blanco
who *relative pron.*   que, quien(es), el (la) cual, los (las) cuales, el (la, los, las) que
  those (the ones) who   quienes, los (las) que
who?   ¿quién(es)?
whom   que, quien(es), a quien(es)
whom?   ¿quién(es)? ¿a quién(es)?
whose *relative adj.*   cuyo, -a (-os, -as)
whose?   ¿de quién(es)?
  whose (bracelet) is this?   ¿de quién es esta (pulsera)?
why?   ¿por qué?
will   querer; *sign of future tense*
  will you (open) . . . ?   ¿quieres (quiere Ud.) (abrir) . . . ?
window   la ventana
windy: be (very)—,   hacer (mucho) viento
wish   querer, desear
  (how) I wish . . . !   ¡ojajá (que) + *subj.!*
  I wish that (would that) . . . !   ¡ojalá (que) . . . !
with   con, de
without *prep.*   sin; *conj.* sin que
woman   la mujer
wonder   *for conjecture use future, cond., future perf., or cond. perf. tense*
word   la palabra
work (*of art*)   la obra; trabajar
  by working   trabajando
  work hard   trabajar mucho
world *adj.*   mundial
worst   peor
  the worst thing   lo peor
would   *sign of imp. ind. or cond. tense*

Louise would like to go   a Luisa le
  gustaría ir
  she would like   le gustaría a ella
  we would like   nos gustaría, quisiéramos
  would that . . . !   ¡ojalá (que) + *subj.!*
wrap (up)   envolver (ue)
write   escribir
writer (*f.*)   la escritora
written   escrito, -a

Y
---

year   el año
  a year ago   hace un año
  every year   todos los años
  for about two years   desde hace unos dos
    años
  last year   el año pasado
  the first year   el primer año
yellow   amarillo, -a
  a yellow one (*m.*)   uno amarillo
yes   sí
  say yes   decir que sí
yesterday   ayer

yesterday afternoon (morning)   ayer por
  la tarde (mañana)
yet   todavía
you   (*fam. sing.*)   tú; *dir. and indir. obj.* te;
    after prep. ti
  with you   contigo
you (*formal*) *subject pron. and after prep.*
    usted (Ud.), ustedes (Uds.); *dir. obj.* lo
    (le), la, los, las; *indir. obj.* le, les, se
  with you (*reflex.*)   consigo
young   joven (*pl.* jóvenes)
  that young man   ese (aquel) joven
  young lady   la joven, la señorita
  young men (people)   los jóvenes
younger   menor, más joven
your *adj.* (*fam. sing.*)   tu(s); (*formal, fam. pl.*)
    su(s)
yours *pron.* (*fam. sing.*)   (el) tuyo, (la) tuya,
    (los) tuyos, (las) tuyas; (*formal, fam. pl.*)
    (el) suyo, (la) suya, (los) suyos, (las)
    suyas *or* (el, la, los, las) de Ud. (Uds.)
  of yours *adj.* (*fam. sing.*)   tuyo(s), -a(s);
    (*formal sing., pl.*) suyo(s), -a(s), de
    Ud. (Uds.)
yourself *reflex.* (*formal sing.*)   sí
  for yourself *reflex.* (*formal sing.*)   para sí

MAPS

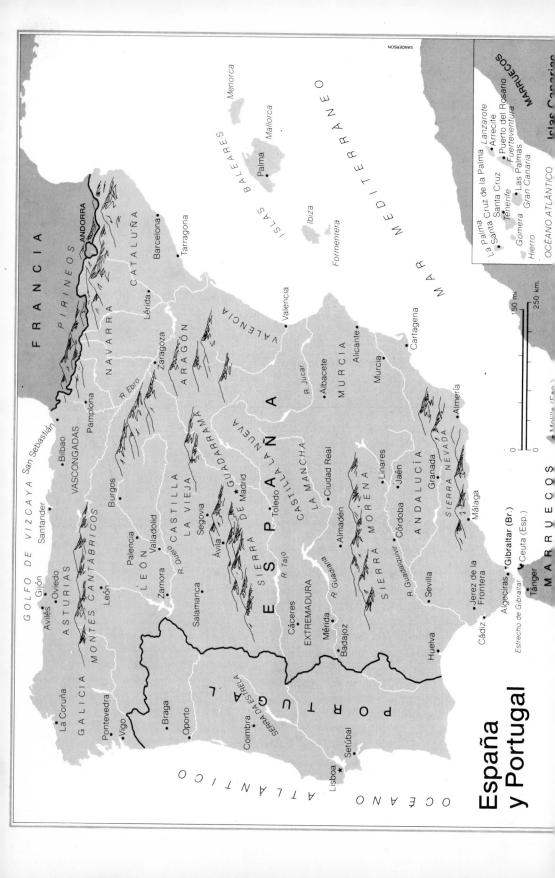

España
y Portugal

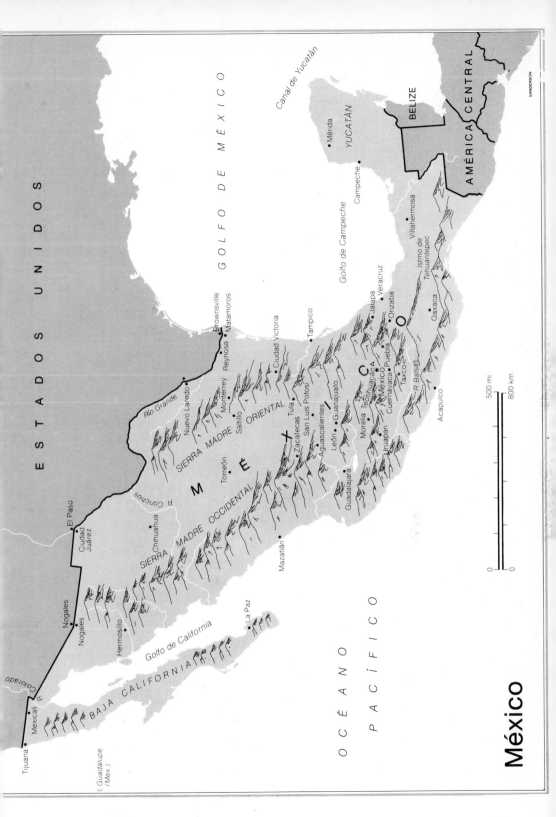

México

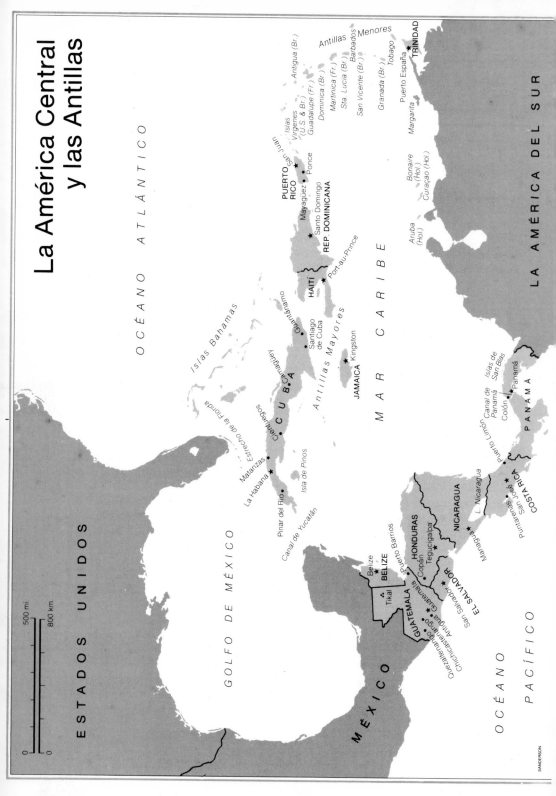

La América Central y las Antillas

ESTADOS UNIDOS

OCÉANO ATLÁNTICO

GOLFO DE MÉXICO

MÉXICO

Estrecho de la Florida

Islas Bahamas

Canal de Yucatán

Pinar del Río ★
La Habana
Matanzas ★
Cienfuegos
Isla de Pinos
C U B A
Camagüey
Santiago de Cuba ★
Guantánamo

Antillas Mayores

Kingston ★
JAMAICA

HAITÍ
Port-au-Prince

REP. DOMINICANA
Santo Domingo ★

PUERTO RICO
Mayagüez
Ponce ★
San Juan ★

Islas Vírgenes (U.S. & Br.)
Antigua (Br.)
Guadalupe (Fr.)
Dominica (Br.)
Martinica (Fr.)
Sta. Lucia (Br.)
San Vicente (Br.)
Barbados (Br.)
Granada (Br.)
Tobago

Antillas Menores

TRINIDAD
Puerto España

Margarita

Bonaire (Hol.)
Curaçao (Hol.)

Aruba (Hol.)

MAR CARIBE

LA AMÉRICA DEL SUR

Belize ★
BELIZE
Puerto Barrios
Tikal
GUATEMALA
Guatemala ★
Chichicastenango
Antigua
Quetzaltenango
Copán
HONDURAS
Tegucigalpa ★
San Salvador ★
EL SALVADOR
NICARAGUA
Managua ★
L. Nicaragua
COSTA RICA
San José ★
Puntarenas
Puerto Limón
Canal de Panamá
Islas de San Blas
Colón
Panamá ★
PANAMÁ

OCÉANO PACÍFICO

500 mi.
800 km

SANDERSON

MAR CARIBE

OCÉANO ATLÁNTICO

Barranquilla
Cartagena
Maracaibo
Caracas
TRINIDAD
Puerto España
VENEZUELA
R. Orinoco
GUAYANA
Georgetown
SURINAM
Paramaribo
GUAYANA FRAN.
Cayenne
Medellín
Bogotá
COLOMBIA
Cali
Quito
ECUADOR
Guayaquil
Iquitos
Manaus
R. Amazonas
Belem
CORDILLERA DE LOS ANDES
R. Madeira
B R A S I L
Recife
PERÚ
Lima
Machu Picchu
Cuzco
BOLIVIA
Titicaca
La Paz
Sucre
Salvador
Arequipa
Brasília
Belo Horizonte
Arica
Iquique
PARAGUAY
Rio de Janeiro
Antofagasta
Asunción
São Paulo
Santos
Trópico de Capricornio
Tucumán
CHILE
ARGENTINA
Córdoba
Pôrto Alegre
Rosario
R. Paraná
URUGUAY
OCÉANO PACÍFICO
Valparaíso
Santiago
Mendoza
Buenos Aires
Montevideo
La Plata
Río de la Plata
Concepción
Bahía Blanca
Puerto Montt
0   1000 mi.
0   1600 km.
Islas Malvinas
Punta Arenas
Estrecho de Magallanes
Tierra del Fuego
Cabo de Hornos

Ecuador

La América del Sur

SANDERSON

287

INDEX

INDEX

Photograph Credits

1 2 3 4 5 6 7 8 9 0